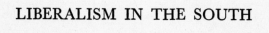

LIBERALISM IN THE SOUTH

The University of North Carolina Press, Chapel Hill, N. C.; The Baker and Taylor Company, New York; Oxford University Press, London; Maruzen-Kabushiki-Kaisha, Tokyo; Edward Evans & Sons, Ltd., Shanghai; D. B. Centen's Wetenschappelijke Boekhandel, Amsterdam

LIBERALISM
IN THE SOUTH

BY

VIRGINIUS DABNEY

CHAPEL HILL
THE UNIVERSITY OF NORTH CAROLINA PRESS
1932

PRINTED IN THE UNITED STATES OF AMERICA BY EDWARDS & BROUGHTON
COMPANY, RALEIGH, N. C.; BOUND BY L. H. JENKINS, INC., RICHMOND, VA.

TO

D. H. D.

ACKNOWLEDGMENTS

I AM UNDER a special debt of gratitude to Dr. Dumas Malone, editor of the *Dictionary of American Biography*, who made many helpful suggestions as to the organization of this study, and who also gave a large part of the manuscript a critical reading. In addition, Dr. Malone made available to me a number of as yet unpublished sketches from the files of the *Dictionary*. My father, Dr. Richard Heath Dabney, of the University of Virginia, examined the entire manuscript and gave me a great deal of sound advice concerning it. Others who read one or two chapters, and whose criticisms were of the highest value, are Miss Ellen Glasgow, Miss Lucy R. Mason, and Mrs. Beverley B. Munford of Richmond and Dr. James Hardy Dillard of Charlottesville.

I desire to express my thanks to Miss Nell Battle Lewis of the Raleigh, N. C., *News and Observer*, for the loan of a file of clippings, and I am greatly indebted to each of the following for invaluable assistance of one sort or another:

Mr. Adolph S. Ochs and Mr. Arthur Krock of the New York *Times*, Dr. Douglas S. Freeman of the Richmond *News Leader*, Mr. Gerald W. Johnson of the Baltimore *Evening Sun*, Mr. Duncan Aikman and Mr. Newton Aiken of the Baltimore *Sun*, Mr. Louis I. Jaffé of the Norfolk *Virginian-Pilot*, Mr. Grover C.

Hall of the Montgomery *Advertiser*, Mr. Mark Ethridge of the Macon *Telegraph*, Mr. Robert Lathan of the Asheville *Citizen* and Mr. Lapsley G. Walker of the Chattanooga *Times*.

I am also under heavy obligations to a number of others who have favored me with their counsel. Among these are Mr. James Branch Cabell, Rabbi Edward N. Calisch, Dr. Beverley D. Tucker, Jr., Dr. B. R. Lacy, Jr., Dr. R. H. Pitt, Miss Adele Clark, and Dr. Orie Latham Hatcher of Richmond; Mr. Clarence E. Cason of the University of Alabama; Mr. Clay Fulks of Commonwealth College, Mena, Arkansas; Dr. W. L. Poteat of Wake Forest, North Carolina; Major Richard F. Burges of El Paso, Texas; Dr. James Southall Wilson and Dr. W. M. Forrest of the University of Virginia; Dr. John R. Sampey of the Southern Baptist Theological Seminary, Louisville; Dr. Yates Snowden of the University of South Carolina and Mr. Langdon Cheves of Charleston, South Carolina; Mr. George A. Sloan, president of the Cotton-Textile Institute, New York City; Dr. Herman Clarence Nixon of Tulane University; Mr. George Clifton Edwards of Dallas; Colonel P. H. Callahan of Louisville, Mr. Richard Reid of the Catholic Laymen's Association of Georgia at Augusta, and Professor Robert D. Meade of the University of Virginia.

I should like to express my appreciation to Professor Addison Hibbard of Northwestern University, who proposed this study on behalf of the University of North Carolina Press while a member of the University of North Carolina faculty; and to Mr. W. T. Couch, Director of the Press, for his penetrating criticisms of the manuscript, particularly in connection with the preparation of the concluding chapter, and his unfailing kindness and courtesy.

The authorities of the Virginia State Library, notably Mr. Wilmer L. Hall, assistant librarian, have coöperated whole-heartedly. I am also indebted to the University of Virginia Library and the Congressional Library for the use of their facilities on several occasions.

I am conscious of an unusual sense of obligation to Dr. John D. Hicks for his excellent study, *The Populist Revolt*, and to Mr. Maynard Shipley for his equally valuable book, *The War on Modern Science*. These works were indispensable to me in the preparation of Chapters XII and XVI, respectively.

And finally I wish to thank my wife for helpful suggestions and for generous assistance in reading the proofs.

V. D.

Richmond, Virginia.
July, 1932.

TABLE OF CONTENTS

1900-1932
THE NEW SOUTH

INTRODUCTION

IN UNDERTAKING a study of liberal tendencies in the Southern States since the American Revolution the author is aware that he has embarked upon a task of formidable proportions. Involving, as it does, an examination of liberal movements in the fields of politics, education, religion, race relations, industry, literature, journalism, and women's rights over a period of more than a century and a half and throughout an area several times as large as any European country except Russia, this inquiry has necessitated rather extensive research in a number of directions.

At the outset the author was confronted with the problem of determining, for the purposes of this volume, the metes and bounds of "the South." Should he limit his study to the eleven states which comprised the Confederacy, or should he include one or two of the border commonwealths? For various reasons Maryland and Kentucky were the only non-seceding states given serious consideration for inclusion. It was decided to omit the former and to admit the latter. This decision was concededly somewhat arbitrary. Both Maryland and Kentucky are below Mason and Dixon's Line. If the one produced the Confederate battle hymn "Maryland! My Maryland!" and is known in song and story for that delectable Southern dish, fried

chicken à la Maryland, the most distinguished citizen
of the other for many years was the picturesque
"Marse Henry" Watterson, a former Confederate
soldier, and prior to the adoption of a certain constitutional amendment, the state was said to have been
largely inhabited by goateed colonels in broad-
brimmed hats engaged for the most part in the pre-
eminently Southern pastime of quaffing mint juleps.
But despite the similarities between the two commonwealths, there appeared to be adequate reasons for
classifying Maryland as primarily Eastern and Kentucky as primarily Southern.

After the territorial limits of the study had been
determined, the next step was the collection of data
bearing upon the state of liberalism, past and present,
in the area under examination. Obviously so broad a
theme as "Liberalism in the South" could be treated
only in its major outlines within the limits prescribed
for the present work. One of the chief obstacles encountered lay in the superfluity of the available material. This necessitated a careful winnowing and
sifting.

Inevitably and unavoidably, readers will discover
omissions which they regard as serious. This man in
Texas or that man in Alabama has not been given
sufficient attention, this movement in Arkansas or
that movement in Florida has been ignored. In anti-
cipation of such criticisms the author, while recognizing
the possible justice of some of them, reiterates that,
in the nature of the case, omissions are necessarily
numerous.

Much confusion and misunderstanding will be

avoided if a definition of the term "liberalism" is presented at the outset.

Liberalism, as Hobhouse has pointed out in his trenchant little book on the subject, is a combination of both constructive and destructive elements. For centuries after the liberal resurgence which accompanied the Renaissance, it was primarily negative and destructive in character. The liberals were largely engaged in tearing down the ancient bulwarks of feudalistic tyranny and clerical despotism. They were the foes of the established order, the enemies of entrenched privilege. It may be said, none the less, that even at this period liberalism enjoyed certain positive attributes, in that one result of the destructive activities of liberalism was a distinct improvement in the status of the average man. As centuries passed and the citadels of Bourbonism capitulated one by one, these destructionists found it possible gradually to devote a larger share of their attention to positive efforts for the benefit of the masses and in the direction of a more democratic system to replace the authoritarian order which was being demolished. A concern for the welfare of the average citizen is, indeed, one of the prime attributes of liberalism. An uncompromising foe of autocracy in whatever shape disguised, it is, as Lord Morley once wrote, an eternal advocate of "the dignity and worth of the individual."

But if liberalism concerns itself in no small measure with the advocacy of democratic as distinguished from aristocratic institutions, it emphasizes to an even greater degree the essential necessity of freedom. That ringing phrase of Voltaire in his letter to Helvetius,

"I wholly disapprove of what you say and will defend to the death your right to say it," epitomizes the creed of the liberal as it relates to freedom. That challenging declaration of Jefferson, "I have sworn upon the altar of God eternal hostility against every form of tyranny over the mind of man," expresses a like attitude in equally imperishable language. To Voltaire and Jefferson and Cobden and Bright and other great liberals of the past, freedom was the very cornerstone of the liberal edifice. Freedom of thought, freedom of speech, freedom of action were the desiderata for which these men fought with impassioned conviction and resolute audacity.

Inevitably the question arises whether that liberty which liberals desire above all else should be absolute or subject to limitations. Obviously the answer is to be found in the fact that there can be no absolute freedom in a civilized society. Freedom under civilization as we know it is a relative term. Few would seriously contend, for example, that men should be left free today to perambulate on Broadway *sans* pantaloons. And since the liberal creed plainly contemplates a certain degree of restriction upon the activities of the individual, we are faced, for the purposes of this study, with the necessity of determining, if possible, where this restriction should begin and where it should end. Unfortunately it is upon this very point that liberals are divided into two opposing camps, and the author consequently approaches the question with trepidation.

The first of these two groups derives in no small measure from the Manchester School in England. Its members agree with the leaders of that school that the activities of government should be reduced to an absolute minimum. They concur in the Jeffersonian dictum that that government is best which governs least. Government, in their view, is "the immemorial enemy of freedom and all sound progress" and "a necessary evil to be kept down at all costs." To this group, many of whom prefer to be known as "libertarians" rather than liberals, all legislation having to do with the liquor traffic, censorship, Sunday observance and matters of personal conduct and morals should be immediately wiped from the statute books. John Stuart Mill sounded the keynote of this libertarian philosophy when he wrote: "The only freedom which deserves the name is that of pursuing our own good in our own way, so long as we do not attempt to deprive others of theirs."

The second group, whose ideals have been rather accurately described as humanitarian rather than libertarian, concerns itself in large measure with the advocacy of laws which it conceives to be for the economic and social welfare of the masses. These laws relate to such matters as regulation of the trusts; improvement of working conditions in industry, particularly for women and children; better educational facilities, improved health regulations, and so on. Many in this group are staunch defenders of prohibition and similar legislation, for it is their sincere belief that such enactments as the Eighteenth Amendment and the Volstead Act have contributed to the social well-being of the people and opened wider doors of opportunity to the workers.

Such, roughly speaking, are the two classes into which present-day liberals may be divided. It should be noted, however, that this classification merely approximates correctness, and that there is considerable overlapping between the groups just described. For example, there are thousands who despise prohibition and at the same time are heartily in favor of child labor legislation. They feel that the drinking habits of the individual lie outside the legitimate sphere of governmental action, and that men and women should be permitted to imbibe what, when, and where they choose. The prohibitionist's idea of freedom seems to them merely the freedom to be dry. Yet these same men take the view that when rapacious employers exploit women and children in mills and factories, the government should step in, even though the enactment of legislation prevents a few individuals who desire to work under unhealthful conditions, from doing so.

Bearing in mind, then, the various shades of liberal belief and the difficulties which confront anyone who seeks to resolve their complexities by dogmatic pronunciamentos or arbitrary ipse dixits, the author feels that members of both groups described in the foregoing paragraphs are entitled to be regarded as liberal. This is not to say, of course, that all prohibitionists are liberal or that all opponents of legislative regulation of child labor are illiberal. The matter is not so simple as that.

No one, indeed, can qualify as a true liberal on either side of any controversial question if he is profoundly intolerant of the views of those on the opposite side. But while tolerance is a highly-important attribute of the liberal-minded man or woman, and although the well-rounded liberal is catholic in his interests, broad in his view of public issues, and receptive to the arguments of those who are in disagreement with him, he is above all true to his own convictions. This cannot be too strongly emphasized. It has been well said by a Southern writer that "the boasted tolerance that is another name for the indifferentism of those who profess not to believe in anything very strongly is of no high value. Things worth while are accomplished by those who believe."

Such, briefly told, is the meaning of the term "liberalism" as used in this volume. If we apply this general definition to each of the specific aspects of Southern life under examination, we shall perhaps be able to fashion a more precise and hence more intelligible picture of the methodology of the present work.

In the field of politics, for instance, it has been the author's view that those Southerners who, without demagoguery, fought such bulwarks of privilege as entails and primogeniture, sought to extend the franchise and the other political rights of the common man, and battled for civil liberty are entitled to be regarded as liberals. The liberals in education are those who advanced the cause of the public schools, and who aided in the establishment and operation of institutions of higher learning which opened the doors of educational opportunity to the people and put the search for truth above all else. In religion the liberals in the early days led the fight for religious freedom and disestablishment, and in subsequent generations buckled on their armor against Fundamentalists, anti-evolutionists and anti-Catholics. In race relations they took part in the ante-bellum movement to rid the republic of the blight of slavery, and after Appomattox they directed their energies to seeking wider opportunities for Negroes and securing justice for the blacks in all their relationships with the whites. In industry they were the employers who displayed a social awareness, in that wages and working conditions in their plants were better and hours shorter than in rival factories and mills. In some industries, however, notably textiles, even these men clung to outmoded paternalistic notions and refused to recognize the unions. Thus liberalism among Southern industrialists up to and including the first six months of 1932 was a diluted brew. There were militant liberals in this field, but nearly all of them were on the faculties of Southern universities and colleges, in editorial sanctums, or engaged in social work. With respect to woman's sphere below the Potomac, there have been many men and women in both the old South and the new who have sought to achieve her emancipation, and these have been given attention in the succeeding pages. In literature those authors have been called liberal whose works have been done in an honest and uncompromising spirit, and have contributed to the building up of freer and more realistic art forms in the South. Authors whose books have furthered liberal movements in other directions, such as politics, religion, industry and so forth, also have been placed in this category, as have editors of newspapers and magazines who have crusaded for like causes.

The foregoing outline of the contents of this study does not pretend to completeness, but it at least adumbrates, in narrow compass, the general nature of the materials treated. In assembling and interpreting those materials, the author has sought to eschew a blind and unreasoning loyalty to his native section on the one hand and a reckless and indiscriminate iconoclasm on the other. He is hopeful that his critical examination of liberal tendencies in the South has been executed in a spirit of sanity and justice.

CHAPTER I

POLITICAL LIBERALISM RESURGENT

WHEN the soldiers of Lord Cornwallis marched out upon the field of Yorktown and laid down their arms on that eventful October day in 1781, their band blared blared forth the martial strains of "The World Turned Upside Down." The commander of His Majesty's forces may have been guided in his choice of music by the thought that an event so singular in its significance and so grievous in its implications called for a selection which would in some degree be appropriate to the occasion. But while Cornwallis and the Tories generally must have felt that the decisive defeat of the British arms was evidence that the world had indeed turned upside down, one may assume, none the less, that they did not at the time grasp the full meaning of the American victory. For the surrender at Yorktown portended not only the loss of thirteen of Great Britain's most important colonies; it also betokened the unleashing of liberal forces which were to shake two continents and lead ultimately to an almost complete *bouleversement* of governmental and religious institutions throughout the whole of America and much of Europe, as well as a far-reaching cataclysm in the social structure here and abroad.

Prior to the American Revolution privilege sat enthroned on both sides of the Atlantic. If the thirteen colonies were without a titled nobility such as controlled the affairs of Great Britain and the Continent, the rich and the well-born were dominant, even on portions of the frontier. They occupied the important offices in church and state and were in virtually complete authority. While social and governmental patterns were more democratic in some colonies than in others, the masses enjoyed comparatively few rights and relatively little influence anywhere.

During the years preceding 1776 there had been, it is true, faint stirrings against the established order, and here and there, as in Bacon's Rebellion, the colonists had risen in armed revolt against their oppressors. But it was not until the American Revolution that the theocracy of the North and the aristocracy of the South felt the full weight of a coördinated movement, under able leadership, looking toward a liberalization of institutions in the interest of the average man.

The time was ripe for such an advance. Submerged elements of the population were rising to power and asserting themselves as never before. While the provisional state governments set up in 1775 did not exhibit startling evidences of reform, and while for the most part they left control in the hands of the aristocracy, the fact that the trend was in the direction of added participation on the part of the masses in the affairs of state was a potent factor in causing the common people to enlist in the Continental armies. Feeling that they had little to lose and much to gain through severance of ties with the mother country, the lower orders in the cities and the frontiersmen of the back country enrolled under the banner of independence. When the war was brought to a successful termination, it was but natural that these urban and frontier groups should have indicated their desire for a larger share in the operations of the government which they had helped to establish.

Of outstanding importance among these underprivileged peoples were the Scotch-Irish. This hardy and adventurous race had emigrated from Scotland to northern Ireland, and then in the seventeenth and eighteenth centuries had come to America to escape persecution at the hands of the English government. Arriving on this side of the water, the vast majority entered the country through the port of Philadelphia. From that point they made for the frontier. The Scotch-Irish not only settled the up country of Pennsylvania, but great numbers traveled southward along the valleys into Virginia and the Carolinas. As the axes of the pioneers bit deeper and deeper into the wilderness, they were in the forefront of the advance. At the outbreak of hostilities with Great Britain, thousands of these tough-thewed Indian fighters and backwoodsmen enlisted eagerly for war on their former oppressors, and to them is accorded a major share of the credit for the subsequent triumph of the American arms.

In addition to the Scotch-Irish, there were two other groups in the South which were liberty-loving, and hence favorable to the cause of reform. At the same time they felt no special fondness for Great Britain. These were the Germans and the French Huguenots.

While they were numerically less important than the Scotch-Irish, they were forces to be reckoned with in certain regions. During the war many of them fought in the armies of Washington, and after the surrender they usually aligned themselves with the apostles of a new order.

These elements were frequently in conflict both during and after the Revolution with a large proportion of the colonists of English birth or descent. When the clatter of musketry at Lexington and Concord signalized the opening of hostilities in 1775, the colonists of English background were in control almost everywhere from New Hampshire to Georgia. A substantial percentage of them remained steadfastly loyal to the mother country, and many left these shores after the close of the war, rather than endure separation from the land of their forefathers. On the other hand, it need hardly be said that a number of the ablest American generals, including Washington himself, were of English descent. After independence was won, the citizens of English stock who remained in the country were sharply divided over matters of reform. Some were prominent in the liberal movement, while others were uncompromising in their support of the status quo.

Below the Potomac, and indeed in the country as a whole, the great liberal of the revolutionary period, the man who led the various progressive elements in a combined assault on the citadel of privilege, was Thomas Jefferson. In an age distinguished above any other in American history for the capacity and statesmanship of its public men, Jefferson stood out above all the rest through the power of his intellect and the catholicity of his genius. In his epochal struggle against the forces of conservatism and reaction, he of course enjoyed the coöperation of powerful leaders in his own and other states. Without the indispensable assistance of these men, some of whom were fired with a zeal as flaming as his own, the liberal movement which followed the Revolution could never have succeeded. But the tawny-haired planter from Albemarle, who moved to the attack in 1776 with the Declaration of Independence and widened the breach the same year by introducing in the Virginia legislature radical measures which startled the wealthy patricians, is rightly regarded as the spearhead of the liberal advance.

Just as South Carolina was to dominate Southern thought half a century later, Virginia dominated the thought of the South, if not of the nation, during and immediately following the Revolution. This is due in large measure to the leadership of Jefferson and the men who fought side by side with him at this critical juncture—Patrick Henry and James Madison, George Mason and George Wythe and John Taylor of Caroline—the most puissant array of liberal statesmen who have sprung from the soil of any American Commonwealth in a like period of time. Washington, it need scarcely be said, also contributed immensely to the prestige of the Old Dominion. But while Washington was a man of heroic mold, he was not often conspicuous as an advocate of liberal causes. True, he expressed strong hostility to the institution of slavery, and he showed, too, that he appreciated the need for a system of universal education, but, on the other hand, he was aligned with the conservative element in politics and usually was found fighting the Jeffersonians.

Prior to the outbreak of the Revolution, the leader of the "up country" Virginians in opposition to the plutocratic tidewater planters was Patrick Henry. This "forest-born Demosthenes" had electrified the colony in 1763 with his championship of the rights of the people against the established church in the "Parson's Cause," and two years later he had defied Great Britain in ringing resolutions in opposition to the Stamp Act. Henry's crusade for civil and religious liberty attracted such upland planters as Jefferson, Madison, Mason, and Taylor, all of whom aligned themselves with him and against the conservatives who lived on the great tobacco plantations along the lowland rivers. When hostilities with Great Britain began, this group was able to direct the trend of affairs in Virginia, and at the same time to exert a powerful influence upon the other colonies.

In his resounding appeal for "liberty or death" in 1775, Henry stated the case for separation in burning words, and the following year Mason with his Bill of Rights and Jefferson with his Declaration of Independence broadcast the doctrines of civil and religious liberty and natural right not only to the farthest corners of America but to Europe as well.

The Bill of Rights, which was adopted by the Virginia Convention on June 12, 1776, and thus antedated the Declaration of Independence by three weeks, was almost entirely the work of Mason. Henry and Madison contributed the clauses which had to do with religious freedom, but otherwise the document was virtually all from Mason's pen. To a considerable degree a recapitulation of English principles, it harks back more than five centuries to Runnymede for some of its fundamental concepts. The right of trial by jury is emphasized, cruel and unusual punishments and the use of general warrants are proscribed, freedom of the press and of religion are stressed as bulwarks of liberty, all men having a permanent interest in and attachment to the country are declared to be entitled to the right of suffrage, and the people are accorded the right to reform or abolish any government which fails to operate for their benefit and security. The conservative patricians of the tidewater counties saw the danger which lurked in this radical paper, and sought by every means in their power to defeat it. But Mason dominated the convention, and the Bill of Rights was adopted. Its importance can scarcely be overemphasized. The first formal declaration of American ideals of liberty by a free American state, it was copied in the Federal Constitution as well as in the constitutions of the states. In addition it was the model for a similar declaration in France, and thus played a part in bringing on the French Revolution.

The Bill of Rights has been called "the original chart by which free governments must steer their course in all coming time," and it was the source of various ideas which Jefferson embodied in his Declaration of Independence. The Declaration, most quoted of all American state papers, also resembled the Bill of Rights in that it was viewed with perturbation by conservatives everywhere, particularly in France, where the doctrines it enunciated synchronized with those of the revolutionary leaders. The Declaration has been the object of severe criticism from various quarters since its adoption more than a century and a half ago, and while some of this criticism is not without justification, the essential vitality of the principles it lays down remains undiminished. Even though the phraseology is at times hackneyed and the content trite and unoriginal, the Declaration of Independence will stand for future generations as a noble expression of the natural rights of man. The English historian Buckle has declared that it "ought to be hung up in the nursery of every king, and blazoned on the porch of every royal palace." Its preamble has been the inspiration of oppressed peoples in many lands.

To almost anyone but Thomas Jefferson, the authorship of such a document would have seemed a completely adequate contribution to the cause of liberty, calling, in so far as he was concerned, for no further exertions in that direction. But for this astonishing man the drafting of the Declaration of Independence was only a beginning. A few months later he introduced in the Virginia assembly legislation designed to tear up the aristocracy, to which he himself belonged, root and branch. To this end he had formulated a four-fold program. It included abolition of the system of entails and primogeniture, which enabled the wealthy planters to keep their estates intact century after century (Jefferson himself was an eldest son); enactment of a statute guaranteeing religious freedom and undermining the established church (into which he had been born); gradual abolition of slavery (he was a slave-owner); and establishment of a system of public education commencing with free elementary schools and culminating in a state university—a system in which educational opportunity for both rich and poor was to be provided.

But Jefferson did not content himself with the mere introduction of this well-nigh revolutionary program. He put his shoulder to the wheel, enlisted the aid of Madison and others, and ultimately obtained its adoption in almost all essential particulars. Within a decade entails and primogeniture had been abolished, the Statute for Religious Freedom had been enacted, and importation of slaves into the state had been forbidden. Subsequently Jefferson's educational plans were brought to a happy conclusion with the establishment of the University of Virginia. Some of these matters will be considered in greater detail in later chapters. For the present suffice it to say that Jefferson's conception and execution of this amazing series of reforms, together with his authorship of the Declaration of Independence, his efforts toward revision of the penal code, and his militant advocacy of free speech and a free press, although he himself was one of the most vilified men of his generation, stamp him as the greatest liberal in American history and as worthy to sit beside the great liberals of all time.

There is no implication here, however, that the liberalism of the Sage of Monticello was of such an exalted variety as to be subject to no criticism whatever. On the contrary, certain of Jefferson's attitudes are to be condemned. He exhibited intolerance toward the political philosophy of the Federalists, for example, and was unwilling to concede that their doctrines were entitled to serious consideration. In fact, when the University of Virginia was established, he went to the extreme of prescribing the textbooks to be used by the law faculty. His purpose was to prevent the heresies of Federalism from taking root at his beloved university. While he may have been so thoroughly convinced that Hamiltonian principles were evil as to regard himself in duty bound to crush them whenever the opportunity presented itself, his position may almost be described as a negation of the very freedom of thought and discussion for which he had fought so valiantly in earlier days.

Jefferson also exhibited a certain provincialism in his notions as to the relative merits of agriculture and industry as bases for civilization. He was unable to perceive any virtue in the concentration of population in urban centers, and regarded manufacturing, shipping, and other concomitants of urban life as almost unmitigated evils. While his attachment to the soil and his enthusiasm for rural joys, especially in the era in which he lived, are quite understandable, one feels that his mind was virtually closed to the arguments of the opposition. But while these and perhaps other criticisms can justly be brought against this many-sided man, it is impossible to deny him the glory of having done more than any other individual to smash the strongholds of American Bourbonism and reaction in the late eighteenth and early nineteenth centuries, and to lay the broad foundations upon which democracy in the republic rests today.

It is a strange fact that Patrick Henry, despite his

fiery attacks on the established order before the Revolution, weakened in the faith a few years later and ended by leaving the cause of reform in Virginia to Jefferson, Wythe, Mason, Taylor, and Madison. Henry had never at any time been stirred by Jefferson's passion for egalitarianism, and when he became governor of Virginia in 1776, his assaults on the strongholds of the aristocracy became gradually less and less vehement. It has been aptly stated that "for Henry the Revolution reached its end in the Declaration; for Jefferson it reached its beginning."

If it appears that undue attention has been focused in the foregoing pages upon political liberalism in the Old Dominion, it is only proper to point out that this was Virginia's golden age. During and immediately after the War for American Independence she showed the way, not only to the South but to the nation. The principles which prevailed in Virginia at this period were, in general, those which prevailed in North Carolina, South Carolina, and Georgia, the only other Southern states in existence until the 1790's. Early in the following century Virginia was to see her leadership below the Potomac pass to South Carolina, but for the time being her position was supreme.

There were, needless to say, political liberals in the other states of the South in the post-revolutionary era, to bear aloft the torch of reform. In North Carolina the tenor of society was more democratic than in the Old Dominion, and for several years after 1776 a radical element consisting mainly of small farmers was in control. This element was led by Willie Jones of Halifax, one of the most remarkable men in the history of the state, a man who has been almost completely ignored by posterity, but a politician of immense influence in his day. Jones belonged to one of the oldest families in North Carolina and his manner of living befitted the aristocracy of his lineage. He had been educated abroad at Eton, and he spent much of his time on this side of the ocean in the society of fox hunters and lovers of horseflesh. Yet Jefferson himself, to whom Jones looked for his political principles, was hardly more advanced in his opinions or more intense in his radicalism. It has been said that Jones "lived like a prince but talked and voted like a Jacobin."

Jones exercised his marked talents as a politician in fighting the conservatives of Eastern North Carolina, who were marshaled under the banner of Johnston, Hooper, and Iredell. His most influential ally in this struggle was Nathaniel Macon, who also was of distinguished ancestry, and combined an aristocratic background with a democratic attitude of mind. Macon rose to prominence somewhat later than Jones. He took over the leadership of the Jeffersonian party in the state shortly before his friend's death in 1801, and held it for thirty years. It was pursuant to the wishes of Jones and Macon that the North Carolina legislature in 1784 made entails illegal and provided for a more equitable distribution of the real property of persons dying intestate.

Down in South Carolina, where the cotton, rice, and indigo planters with their vast lowland estates were dominant, the rich and the well-born enjoyed a virtual monopoly of all the important positions in church and state when hostilities with Great Britain began. The social and intellectual life of the colony revolved about Charleston, the stronghold of the patricians. But despite the conservatism of most of the leading South Carolinians, political liberals came forward to spread the new gospel of democracy and egalitarianism.

Among these was Christopher Gadsden, fiery and impetuous critic of Great Britain before independence was won, and afterward outspoken in his advocacy of democratic principles. A liberal of a rather different type was Henry Laurens. In one of the crises of the war, when bitterness was at its height, Laurens delivered a noble and courageous defense of "the sacredness of individual freedom in thought, spoken word and action." It is also noteworthy that at a time when religious intolerance was more common than it is today, he exhibited a freedom from bigotry and narrowness which was in refreshing contrast to the attitude of many of his contemporaries. Two of the greatest and most powerful families in South Carolina were the Rutledges and the Pinckneys. Yet Charles Pinckney and Edward Rutledge joined hands to accomplish the abolition of primogeniture in the state. Pinckney, who is not to be confused with his cousin, Charles Cotesworth Pinckney, had served with marked distinction in the Continental Congress and the Federal Constitutional Convention while still in his twenties. It was during one of his three terms as governor that the revised South Carolina Constitution of 1790 was adopted. He urged that a section instructing the legislature to abolish primogeniture be included. His proposal met with approval and the clause was inserted. The next year Rutledge drew the legislative bill which carried this constitutional mandate into effect.

The sparsely populated frontier state of Georgia also felt the force of the post-revolutionary upheaval, and its Constitution of 1777 did away with both entails and primogeniture. Georgia was thus the first among all the states to abrogate these two bulwarks of the *ancien régime*.

The fifteen years which followed the adoption of the Declaration of Independence witnessed their abrogation throughout the South and in most of the North as well. This was a movement in which the South had been the pioneer. Its far-reaching importance may be grasped from the words of Professor Charles A. Beard: "Considered relatively . . . the destruction of landed privilege in America by the forces unchained in the War for Independence was perhaps as great and as significant as the change wrought in the economic status of the clergy and nobility during the holocaust of the French Revolution."

The economic and social questions which played so large a part in the struggle over entails and primogeniture also were factors in the framing and adoption of the Federal Constitution. While the convention which framed it was on the whole a distinctly conservative body, some of its members were rather less conservative than others. Madison, the "Father of the Constitution," was the outstanding spokesman for the comparatively liberal element, while Hamilton was the champion of the reactionaries. When the final draft was submitted to the states after nearly four months of deliberation, the voters, North and South, divided at once into proponents and opponents of ratification. In general, those who favored adoption were the well-to-do merchants and manufacturers of the seaboard and the holders of public securities, while the small farmers of the interior formed the backbone of the opposition. In fact these up country farmers were so numerous and powerful in North Carolina that Willie Jones and his allies were able to prevent that state from ratifying until the end of 1789, more than a year after the Constitution had gone into effect.

Shortly after Washington took office as the first president, opposition to the comprehensive legislative program sponsored by Hamilton began to develop. This program included the funding of the national debt, assumption at face value by the national government of the revolutionary obligations of the states, establishment of a United States Bank, and the levying of a tariff for the benefit of the manufacturers. These measures were debated in heated fashion in the Congress. Their enactment did much to crystallize opinion throughout the country among planters, farmers, and laborers against the policies of the Federalists. Jefferson, the leader of the protesting group, saw in Hamilton's fiscal measures an elaborate scheme for the exploitation of the masses for the benefit of the classes. In his fight on the Federalists he had the assistance of John Taylor of Caroline, "the philosopher and statesman of agrarianism," whom Parrington has called "the most penetrating critic of Hamiltonian finance and the most original economist of his generation." Taylor joined Jefferson in declaring war on special privilege.

Popular resentment against the Federalist program, which included the Alien and Sedition Acts, swept Jefferson into the presidency in 1800. His party in two Southern states had expressed its unqualified disapproval of the Alien and Sedition Laws in the famous Kentucky and Virginia Resolutions of 1798 and 1799. The Alien Act conferred upon the president the power, in the event of war, to fix the conditions under which alien enemies might be ordered out of the country or imprisoned, while the Sedition Act prescribed a fine and imprisonment for persons who unlawfully combined or conspired against the government at any time, or who wrote or published anything deemed by the authorities to be false, scandalous or malicious and calculated to bring the United States government or its officers into disrepute. This grossly arbitrary and despotic legislation was not passed under the stress of any great national emergency. On the contrary there is reason to believe that in sponsoring these laws, the Federalists were actuated largely by a desire to silence all criticism of their acts. Republican newspapers and individuals had been harassing them unmercifully, and they chose this method of abrogating the constitutional rights of free speech and a free press. The Kentucky Resolutions were the work of Jefferson and his disciple, John Breckinridge, while Jefferson and Madison drew the Virginia Resolutions. As indicated above, the resentment which these resolutions expressed was widely felt, and was reflected at the polls in 1800.

When Jefferson entered the presidency the following year, his party had established its right to recognition as the liberal party of the nation. True, it was to forfeit that right not many decades in the future, with its repudiation of the principles of its founder. At the opening of the nineteenth century, however, no one could justly deny the claim of the Republicans* to liberal leadership.

Throughout his eight years as president, and for the succeeding fifteen years he spent in retirement, the ire of Jefferson and that of his party was constantly aroused by the judicial decisions of an able and aggressive Southerner who, during practically the entire period, was the most influential figure in the Federalist ranks. John Marshall served as chief justice of the United States Supreme Court from 1801 until 1835. His legal judgments were invariably in the Hamiltonian tradition and tended always toward increased concentration of authority at Washington. Extreme Jeffersonian theories of state rights held no validity for Marshall, nor was he particularly concerned for the welfare of the average man. His predilections were to a much greater degree in favor of the possessor of property and wealth. One of the world's great jurists, who did much to strengthen the Federal fabric at a time when it needed strengthening, he was nevertheless at heart a rock-ribbed conservative, fundamentally reactionary in outlook and intent on maintaining the status quo.

But while Marshall's decisions as chief justice did much to further the Federalist cause, the vitality of

* The party founded by Jefferson took the name of "Republican" or "Democratic-Republican." After the election of Jackson, it became the "Democratic" party. The present Republican party was founded about six years before the Civil War.

the opposition party remained undiminished. Jefferson died in 1826, but two years later Andrew Jackson of Tennessee, the first man of humble birth to enter the White House, was elected to the presidency. Consequently, despite the steady bolstering of the central government through the judicial process, the common people came into their own as never before. Jackson had grown up on the frontier and was the idol of the rapidly-expanding West. A two-fisted Indian fighter and backwoodsman who had won national renown at the Battle of New Orleans, he was a type of popular leader new to Washington. Many a *grande dame* arched her eyebrows in disdain when she saw the horde of frontiersmen in leather breeches and coonskin caps which trampled the White House carpets and upset the furniture at Jackson's inaugural reception. Yet those who looked behind the boorish behavior of the new president's partisans saw that the entrance of "Old Hickory" upon the political stage was an event of profound importance. It signified not only the emergence of the West to a position of great influence in the national councils, but it also betokened new leveling processes throughout the country as a whole. Under Jackson the Democratic party became democratic in name and also in fact.

Since the turn of the century the struggle in the Southern states between the great seaboard planters on the one hand and the mechanics of the cities and the small farmers of the uplands on the other, had grown increasingly acute. The planters had always held the upper hand in colonial times, and many of them were severely pained by the demands of the farmers and mechanics for an equal share in the government. Seldom, if ever, has a single class in any country voluntarily relinquished control of governmental affairs and admitted another class to a position of equal influence. It is not surprising, therefore, that the Southern planters defended their ancient prerogatives with stubborn persistence and made concessions grudgingly. While the urban mechanics were by no means negligible factors in this contest below the Potomac, the battle for supremacy between the large slaveholders and the up country farmers held the center of the stage. As the Scotch-Irish, the Germans, and others poured into the piedmont and transmontane region in ever greater numbers, the white population of the Southern back country soon exceeded that of the lowlands. This naturally led to a movement by the upland leaders to obtain the rights of suffrage and representation to which they considered their constituencies entitled.

Virginia and South Carolina fixed the patterns of Southern thought from the Revolution to the Civil War, and the struggle between patrician and plebeian in those two states during the post-revolutionary years will therefore be examined in some detail. Speaking in terms of rough approximation only, the social and political concepts which were to govern the thinking of Kentucky and Tennessee sprang from the Old Dominion, while those which were to become dominant in Alabama and Mississippi had their origins in the Palmetto State.

An idea of the power wielded by the seaboard parishes in South Carolina during the early years of statehood may be gathered from the fact that the first nineteen governors came from Charleston or its immediate vicinity. The system of representation was grossly unfair to the interior, and the restrictions which surrounded the holding of office and the exercise of the suffrage were such as to disqualify the great majority of its inhabitants. Slight concessions were made by the slaveholders of the lowlands in the constitutions of 1776, 1778, and 1790, but much remained to be done. In 1790 the planters agreed, after lengthy debate, to move the capitol up state from Charleston to Columbia, but under the constitution adopted in that year, they retained a majority of the members of both branches of the legislature, although the white population of the up country was approximately four times that of the low country.

There were, however, influential lowland planters who championed the cause of the small farmers. Among these was Joseph Alston, said to have been the wealthiest slaveowner in the state, who for many years urged that the system of representation be liberalized in the interest of justice to the interior. Alston favored a system of representation based on white population. The agitation which he and others carried on led to rather substantial concessions in the constitutional convention of 1808, during the gubernatorial administration of Charles Pinckney. Not only was there a compromise between population and wealth which gave the uplanders a more substantial share in the government, but the suffrage was extended to all white persons. After 1808 the sectional struggle within the state became relatively quiescent. In the Nullification Convention of 1832, Henry Middleton, of the famous Middleton family, condemned the existing system of representation and offered a resolution to the effect that sovereignty should rightly reside in the free white inhabitants, and that it was not fair to apportion representation in the convention on the basis of taxation and wealth. The gesture was futile, however, as the convention voted down this and all other similar proposals.

Virginia, like South Carolina, was at this period in the throes of a struggle between the tidewater, with its small white population and great tobacco plantations, on the one hand, and the Piedmont, the Shenandoah Valley and what is now West Virginia, with their sturdy yeomanry, on the other. Since the Virginia convention of 1776, in which the Eastern aristocracy had defeated the greater part of Jefferson's progressive political program, the slaveowners of the Old Dominion had enjoyed undue prestige. They had arranged the representation and the suffrage to their own advantage, with as few concessions as possible to the Scotch-Irish and German population of the frontier counties. During the early years of the nineteenth century expressions of discontent from the up country had become louder and louder until toward the close of the century's third decade sentiment for constitutional revision reached such proportions that a constitutional convention was called. It met in 1829 and did not adjourn until late in the following year.

The redistricting of the state, with a view to providing the back country with something approaching equitable representation in the legislature, and extension of the franchise were the two great objectives of the advocates of change. Chapman Johnson of Augusta County and Richmond, and Philip Doddridge of Wheeling were the leaders in this movement, while Benjamin Watkins Leigh and John Marshall of Richmond and John Randolph of Roanoke were powerful spokesmen for the conservatives. The liberals called attention to the fact that twenty-two of the twenty-four states had general suffrage, but Leigh "classed general suffrage with the other plagues: the Hessian fly, the varioloid, etc., which had arisen in the North and later spread to the South." The scintillating and eccentric Randolph, then nearing the close of his earthly pilgrimage, proclaimed his refusal to live under the dominion of "King Numbers." Abel P. Upshur of the Eastern Shore, in what was perhaps the most important address of the convention, enunciated the familiar doctrine that the people of wealth were entitled to rule. So firmly did this philosophy take hold of the delegates that even the venerable Madison, after a lifetime spent in serving liberal causes, succumbed to the advocates of reaction. The convention ended by making concessions in both representation and the suffrage, but these concessions were inadequate, and the final outcome of its deliberations was distinctly disappointing to Virginians of democratic leanings.

But while twenty years were to pass before white manhood suffrage was to become a reality in the Old Dominion, a majority of the more momentous controversies between the Southern slaveholders and nonslaveholders over representation and the ballot were settled by 1835. The democratization of Southern institutions had been greatly hastened by the admission of the frontier states. Kentucky, for example, had entered the Union in 1792 with white manhood suffrage, and four years later Tennessee had come in with a constitution embodying more equitable provisions as to the franchise than were to be found in that of North Carolina, which had served as its model. Tennessee's constitution was liberalized still further under William Carroll, the state's great reform governor of the ante-bellum period. While several decades were to elapse before qualifications for voting and holding office in some of the states could be reduced to reasonable levels, and inequalities in legislative apportionment could be corrected, the first third of the century saw a removal of the bulk of the more glaring evidences of discrimination against the common people. It was an era during which the cause of political liberalism moved forward with a firm and steady stride.

CHAPTER II

THE FIGHT FOR RELIGIOUS FREEDOM

AT THE opening of the American Revolution, the Episcopal church had long been established by legislative sanction in all four of the Southern colonies. A similar union of church and state obtained in Massachusetts, Connecticut, and New Hampshire, where Congregationalism was the official creed. Of the thirteen colonies, nine had established churches and imposed a general tax for the benefit of those churches. Dissenters were keenly resentful of the necessity for contributing to the support of a faith which they did not profess, but while mutterings of discontent were heard here and there, concerted and effective movements against the system had been few in colonial America.

When Lord Baltimore, a Roman Catholic, established the colony of Maryland in 1634, he decreed that the principle of religious toleration should be observed within its bounds. Subsequently, under the terms of the Toleration Act of 1649, persons professing to believe in Jesus Christ were left free to worship as they chose, but those who did not so profess or who denied the Holy Trinity, were punishable with death. If this law placed non-Christians within reach of the executioner, it marked, nevertheless, a decided advance over the religious polity which prevailed at that time in almost all other countries. Toward the end of the century, however, Maryland fell under the sway of the Anglican communion, and Catholics were harshly persecuted.

The real pioneer in America in the field of religious *freedom*, as distinguished from religious *toleration*, was Roger Williams. A bold and original thinker whose heterodox opinions soon made him anathema to the Puritan theocracy in Massachusetts, Williams was banished in 1636 to the snow-covered wilderness which is now Rhode Island. He proceeded at once to found that colony on a basis of absolute freedom of worship. Rhode Island was the first colony to grant complete religious liberty, and Williams is entitled, in consequence, to a place among the great liberals of America. It should be noted, however, that the colony repudiated one of the cardinal principles of its founder when it disfranchised all persons of Catholic faith in 1719.

Thus when the Revolution began, unqualified freedom of religion was not permitted by any American state. Catholics suffered universally from disabilities of one sort or another, and in most of the thirteen states there were also other important restrictions. The harsh treatment of Catholics in some of the Protestant-controlled commonwealths contrasted with the treatment of Protestants in the Spanish settlements along the Gulf of Mexico at the close of the eighteenth century. The commandants at Natchez and the governors-general of Louisiana were Spanish Catholics, but under their beneficent rule, persons of other faiths enjoyed the right of family worship, and no effort was made to proselyte among them or to interfere with them in the private practice of their religious rites.

The position of dominance occupied by the Anglican church in the four Southern colonies in 1776 was analogous to that enjoyed in civil affairs by the aristocracy of those colonies at the same period. Episcopalians held most of the important political offices, and there was thus to a large extent an identity of interests between the leaders in church and state. The church, on the whole, was distinctly reactionary and strongly opposed to any important change in the existing ecclesiastical order, just as many of its communicants were bitterly against any plan for disturbing the existing political alignment. But although this combination of civil and ecclesiastical authority was a formidable one, the same liberal forces which were to secure for the middle and lower classes a reasonable share in the affairs of government stood ready to drive a wedge between church and state and force from a recalcitrant hierarchy an acknowledgment of every citizen's right to liberty of conscience.

Until the coming of the Great Awakening in the 1730's, America contained a larger percentage of unchurched persons than any other country in Christendom. But the evangelical renascence which accompanied the Pietist movement in Germany and the Methodist revival in England had its counterpart on this side of the water in the wave of religious emotionalism which began with Jonathan Edwards' revival in Northampton, Massachusetts, in 1734 and swept the colonies from end to end. During this evangelical quickening the masses were attracted to the participating churches as never before. The new revivalistic technique employed by the dissenting denominations appealed to the urban mechanics and backwoods frontiersmen, and thousands affiliated with these churches who previously had exhibited no interest in such matters.

In the South, where the Anglican church was supreme, the Great Awakening raised up an aggressive group of evangelicals bent on undermining the prestige of that dignified communion. The Baptists and the Presbyterians were particularly vigorous in their opposition. The former denomination, which at the period stood for an unpaid and uneducated ministry, appealed especially to the lower orders, while the latter, with its splendidly equipped clergy, attracted the upper classes. As the Revolution neared, the fact that the Baptists had separation of church and state as one of their cardinal tenets led many who desired independence from Great Britain to look upon them with favor. For there was a rather striking analogy between the contention of the Baptists that they should not be taxed to support the Episcopal church and the argument of the colonials that they should not be taxed by the mother country without representation. At this period the Baptists were the only large body of Southern dissenters demanding separation of church and state. The Presbyterians, who were to join forces with them after Yorktown, contented themselves for the time being with seeking their rights under the English Toleration Act of 1689.

But the established church not only was under assault from the evangels; it was also a target for the

Unitarians and deists who swarmed in the land, and whose unorthodox ideas were traceable to the English and French deists, particularly the latter. Such powerful leaders as Franklin, Washington, John Adams, Paine, Jefferson and Madison were either Unitarians or deists, and their combined influence was potent in the cause of ecclesiastical and theological reform.

First among the Southern states to reduce the Anglicans to a position of complete parity with members of all other creeds, was North Carolina. As early as the fall of 1776 this democratic commonwealth adopted a constitution and bill of rights which provided for disestablishment. Almost complete religious freedom was also granted, the only exceptions being that persons who denied the existence of God or questioned the authenticity of the Protestant religion were prohibited from holding office. Disestablishment came practically without a struggle in North Carolina, owing to the fact that a large percentage of the Episcopal clergy and communicants remained loyal to the crown. This naturally did not strengthen the church in the eyes of the Scotch-Irish and the other strong groups who felt intense hostility toward the mother country. They accordingly seized the first opportunity to deprive it of its privileged position.

A few months later Georgia followed the example of North Carolina. The establishment there was of comparatively recent standing and consequently was less firmly entrenched than in some of the older states. It was therefore a fairly simple matter to write into the new constitution, adopted in February, 1777, a clause providing that all Georgians should have the free exercise of their religion, where such freedom did not endanger the peace and safety of the state.

The Episcopalians were much stronger in South Carolina than in either North Carolina or Georgia, and they accordingly were able to put up a formidable fight against the dissenters and their allies. The Anglican priesthood was nowhere more highly respected than in South Carolina. In addition to the fact that its members were culturally distinguished, there had been few, if any, complaints of undue bibulosity or other moral laxity against them, such as had been heard against their *confrères* in Virginia and Maryland.

With the opening of the legislative session late in 1776, the question of disestablishment was brought forward almost immediately as a major issue. Leading the assault on the battlements of ecclesiasticism was the Rev. William Tennent, a native of New Jersey who had been ordained to the Presbyterian ministry but had come to Charleston a few years before as pastor of the Independent Congregational Church. This accomplished theologian and able political strategist had taken an active part in rousing the up country against Great Britain. Shortly after the commencement of hostilities he circulated in the chief strongholds of the dissenters a memorial to the General Assembly urging disestablishment. By the time that body began its deliberations, many thousands of signatures had been secured.

Tennent, himself a member of the legislature, found a valuable confederate in Christopher Gadsden, one of the few revolutionary leaders in the state who was

not an Episcopalian. Gadsden presented the petition
and gave cordial support to the movement. Tennent
delivered an eloquent address in which he denounced
"ecclesiastical establishments" and demanded "free
and equal religious liberty" as against mere toleration. He was opposed by Charles Pinckney and Raw-
lins Lowndes, who "felt that the established church
should be retained in order to care for the poor and
to manage the elections of members of the general
assembly." They concurred, however, in the thesis of
the dissenters that the people as a whole should not
be taxed for the benefit of a single denomination.

The Charleston cleric conducted the fight on the
established church during the first six months of 1777,
but in the summer of that year he was seized with a
"violent fever." Although in the prime of life, he succumbed to this malady within a few days. Gadsden
and others carried on after his death, and brought
the struggle to a successful conclusion in 1778, with
the adoption of a constitution which placed all Protestant sects in a position of equality before the law.

With the promulgation of this South Carolina constitution, the agitation for disestablishment came to
an end in the Southern states, with the exception of
Virginia. There the most spectacular contest of all
was as yet undecided. The Presbyterians and Baptists
had opened the onslaught upon the embattled Anglicans before the Revolution, and the latter had re-
torted with brutally repressive measures. More than
thirty Baptist ministers had been thrown into jail between 1768 and 1770. Such tactics had had the effect
of augmenting the resentment of the dissenters and

goading them to still greater heights of desperation. They had found an able and influential champion in Patrick Henry, who had assailed the establishment in the "Parson's Cause," and who subsequently had given his legal services without charge to a number of persecuted Baptist ministers.

After the outbreak of the Revolution, the Episcopal church suffered in prestige from its long association with England and from the fact that some of its ministry and membership were Loyalist in their sympathies. It likewise was under attack for the convivial habits of its parsons, a goodly number of whom are reputed to have been gluttons and winebibbers. Fondness for the bottle was not, however, a peculiarity of clerics of the Anglican persuasion. The dour-faced Congregationalists of New England found nothing in the rigorous Puritan creed to inhibit their offering up frequent libations of rum and usquebaugh to the deity. One of their number complained during the eighteenth century that he personally knew forty ministers who were "intemperate" and another announced that he had compiled a list of "123 intemperate deacons in Massachusetts, 43 of whom became sots."

The cause of religious liberty in Virginia received a great impetus in 1776, with the adoption of the Bill of Rights. The clause relative to freedom of conscience, as originally drawn by George Mason, provided for "toleration" only. James Madison, then a youth of twenty-five, was almost the only member of the convention who realized the importance of going still further and declaring for religious freedom. He offered a substitute which provided that "no class of men ought on account of religion to be invested with peculiar emoluments or privileges, nor subjected to any penalties or disabilities, unless under color of religion the preservation of equal liberty and the existence of the state be manifestly endangered." If this had been approved by the delegates, subsequent enactment of the Statute for Religious Freedom would have been almost superfluous. The convention contented itself, however, with a declaration that all men are entitled to the free exercise of religion "according to the dictates of conscience," an extremely valuable pronouncement, but less revolutionary in its implications than that suggested by Madison.

Later in the same year Jefferson appeared in the legislature with his now famous statute in his pocket. Its introduction was the signal for increased activity on the part of the established church, looking toward the maintenance of its privileges and emoluments. And, indeed, the Episcopalians were successful for some years in frustrating the plans of Jefferson, Madison, and the dissenters. This despite the fact that the Methodists had now joined with the Presbyterians and the Baptists in the clamor for disestablishment. The Wesleyans had not broken with the Anglicans until after the Revolution, too late for them to take a conspicuous part in the battle for religious freedom in any Southern state except Virginia. But in the Old Dominion during the post-revolutionary years they added their voices to the rising chorus of dissent, and played an important part in determining the outcome of the struggle.

One of the last maneuvers of the reactionaries was

the introduction in 1784 by Patrick Henry, who by
that time had been metamorphosed from a flaming
radical into a hidebound conservative, of a bill providing for a general assessment by the civil authority
for the support of various religious denominations.
Under the terms of this measure, each citizen was to
allot his tax to the Christian church of his choice, but
there were to be no exemptions. Thus persons of Jewish faith or of no faith were to be compelled to contribute to the support of an ecclesiastical establishment whose tenets they did not profess. Washington
and Marshall joined Henry in support of this legislation, while Jefferson and Madison, who were desirous
of according "an equal liberty to all varieties of belief
and unbelief," took charge of the opposition. Madison
was greatly incensed with the Presbyterians, who
joined the Episcopalians in advocating the bill. He
commented acrimoniously that the Presbyterians
"seem as ready to set up an establishment which is
to take them in as they were to pull down that which
shut them out," and added: "I do not know of a more
shameful contrast than might be found in their memorials on the latter and former occasions."

Jefferson sailed for France in 1784 on a diplomatic
mission of five years' duration, and the leadership of
the liberal element in the legislature passed into the
hands of Madison. When Patrick Henry's bill came
to a vote in the assembly of 1785, public sentiment
had been shown to be distinctly hostile, and it was
defeated. Madison thereupon seized the opportunity to
press for the passage of the Statute for Religious Freedom. The powerful forces massed in opposition had

3

gradually been worn down during the preceding decade, and the long-awaited moment had arrived. Gathering all their energies for one final stroke, the proponents of Jefferson's statute put it through both houses at the session of 1786. In enacting this, the "first detailed law in all human ordinances giving perfect freedom of conscience," the Virginia legislature not only provided a legal sanction for the exercise of complete spiritual and intellectual liberty, but it declared further that the enjoyment of such liberty was a natural right which ought not to be disturbed by any subsequent assembly. With the passage of this statute, the last stronghold of the Episcopal church in the Southern states capitulated. Some years later that denomination's humiliation was made still more complete with the enactment of legislation depriving it of its endowments and glebe lands.

Owing to the sharpness with which the issue had been drawn in Virginia, the bitterness and duration of the contest, and the prominence of the leaders on both sides, the final victory for liberalism had a tremendous effect throughout the country. When the Federal Constitutional Convention met a few years later, religious establishments had been done away with everywhere in the South and in various middle states as well. This fact, coupled with the decisive triumph of the dissenters in the Old Dominion shortly before, had a potent influence upon the decision of the delegates to write religious freedom into the organic law of the nation. The constitutional provision relative to the free exercise of religion did not, however, prevent the enactment of restrictive legislation by several of the states.

But despite the victories for liberty of conscience in the Federal convention and in numerous individual states, the Congregational church managed to maintain its privileged position in most of New England until well into the nineteenth century. New Hampshire finally broke its grip in 1817, and Connecticut followed suit in 1818. Massachusetts, last among the original thirteen states to abandon the levying of a general tax for the support of a single denomination, did not completely disestablish Congregationalism until 1833.

While Episcopalians and dissenters were struggling for supremacy in Virginia, the Carolinas, and Georgia during and after the Revolution, restless pioneers were pushing on into the Western back country. This movement was led during the latter part of the eighteenth century by the Scotch-Irish Presbyterians, who seemed destined to achieve a position of ascendancy on the frontier. This was a period of great "spiritual deadness" in all the churches, and the frontier Presbyterians led in bringing about the "Second Awakening." James McGready, who had removed from North Carolina to Kentucky in 1796, established a reputation as a revivalist in Logan County, and in the summer of 1800 he held the first camp meeting in this or any other country. From Logan County as a focal point the movement spread throughout the South and Southwest, and in a short time the "Second Awakening" was under way. This revival of evangelical religion took hold of the Presbyterians, the Methodists, and the Baptists, and was characterized by the most grotesque emotional excesses. Vast audiences listening under the trees to renowned exhorters were suddenly seized with the "jerks," would bark and sway from side to side, leap hither and yon, or fall prostrate on the ground and remain motionless for hours, sobbing and moaning.

This religious orgy was at its height during the first decade of the nineteenth century, and it was during that period that the Presbyterians lost their position of preëminence in the West. Failure to adapt themselves to frontier conditions cost them many thousands of adherents, and undermined their influence in the region. The Calvinist creed was harsh enough at best, but the Presbyterian authorities made it doubly onerous to persons with Arminian inclinations by undue severity in its enforcement. Exacting educational requirements for those who desired to enter the Presbyterian ministry likewise made scant appeal to the comparatively crude type of citizenry living on what was then the fringe of American civilization. This situation led to dissensions within the ranks of Presbyterianism. Meanwhile, rival denominations were careful to pitch their theology and their religious polity on levels suited to conditions prevailing on the frontier.

The first serious split in the Presbyterian ranks came in 1803, when a group of members in Kentucky and Tennessee joined in a revolt against ecclesiastical and creedal authority. Almost simultaneously the Rev. James O'Kelley led a similar movement among the Methodists of North Carolina and Virginia. These two seceding groups united with a third, composed of New England Baptists, and formed the Christian church, in which the Bible was made the "only rule of faith and practice" and every individual interpreted the Bible for himself.

Another schism which exemplified what a distinguished church historian has termed "frontier liberalism contending against the narrow control of the older settled regions," resulted in the organization of the Cumberland Presbyterian church. The initial break came in 1810, with the formation of the Cumberland presbytery, following disagreements with the Presbyterian authorities over doctrinal matters, the licensure of uneducated laymen, and emotionalistic methods of revivalism. The dignified Presbyterian clergy from the East had come to look upon camp meetings with a fishy eye, although one of their number had inaugurated these gatherings not many years before. The Cumberland presbytery was situated on the remote frontier, where revivalistic technique was widely employed. For this and other reasons the presbytery separated definitely from the parent denomination in 1813, and became the Cumberland Presbyterian church.

The organization of the Disciples of Christ by Thomas and Alexander Campbell was another significant movement of the period. Like the Christians, the Disciples rejected formal creeds and harked back to the Bible as the standard of faith and morals, and like them again, they drew many of their adherents from Kentucky and Tennessee, rather than from the seaboard. Although Alexander Campbell was a literalist in some respects, he declared that the Old Testament had no binding force, except such portions of it as were reënacted in the New Testament. This, in the early nineteenth century, was decidedly unorthodox doctrine.

As the century advanced, dominance on the frontier passed steadily into the hands of the Methodists, the Baptists, and the Disciples. Strongest of all were the Methodists, whose emotionalistic appeal and hell-fire theology was admirably adapted to the back-woods. Under the leadership of the indomitable Francis Asbury, who gave the last forty-four years of his life to the cause, this denomination throve mightily. Although weakened to some extent in 1830, when a group calling itself the Methodist Protestant church seceded in protest against the refusal of the Methodists to grant laymen a voice in their legislative councils, its progress was rapid.

The growth of the Baptists was likewise rapid, and in later years they were to become much more numerous in the Southern states than the Methodists. Even at this early date, these two denominations were numerically superior to the Episcopalians and Presbyterians, and their stern moral standards were markedly influential in modifying the tone of Southern society. It was partly due to the rise of these evangelical churches that the gay, rollicking, carefree life of the eighteenth century gave way in the nineteenth to more rigorous, pietistic, and Sabbatarian social usages. It is a strange fact, however, that despite the similarities between the Baptists and the Methodists, cordiality between them was sadly lacking at times. Dr. John D. Wade has called attention to the decidedly strained relations between these denominational groups in

THE FIGHT FOR RELIGIOUS FREEDOM

Georgia in the 1820's: "A Methodist called upon to testify in court as to his neighbor's character, said that he knew of no fault in the man, further than that he was a Baptist. . . . A Baptist matriarch whose son actually . . . married a Methodist, found herself for once speechless. Drawing her chair up before a low fire, she sat down and . . . remained there through the long night in abysmal silence, dumb before an affliction too stupendous for her conceiving."

This was the period when Sunday schools and foreign missions were coming more and more to occupy the attention of the churches. In the Southwest the Primitive Baptists opposed these innovations. They also objected to the establishment of theological seminaries. Their stand on these issues was predicated upon the thesis that God did not regard such activities as necessary to convince men of sin or to show them the way of salvation. While there were individuals with similar views in other Southern churches, no denomination of consequence, except the "Hardshell" Baptists, went to such lengths as this. The Archbishop of Canterbury and the Bishop of Rochester had denounced the Sunday schools upon their emergence in England some decades before, and now there were clerics and churchmen on this side of the Atlantic to echo their sentiments. Similar opposition arose here and there to foreign missions and theological seminaries. In general, however, the American churches, North and South, were interesting themselves actively in the promotion of Sabbath schools, missions, and seminaries during the first half of the nineteenth century.

Another noteworthy development of these years was the launching of the Jewish Reform movement in Charleston, the first movement of the kind in this country. It was led by Isaac Harby, prominent journalist and playwright, who was instrumental in 1824 in persuading a large percentage of the members of Congregation Beth Elohim at Charleston to petition the trustees to shorten the service and to introduce the English language. When the request was refused, they withdrew and organized the Reform Society of Israelites. With this as a beginning, the Reform movement spread to all parts of the United States, and affected American Judaism profoundly. Distinctly liberal in tone, it represented not only a reaction against "the external accessories of worship, the fixed formalism of litany and liturgy," but it also dealt a fatal blow to the exercise of rabbinical authority in civil matters and thus was an important forward step in the age-long battle for the separation of church and state.

CHAPTER III

EARLY EDUCATIONAL ADVANCES

WHEN George Washington entered upon his duties as first president of the United States there was no system of secondary or higher education anywhere in this country remotely resembling those which we now enjoy. Such secondary institutions as were then in operation were largely subject to ecclesiastical control, and a similar situation obtained in the field of the higher learning. Even in Massachusetts, with its celebrated system of schools and its widely-touted Harvard College, the entire educational process was closely bound up with the Puritan theocracy. Benjamin Franklin had established the College of Philadelphia on genuinely liberal principles in 1755, but one looks in vain for any other similar manifestation of enlightenment in colonial America.

The South was educationally the most backward section of the Union, as far as the masses of the population were concerned, when the republic was born. If the system of public schools then functioning in New England was far from adequate, judged by twentieth-century standards, this was doubly true of Virginia, the Carolinas, and Georgia. As for institutions of higher education, William and Mary in Virginia was the only college established in any of these four colonies until just prior to the Revolution, and, like every other college in pre-revolutionary America, with the single exception of Franklin's school at Philadelphia, it had been founded for the primary purpose of training clergymen.

But the fact that the masses in the South were not provided with adequate educational opportunities at this period should under no circumstances be interpreted as indicating that there was a dearth of educated leaders in the four Southern states during and immediately following the Revolution. Very much to the contrary, the upper classes enjoyed educational facilities of the highest excellence. The private academies in which they received their early training were among the most thorough in the world, and Southerners who did not care to enter William and Mary or one of the Northern institutions upon the completion of their preliminary studies, were frequently matriculated in the universities of Great Britain or the Continent. The planters of South Carolina were especially strong in their predilection for European modes of education. Of the more than one hundred Americans who were admitted to the Inns of Court in London between 1759 and 1786, almost fifty per cent were South Carolinians.

But if a small group of upper class Southerners was superbly trained, the opportunity to attend college was limited almost entirely to this exclusive circle. Interest in popular education was less lively in the South than in the North. There are various reasons for this. In the first place, the population of the North was much more compact. The people lived in towns or on small farms where communication was readier and the strata of society were less sharply differentiated. In the second place, the Puritan clergy concerned themselves to a considerable degree with the promotion of both secondary and higher education. This was in contrast to the ministers of the established church in the South, who took comparatively little interest in such matters. It was not until the Rev. James Blair arrived in Virginia in 1685, that an Anglican cleric of broad educational vision appeared below the Potomac. Blair took a prominent part in the founding of the College of William and Mary and served as its first president. Unfortunately for the South, few of the clerics of the Episcopal persuasion exhibited a desire to emulate him. A third factor in the South's failure to concern itself actively with popular education is to be found in the individualistic ideas of a large percentage of its population.

With the rise of the Presbyterians to strength and influence shortly before the Revolution, however, the cause of Southern education received a decided impetus. They founded Queen's College at Charlotte, North Carolina, which was second only to William and Mary in the colonial South, and they are said to have been instrumental in inserting in the North Carolina constitution the clause providing for a state university. In Virginia the Presbyterians established Hampden-Sidney College in 1776, and in the same year opened Liberty Hall Academy, which subsequently became Washington College and later still, Washington and Lee University. Standing, as they

44 LIBERALISM IN THE SOUTH

did, for a highly trained ministry and for the democratization of the educational process, the Presbyterians were the greatest single force for educational progress in the Southern states during the late eighteenth and early nineteenth centuries. It must be said, on the other hand, that their contribution would have been of still greater value if the denominational leaders had been less narrow in their educational concepts and less insistent upon the maintenance of rigorous doctrinal standards in the institutions under their control.

The individual who exercised the profoundest influence on behalf of a more liberal and democratic system of both secondary and higher education in the South is Thomas Jefferson. His plan for universal free education in Virginia, embodied in the bill which he introduced in the state legislature in 1779, was in advance of anything known in this country at the time. Almost simultaneously he turned his attention to his alma mater, William and Mary. As a trustee of the institution, he virtually made over the curriculum, emphasizing scientific and social studies, then almost universally neglected, and arranged to allow the students a larger degree of freedom in choosing their subjects. The reforms he instituted at William and Mary while Continentals and Redcoats were still struggling for supremacy were in many ways similar to those he was to make effective on a larger scale some forty years later with the establishment of the University of Virginia.

George Washington demonstrated, too, that he was a statesman in the field of education as well as in that of public affairs, by his advocacy of a great national university, with standards unsurpassed in Europe or elsewhere, which would bring together young men from all parts of the country, and thus help to allay sectional prejudice. He desired Congress to support the institution with funds from the national treasury, and included in his will a bequest for its endowment, in the event that it should at any time be established. Such a plan, however, was inimical to the policies of the Jeffersonians, with their emphasis upon state rights, and it was also incompatible with the ambitions of certain colleges already in operation. It accordingly failed of adoption.

The booming of the guns at Yorktown had hardly died away before forces were set in motion in Georgia, North Carolina, and Virginia looking toward the establishment of state universities. The educational renaissance in the first of these commonwealths was promoted in large measure by two natives of Connecticut. One of them was Dr. Lyman Hall, who was elected governor of Georgia in 1783, and who recommended in his opening message to the legislature that "seminaries of learning" be endowed and that sufficient tracts of land be set aside for their support. The other was Abraham Baldwin, author of the charter adopted by the assembly in 1785 for Franklin College, afterwards the University of Georgia, the second state college chartered in America, the University of Pennsylvania, incorporated in 1779, being the first. Baldwin, who deserves his title, "father of the University of Georgia," was elected the first president of the institution, and subsequently served as chairman of the board of trustees until his death. The charter he drafted for Franklin College indicates that he was a man of broad educational statesmanship. It forbade the trustees to "exclude any person, of any religious denomination whatsoever, from free and equal liberty and advantages of education, or from any of the liberties, privileges and immunities of the university in his education, on account of his or their speculative sentiments in religion, or being of a different religious profession." The clumsiness of the language here quoted should not blind us to the significance of the liberal sentiments it expresses.

The college enjoyed marked expansion during this early era under the presidency of Dr. Moses Waddel, whose régime began in 1819 and lasted for a decade. Dr. Waddel, a Presbyterian minister, had for the preceding fifteen years conducted one of the most famous of the private academies in the ante-bellum South. This school, situated at Willington, South Carolina, numbered among its alumni John C. Calhoun, William H. Crawford, Hugh Swinton Legaré, George McDuffie, James L. Petigru, and A. B. Longstreet. Calhoun called Dr. Waddel "the father of classical education in the upper country of South Carolina and Georgia." After bringing to Franklin College what Longstreet described as "a measure of prosperity altogether unequalled in its previous history," he resigned in 1829 and reopened his academy at Willington.

Georgia's example in granting a charter to its state college was followed shortly afterward by North Carolina, which chartered the University of North Carolina in 1789. Owing to the fact that Georgia did not provide sufficient funds until after the adoption of its constitution in 1798 to enable Franklin College to open its doors, the University of North Carolina, which opened in 1795, was the first state university in the South and the second in the country to begin actual operations. It was antedated by the University of Pennsylvania, but by no other state institution of higher learning. The University of Pennsylvania remained a state institution for only a few years, however.

William Richardson Davie, a native Englishman who fought in the Continental army and then settled in North Carolina, was mainly instrumental in establishing the university at Chapel Hill. Davie was a Bourbon in politics who distrusted democracy and adhered to Hamiltonian concepts of government, but he exhibited liberalism in the field of higher education. He chose the site for the new university, took the leading part in raising the endowment, and, even more important, furnished the institution with a broad and elastic scheme of instruction which comprised literary and social subjects as well as the familiar Latin, Greek, and mathematics. The Rev. David Caldwell, a Presbyterian cleric who conducted a celebrated classical school in Guilford County, North Carolina, for three decades, beginning some ten years before the Revolution, declined an offer of the first presidency of the university because of his advanced age. The trustees subsequently chose the Rev. Joseph Caldwell, another Presbyterian, who, like most of the other ecclesiastics of that faith during the period under examination, was a graduate of Princeton. After serving for some years as chairman of the faculty he was elected president in 1804, which post he held until his death in 1835, with the exception of a brief interregnum of four years when he relinquished the office to devote additional time to study. Dr. Caldwell's régime at Chapel Hill was productive of much good to the cause of both secondary and higher education in the state. He built the first astronomical observatory in the United States at the university and promoted the growth of the institution in many ways. He was also a staunch advocate of more comprehensive methods of educating the masses through the medium of public schools.

Strangely enough, the movement for a state university in Virginia first approached fruition on the frontier, in what is now Kentucky. Transylvania Seminary at Lexington, Kentucky, was endowed by the Virginia assembly as early as 1780, largely through the efforts of the Rev. John Todd, a Presbyterian divine, and his nephew, Colonel John Todd, a member of the legislature. It was not until Kentucky had been admitted to the Union as a separate state, however, that Transylvania University was established by legislative act. Its charter provided that the university was to be the capstone of a state educational system which was to include preparatory academies in every Kentucky county. For this grandly comprehensive program, Kentucky is chiefly indebted to Judge Caleb Wallace, of the state supreme court. The plan was launched auspiciously at the turn of the century, but it was apparently doomed to failure from the first, owing to the fact that it was too closely bound up with the Presbyterian church. The Presbyterians had been far more active in promoting the cause of education in Kentucky than the members of any other denomination, and Transylvania University, whose board of trustees was largely Presbyterian, had been opened under their auspices. But this partial union of church and state proved to be an insurmountable handicap to the proper development of the scheme, and led to the state's withdrawal of much of its financial support.

Transylvania University remained at first in comparative obscurity, but its position in the educational life of the West became gradually more and more commanding until 1818, when, with the election of the Rev. Horace Holley, a Unitarian clergyman, as President, it assumed a place of undisputed leadership beyond the Alleghanies. Under Holley, Transylvania developed into a great institution of higher learning which rivaled Harvard and Yale in curriculum and enrollment. But the Presbyterians, who had done so much to found it, now discovered to their horror that its president actually denied the "real personality of the devil" and professed himself as skeptical as to the authenticity of the Biblical account of the creation. They accordingly made it so unpleasant for him that he resigned in 1826. Within a short time the university lost much of its prestige. In 1856 it became a state normal school and immediately following the Civil War it disappeared from view upon being merged with the University of Kentucky. Subsequently it resumed its original name. The unfortunate experience of Transylvania illustrates excellently the strength

4

as well as the weakness of the Presbyterian church in its relationship to the development of education in the South. It exemplifies the splendid educational pioneering of that church, but at the same time it shows how narrow the Presbyterian conception of higher learning often was, and how Presbyterian-controlled educators frequently found themselves hedged about with theological tabus.

It is a rather anomalous circumstance that South Carolina, which sent more students to European universities than any other colony during the late eighteenth century, should have been last among the four original Southern states to take definite steps looking toward the foundation of a college supported from its own state treasury. South Carolina College was established in 1801 at Columbia, thanks to the efforts of three members of the lowland aristocracy. The first of this triumvirate was Governor John Drayton, whose appeal to the legislature led to the passage of the bill incorporating the institution. The others were Henry William DeSaussure and Paul Hamilton, who did much to place the college on a sound operating basis and to secure the support of the various sections of the commonwealth for the venture. The Rev. Jonathan Maxcy of Massachusetts was elected the first president when the institution opened its doors in 1805, and he served until his death in 1820. Dr. Maxcy guided the affairs of the college with such ability, energy and foresight that the entire state was his debtor when his administration came to a close. He is one of a number of New Englanders who have rendered valuable service to the cause of Southern education.

Maxcy was succeeded as head of the college by Thomas Cooper, a native of England, who Jefferson said was "acknowledged by every enlightened man who knows him, to be the greatest man in America, in the powers of mind and in acquired information." As we have seen, many college presidents of that era were clergymen. Cooper, on the other hand, not only was no clergyman; he distrusted ecclesiastics, and his views concerning the Bible were such as to lay him open to grave suspicion on the part of the orthodox. It was inevitable that a man of his independence and bellicosity should have locked horns with the Presbyterians early in his administration as president of South Carolina College. Before he had been in office two years the members of that church were holding meetings throughout the state and demanding his expulsion. He, in turn, was hysterically abusive of his clerical critics. Governor John L. Wilson and divers powerful politicians came to his rescue, and this storm blew over, but there were numerous others. Finally his foes assailed him with such power and ferocity that he found it necessary to resign in 1833.

Despite the scurrility of some of Cooper's controversial utterances, his influence as president of the college was exercised on behalf of a better-articulated educational system. In one of his last reports he called attention to the serious "want of a better and more diffused education" among the population of South Carolina. Cooper's biographer, Dr. Dumas Malone, declares that he was not only "a pioneer in Southern education" but that he is entitled to "a conspicuous place in the history of intellectual liberty in America." As

president of the college at Columbia he "broadened
and enriched the curriculum," "lectured with un-
rivaled brilliance," "played a direct part in the promotion of professional training" and "probably did
more to stimulate the intellectual life of the community
than any other man of his day." Cooper's views on
slavery and the vast influence he wielded as a political
thinker will be examined in another chapter.

At about the time that this versatile Briton joined
the faculty of the college at Columbia, his friend
Thomas Jefferson, in retirement at Monticello, was
bringing to a successful culmination his long-cherished
dream of a state university at Charlottesville. Nearly
forty years before as we have seen, the Virginia assembly had taken steps looking toward the founding of
Transylvania Seminary in what was shortly to become
Kentucky. Then in 1786 the Chevalier Quesnay de
Beaurepaire, a Frenchman, had laid plans for an
Academy of the Arts and Sciences at Richmond, a
conception which Dr. C. F. Thwing has termed "the
most brilliant and daring project of the higher education ever put forth by a foreigner, or possibly a
native, in the new world." A total of 60,000 francs
were subscribed by Virginians and others, "the first
contributors to university education in the South,"
but the onrush of the French Revolution prevented
the consummation of the scheme.

French influences were again to the fore in the plan
for a university which Jefferson was actively engaged
in promoting during the second decade of the nineteenth century. With the invaluable aid of Joseph C.
Cabell, a member of the legislature who worked in-

defatigably on the project at the risk of serious impairment to his health, the venerable master of Monticello was successful in obtaining a charter for the University of Virginia in 1819. Six years later his life work was happily crowned with the university's opening. He had devoted his declining years to its establishment, and had provided it with one of the ablest faculties ever assembled in this country, a broad and comprehensive curriculum which permitted students a wide choice of subjects, genuine standards of scholarship, and the most beautiful campus in America. Whether or not one agrees with Herbert Baxter Adams of Massachusetts in his dictum that the university was "the noblest work of Jefferson's life," it is impossible to dispute the virtually unanimous opinion of scholars that from the time of its opening in 1825 until the end of the century, this institution exerted a more potent and more salutary influence upon the development of higher education in the South than any other college or university below Mason and Dixon's Line. Its high standards were an unfailing stimulus to other institutions, while its division of the curriculum into distinct "schools" and its inauguration of the elective system were widely imitated.

During the initial session of the University of Virginia, the cause of higher learning in the Southwest received a powerful impetus through the acceptance by the Rev. Phillip Lindsley of the presidency of Cumberland College, Nashville. Dr. Lindsley, a Presbyterian minister, already had declined the presidency of Princeton University and other large institutions, but his desire to build up a university in Tennessee which would rank with the best led him to assume charge of the Nashville college. He soon changed its name to the University of Nashville and formulated splendid plans for its development. A man of broad vision and liberal outlook, he "did not see why colleges should be denominational any more than penitentiaries or banks." But although Dr. Lindsley remained as head of the university for a quarter of a century, and administered its affairs with conspicuous ability, lack of adequate finances handicapped him fatally in the execution of his program. Few will deny, however, that during his sojourn in Tennessee he exerted a profound influence for sounder scholastic standards in the Southwest.

The whole future of education in the South and Southwest, as well as in the North and East, had been materially affected shortly before Lindsley went to Nashville by John Marshall's decision in the Dartmouth College Case. Ruling, as was his wont, contrary to the wishes of the Jeffersonians, Marshall held that the charter granted by the British crown to Dartmouth College was a contract, and that the New Hampshire legislature could not legally impair that contract by converting the college into a state institution. In the long perspective of time it is apparent that Marshall's decision was highly beneficial to the cause of education in America. State institutions ultimately were founded in sufficient numbers, despite his adverse ruling, and at the same time his action in securing private institutions against political interference not only enabled existing colleges and universities to obtain substantial increases in their endowments, but also resulted in the establishment of many new ones, both sectarian and non-sectarian.

Such are some of the more significant developments in the field of higher education below the Potomac from the Revolution down to 1830. While this was an era in which vigorous and widespread sentiment on behalf of tax-supported public schools wholly free from clerical control had not been aroused in any large portion of the republic, and while this was especially true of the South, certain individuals and certain trends in that section are none the less worthy of scrutiny.

Prior to the War for American Independence the educational scene in the Southern states bore the stigmata of long years of domination by the Anglican communion. In other sections Puritans, Calvinists, Lutherans, Quakers, or Dutch Reformers were influential in arousing a fairly general interest in free schools, although these schools were nowhere of the type which prevail universally at present. But in the sub-Potomac region the failure of the Episcopalians to concern themselves with such matters had a repressive effect and hindered the development of secondary education. There were a few so-called "free schools" in each of the Southern colonies, but almost all of them were privately endowed or operated as charitable institutions. The charitable aspect of the movement was particularly unfortunate, for Southern pride rebelled at the idea of accepting anything which resembled a gratuity, whether from an individual or an institution. It was to be many decades before this prejudice against state-supported schools could be completely eradicated.

The statement already has been made that the coming of the Scotch-Irish to the South in substantial numbers resulted in a quickening of interest in both secondary and higher education. Establishment of schools on the frontier by the Presbyterian dominies helped to offset the indifference of the Anglicans and was a potent factor in rousing the denizens of the up country to the need for adequate educational facilities. Diffusion of education among the underprivileged was further promoted at the end of the eighteenth century by the advent of the Sunday schools from England. The curricula of these schools were much more comprehensive in scope at that time than they later became. Students in the early Sunday schools were given elementary instruction in secular subjects, as well as in matters pertaining to Holy Writ. Still a third factor in the democratization of educational ideas in the South at this period was the establishment in the West, notably Kentucky, of Pestalozzian schools, operated upon principles laid down by the famous Swiss pedagogue, Pestalozzi.

As heretofore indicated, the caste system operated in the slave states to hamper the growth of popular education. The planters, as a group, were not receptive to arguments in favor of free schools. This is not to say, however, that their attitude was invariably one of active hostility, for perhaps a majority of them should be described as indifferent rather than hostile. So eminent an historian as Dr. Philip Alexander Bruce has stated that "there is no record of a single public man of high standing in the South under the old system who planted himself in open hostility to the different measures which, from decade to decade, were adopted by Southern legislatures for the instruction of the bulk of the white population at the public expense." It is also true that not a few members of the aristocracy took a lively interest in popular education and exerted their influence in its behalf.

Jefferson's famous "Bill for a More General Diffusion of Knowledge," introduced in the Virginia assembly in 1779, embodied a notably progressive scheme for a state-wide system of primary and secondary schools, sustained by general taxation and open to the public without charge for the first three years. Unlike the public schools of the present day, these institutions were to operate upon a principle of rigid selection after the primary grades had been passed. Students with exceptional capacity were to be trained without cost in the higher grades, but the others were to be required to pay a fixed fee. The ablest of those who completed this secondary course were then to be given three years at William and Mary College. It will readily be seen that this plan differs in several fundamental particulars from that under which the twentieth-century system of elementary, secondary, and higher education is operated. Not only so, but there are those who regard it as distinctly superior to the modern plan, since it provides free educational facilities for those whose mental endowments justify it, while eliminating the others after a brief period of primary instruction.

The Virginia legislature failed to act on Jefferson's bill until 1796, when it adopted the measure in modified form. Unfortunately a clause was inserted which made it optional with the court of any county as to whether that county should make the system operative within its borders. This provision of the act so vitiated its effectiveness that its passage, although significant, was of little practical value. Legislation adopted in 1818 set aside part of the revenue from the literary fund for the education of indigent children, but this was a poor substitute for the magnificently-conceived plan of 1779. Its principal result was the establishment of the "pauper" school system, which was not abandoned in the Old Dominion until after the Civil War.

But if Thomas Jefferson presented the most carefully wrought out educational program of the post-revolutionary era, there were others of the planter class in the South to follow the general outlines of his formula. Prominent among these were Willie Jones and Nathaniel Macon of North Carolina, whose platform for that state, promulgated in the 1780's, emphasized better educational facilities for the people as one of its cardinal points. While Jones and Macon were important pioneers in this field, the commonwealth owes a still greater debt to Judge Archibald D. Murphey, whose more significant work was done in the early years of the succeeding century. Judge Murphey was chairman of a committee created by the state legislature in 1816 to consider the need for public schools in North Carolina. He visited New England and Europe in his quest for data, and on his return presented a highly competent report. Unluckily the legislature did not feel financially able to put his recommendations into effect, and the setting up of a genuine system of public education in the state was accordingly delayed for several decades.

In South Carolina as early as 1795 General Francis Marion, the "Swamp Fox" of the Revolution, advocated additional state support for both free schools and higher education. No important step in the direction of equitable appropriations to free schools was taken, however, until 1811. In that year Governor Henry Middleton urged the establishment of these schools "in all those parts of the state where such institutions are wanted" in order to "diffuse the benefits of education as widely as possible." With the aid of Stephen Elliott of Charleston, the Free School Act was gotten through the assembly. While the system which this legislation created cannot be described as adequate, on the basis of present-day standards, it was nevertheless a step forward.

Governor William Carroll of Tennessee was another far-seeing educational statesman of this period. He urged the legislature in 1823 to set aside additional funds for both secondary and higher education, and some years later was successful in securing the inauguration of Tennessee's common schools.

Thus the half century which followed the War for American Independence witnessed the founding of free school systems in various Southern states, as well as the establishment of a number of important colleges and universities. True, the school systems set up during those years were merely embryonic foreshadowings of the elaborate organizations for public instruction which were to cover the South after the Civil War. It was in the realm of the higher learning that the greatest progress was achieved in the era under examination.

CHAPTER IV

OF HUMAN BONDAGE

" ABOUT the last of August came in a Dutch man
of warre that sold us twenty negars."
These fateful words, penned by John Rolfe,
husband of Pocahontas, early in 1620 concerning an
episode of the preceding year in Virginia, were of far-
reaching and catastrophic significance. Little did
Rolfe or the other colonials of the early seventeenth
century realize, however, that implicit in the coming
of these first Africans to American shores were the
seeds of internecine strife and sundering conflict between the sections. There was no prophet among them
to foretell the future, no seer to discern far down the
centuries the glint of sunlight on Confederate bayonets,
the clash of steel on steel at Sumter, Chickamauga and
Gettysburg.

Once the importation of Negroes was begun, there
was no stopping it. The number increased only gradually at first, but by the end of the century the slave
trade had become well organized, and the dark tide
was pouring into the colonies in a steady stream.
While the agricultural economy prevalent in the South
created a much more insistent demand for Negroes in
that section than in the North, blacks were imported
everywhere. New England mercantile interests soon

managed to obtain a position of supremacy in the trade, so that although Georgia and South Carolina imported far more Africans than Massachusetts or Rhode Island, many of the slaves unloaded at Savannah and Charleston came in vessels flying the flag of New England shipowners. And if the flower of the Southern aristocracy purchased these unfortunate creatures for work on the tobacco plantations and in the cotton fields, the flower of the New England aristocracy was financially interested in the process whereby they were captured with barbarous brutality in Guinean jungles and transported like wild beasts in loathsome, foul, and verminous dens to the coasts of America, there to be sold into bondage. In New England many leading churchmen invested in slave ships, and numbers of the most influential Congregational ministers, including Jonathan Edwards and President Ezra Stiles of Yale, were slaveowners. In the South, where the Anglican communion claimed a majority of the large planters, the easy-going parsons of that denomination were well content to leave consideration of disturbing social questions to others.

Such was the situation in colonial America during the first century and a half after the settlement of Jamestown. But with the rise of liberal thought during the decades immediately preceding the Revolution, grave questions as to the moral propriety of chattel slavery began to trouble the minds of humanitarians. Christopher Gadsden of South Carolina exemplified this trend when he declared in 1766 that slavery was a crime. There were others of like mind at the period, although they often remained inarticulate in the face of what seemed to be an overwhelming adverse sentiment.

Shortly before the outbreak of the war with Great Britain, however, leading colonials were vigorous in their denunciation of the slave trade. Several of the colonies sought to prohibit or restrict the ghastly traffic, but they always found themselves thwarted by the British crown. Thomas Jefferson drafted a blistering paragraph for the Declaration of Independence, in which he condemned George III in unsparing fashion for his protection of the slave traders, many of whom were Englishmen, but the paragraph was stricken out as a concession to South Carolina and Georgia on the one hand and to New England on the other.

With the commencement of the Revolution there arose in a number of the colonies a rather general feeling of revulsion against the slave trade, and against the institution of slavery as well. The opinion became more or less widespread that a people who were proclaiming the doctrines of equality and human brotherhood could not consistently hold another race in bondage. With the exception of Bernard Romans, a native of Holland who came to America in 1755, scarcely a writer during the revolutionary era defended slavery in uncompromising fashion. At the same time, leading statesmen pronounced the institution a curse and sought to devise means of getting rid of it.

Foremost among the anti-slavery spokesmen was Jefferson. His excoriation of King George's position on the slave traffic was deleted from the Declaration, but shortly thereafter he introduced in the Virginia assembly a bill for the gradual abolition of slavery in that state. While he was unsuccessful in accomplishing this design, it was due in no small measure to his influence that the Old Dominion prohibited the slave trade in 1778. North Carolina followed suit in 1787 with the imposition of a prohibitive duty upon further importations, and almost simultaneously South Carolina enacted the first of a series of temporary laws which put an end to the traffic for the next sixteen years. In 1798 Georgia abolished the trade, but South Carolina reopened it five years later. Not until the prohibition in the Federal constitution became effective in 1808 was there a permanent stoppage in the legal flow of Negroes into the Palmetto State.

But Jefferson's statesmanship with regard to slavery was even more strikingly exemplified in connection with his proposed ordinance of 1784. Under the terms of this document, as drafted by him, slavery was to be excluded after 1800 from the entire region from which the states of Kentucky, Tennessee, Alabama, and Mississippi were subsequently carved, as well as from the Northwest Territory. The portion of the ordinance which had to do with slavery failed of adoption by a single vote. "Thus we see the fate of millions unborn hanging on the tongue of one man," Jefferson wrote, "and Heaven was silent in that awful moment." Under the subsequent Ordinance of 1787, slavery was banished from the Northwest Territory, but "this abominable crime," as Jefferson termed it, was permitted to fasten itself on the entire region south of the Ohio and east of the Mississippi. Few more dreadful calamities have occured in the history of America than the defeat of the anti-slavery clause contained in the Ordinance of 1784. Its adoption and strict enforcement would have reduced the slave territory to such an extent that the institution probably would have died out within a comparatively short time in those states where it still existed. There would almost certainly have been no Civil War.

But the states were not only unwilling to prohibit slavery from entering the territory covered by the Ordinance of 1784; they were also unwilling to abolish the foreign slave trade immediately. Thanks to a bargain between Massachusetts, Connecticut, and New Hampshire on the north and Georgia and South Carolina on the south, the Federal constitutional convention of 1787 legalized the traffic for twenty years more, or until 1808. Congress was empowered to prohibit it after that date. In the Congressional debates of 1806-07, pursuant to the enactment of legislation putting an end to the trade on and after January 1, 1808, Congressmen G. M. Bedinger of Kentucky, John Morrow of Virginia, and Marmaduke Williams of North Carolina were notably liberal in their attitude.

We have seen that the master of Monticello was the most conspicuous of the foes of slavery during the post-revolutionary era. It need hardly be said that other men of influence and standing came forward in the late eighteenth century to promulgate sentiments similar to his. At the same time several of the principal religious denominations went on record as vigorously opposing the institution. At this period, when so large a percentage of the Southern slaveholders were Epis-

5

66 LIBERALISM IN THE SOUTH

copalians, the Methodists, Baptists, and Presbyterians
had little hesitancy in taking a liberal stand. Later,
when their own membership came to include many
slaveholders, they conveniently forgot their early pro-
testations and became ardent apologists for the slave
system. The Quakers, on the other hand, maintained
a consistent position throughout. They were among
the first to express opposition to African slavery, and
they continued to do so until it was abolished. In addition, thousands of Quakers left the South rather
than live in a region where human beings were held
in subjection by a more powerful race.

Reference has been made to the fact that various
prominent Southerners were loud in their denunciations of slavery during the years which followed the
War for American Independence. Among them was
Henry Laurens of South Carolina, a man of exalted
character who was genuinely desirous of emancipating
his hundreds of Negroes, but who found that his environment made such a step virtually impossible. He
nevertheless joined with Christopher Gadsden in proclaiming his abhorrence of the institution. At a somewhat later date, Charles Pinckney and Edward Rutledge bitterly opposed the proposal to reopen the
African slave trade in South Carolina.

In Georgia and North Carolina, on the other hand,
few voices were raised in criticism of the enslavement
of the blacks. Georgia was still a frontier state, and its
small white population apparently was strongly convinced that chattels were a necessary component of
the agricultural scene in the far South. North Carolina,
which in the nineteenth century was to be the pro-

genitrix of not a few liberals on the slave question, was at this time under the sway of Willie Jones and Nathaniel Macon. Jones and Macon, as heretofore noted, were democrats in politics and progressives in education. On the slavery issue, however, they were reactionary. Macon, it is true, considered the institution "a curse," but he regarded its abolition as impossible and even went to the length of defending the system as essential to Southern prosperity.

In 1785 Thomas Jefferson declared that anti-slavery men were as scarce to the south of Chesapeake Bay as they were numerous to the north of it. In his own state of Virginia anti-slavery sentiment was more vocal at the period than in any other Southern commonwealth. Richard Henry Lee, Patrick Henry, George Washington, George Mason, James Madison, and, of course, Jefferson himself, were among the Virginians who condemned the system unsparingly. Characterizing it as a colossal evil, wholly out of place in a republic founded upon the principles of liberty and equality, these men were anxious to abolish it by any practicable means. The weight of such great names thrown into the scales in opposition to the institution not only was a decisive factor in accomplishing the abolition of the slave trade in Virginia in 1778, but it also stimulated the growth of abolitionist or emancipationist sentiment throughout the republic.

In the South as a whole, however, there is reason to believe that the bulk of the people and their legislative representatives in the late eighteenth century were unconvinced that abolition, whether immediate or gradual, was either feasible or advisable. The enormous investment in slaves, together with the widely prevalent belief that slave labor was essential to the production of certain crops, were regarded by many as almost insuperable difficulties in the way of any plan to free the blacks. This is not to say, however, that popular sentiment favorable to the elimination of slavery from the Southern economy could not have been developed under more favorable conditions. As a matter of fact, the system was gradually being put on the defensive in both North and South, owing to a combination of circumstances. Already the farmers of New England and the middle states had concluded that slavery was unsuited to their needs, and forces had been set in motion leading to the gradual extinction of the institution in the region. At the same time there was a severe depression in the Southern tobacco industry, while indigo production was dying out and the cultivators of rice were in difficulties, owing to the introduction of new methods of rice culture. To make matters worse, slave prices had gone into a rapid decline. All these factors combined to create a state of mind among Southern planters which, given proper direction, might have eventuated in a comparatively brief period in the complete abolition of slavery.

But in 1793 Eli Whitney came forward with his cotton gin, and within a few years there was a decided shift in sentiment. The gin worked an almost immediate transformation in the South's agricultural system, vastly increasing the production of cotton and sending the price of slaves skyrocketing. Whereas separation of the cotton from the seed by hand had been a slow and clumsy process, the new machine solved the problem with complete adequacy, and opened up new vistas of prosperity to the discouraged planters. An idea of the tremendous change wrought by the advent of Whitney's device may be obtained from the fact that the South's cotton crop jumped from 2,000,-000 pounds in 1790 to 40,000,000 in 1800 and 160,-000,000 in 1820. Cotton became the South's absorbing interest.

Under the new dispensation, agriculturists below the Mason and Dixon Line found that the obstacles in the way of emancipation had been greatly multiplied. When crops were bad and prime field hands were quoted at $300, these men had entertained suggestions for freeing their slaves and even for abolishing the slave system, but when production mounted and the value of Negroes doubled and trebled, the problem became rather more complicated. There were still many planters who managed to preserve their humanitarian principles in the face of rising profits, and who were willing to coöperate in the formulation of plans for the elimination of slavery from the Southern scene, but the invention of the cotton gin unquestionably made the realization of any such ideal much more difficult than ever before.

Another factor discouraging to liberals was the gradual replacement of Virginia by South Carolina as the arbiter of Southern thought. During the 1820's the supremacy of the Old Dominion was becoming definitely a thing of the past, and the egalitarianism of the Jeffersonian school was giving way before the feudalistic notions of the South Carolinians. True, voices

still were raised here and there in the Palmetto State
and other parts of the deep South in opposition to
chattel servitude. In Charleston the Grimké sisters,
Sarah and Angelina, daughters of Judge John Fauch-
eraud Grimké, a wealthy and influential planter, became profoundly convinced of the iniquity of slavery.
Following the death of their father in 1819, they freed
the Negroes they had inherited, moved to Philadelphia, and became nationally prominent in the anti-
slavery movement. Governor Bennett of South Carolina showed in 1821 that he too was aware of the in-
defensible nature of the South's "peculiar institution."
In that year he delivered a fierce arraignment of the
domestic slave trade. But in 1822 the growth of such
emancipationist sentiment as had been slowly built up
in the state by Bennett and others sustained a severe
reversal with the discovery of a well organized plot
for a widespread slave revolt in and near Charleston.
Denmark Vesey, a free Negro, had spent several years
in perfecting plans for the insurrection, and it was
only through information received from a loyal body-
servant that the conspiracy was thwarted. Detection
of this deep-laid scheme led many whites in South
Carolina and elsewhere to the conclusion that the
safety of their families and firesides required the abandonment of plans for emancipation and the enactment
of stricter regulations affecting the blacks. It seemed
to them deeply significant that a free Negro had plot-
ted this insurrection.

Undismayed by these disheartening developments,
Governor Brandon of Mississippi took occasion in
1828 to criticise slavery severely in his message to the

legislature, but shortly thereafter the influential S. S. Prentiss of Natchez, while acknowledging the evils of the system, declared that it was "too deep-rooted to be eradicated." At the same period James G. Birney of Kentucky, later one of the greatest of the anti-slavery leaders, was prominently identified with abolitionist activities in Alabama, whence he had removed some years before. Not long afterward he returned to his native state. There he besought Henry Clay to launch a crusade to drive slavery beyond the confines of Kentucky, but the Great Compromiser, although recognizing the iniquitous aspects of the institution, compromised with his conscience and declined. Birney, the son of well-to-do slaveowning parents, accordingly took charge of the movement himself in the early thirties, but he encountered such implacable opposition that he soon found that the exigencies of the situation required his migration to more congenial regions beyond the Ohio.

As a general rule, however, there was greater freedom of utterance on the slave question in the states near the border than in those farther South. Benjamin Lundy, the mentor of William Lloyd Garrison, traveled about freely in the 1820's organizing anti-slavery societies. He declared that in 1827 a total of 130 such societies with 6,625 members had been formed in the country as a whole, of which 106 societies with 5,150 members were in slave territory. There were fifty of these organizations with 3,000 members in North Carolina alone, nearly half the total for the entire United States. Tennessee had twenty-five more with 1,000 members, while Virginia, with eight societies,

had a much smaller enrollment. Quakers were particularly zealous in the promotion of these societies.
In North Carolina they produced such notable agitators as Charles Osborn, Vestal Coffin, and Levi
Coffin. Osborn, who settled in Tennessee in the late
eighteenth century, was "the first man in America to
proclaim the doctrine of immediate and unconditional
emancipation." The Underground Railroad, whereby
runaway slaves were speeded on their way to freedom,
was established by Vestal Coffin near the present
Guilford College in 1819, and his cousin, Levi Coffin,
who removed from North Carolina to Indiana in
1826, is said to have served as its president for thirty
years.

But while the upper South was still more or less
receptive to anti-slavery arguments, leaders of thought
in South Carolina were gradually veering away from
the principles of liberty and equality enunciated in
the Declaration of Independence. As a substitute for
the humanitarian concepts so widely proclaimed in
the post-revolutionary era they celebrated the virtues
of the authoritarian order prevalent in ancient Greece.
One of their earliest spokesmen was George McDuffie,
who expressed the conviction in 1825 that slavery was
morally defensible. The following year President
Thomas Cooper of South Carolina College published
an article on "Coloured Marriages" which was immensely influential in setting the pattern of Southern
thought on the slave question. Cooper, a former disciple of Jefferson, publicly repudiated the Jeffersonian
philosophy and revealed himself as a thoroughgoing
believer in the equity of chattel servitude. Many of the

ideas subsequently put forward by Dew, Harper, Hammond, and other outstanding apologists for the slave system in the Southern states are traceable to Cooper. His biographer feels that "his right to be regarded as a pioneer in the philosophical defense of slavery is indubitable."

Such was the status of slavery in the South as the third decade of the nineteenth century came to a close. But before bringing this chapter to a conclusion, let us glance briefly at the slave system as it existed below the Potomac a hundred years ago.

It is unnecessary to state that the South's "peculiar institution" was intimately bound up with the general agricultural scheme in the region. In the upper tier of States—Virginia, North Carolina, Kentucky, and Tennessee—chattels were occupied mainly in the cultivation of tobacco. In South Carolina and Georgia cotton and rice were the staple crops, while cotton was supreme in Alabama and Mississippi. In the lower Mississippi Valley, on both sides of the river, great gangs of slaves toiled in the cotton fields and on the sugar plantations, while farther on to the westward in the United States territory of Arkansas and the Mexican state of Texas, cotton was the principal crop.

Hundreds of volumes have been written concerning the ante-bellum South, many of them highly partisan. On the one hand we have the richly colored narrative, frequently emanating from sources close to the Northern abolitionists, which depicts the Southern slaveholder as a fiend in human shape, flogging his Negroes unmercifully on the slightest excuse and no excuse, cutting off their ears, searing them with branding irons, keeping a seraglio of slave women, and otherwise conducting himself in a manner brutal, arrogant, and bestial. On the other hand we have the rose-tinted picture from the pen of the Southern apologist who would have us believe that Dixie was a land inhabited exclusively by handsome men and beautiful women who always lived in great pillared mansions, amid the perfume of magnolias and the songs of birds, surrounded by happy Negroes who were invariably treated with the utmost kindness and who spent their time devouring fried chicken and strumming on banjos.

Neither of these familiar formulæ is adequate, of course. While there were floggings, brandings, and similar barbarities on Southern plantations, it is preposterous that such practices should ever have been regarded as universal. Even to those who feel that the average slaveholder was not above such indecencies, it should be obvious that it was to his own advantage to treat his Negroes reasonably well. An able-bodied field hand was worth at times during the ante-bellum period as much as $2,000. Certainly the Southern planters, as a class, were not so stupid as to wish to depreciate the value of their slaves by rendering them unfit for work through cruel and inhuman treatment. True, the movements of slaves were severely restricted by statute, especially during the three decades immediately preceding the Civil War, and in some respects a Negro's status at law was no better than that of a beast. Marriages between slaves were not recognized as legally valid, except in the event of subsequent emancipation, and the white man who raped a female slave was not guilty of a crime against her. Under the law, he was merely liable for trespassing upon the property of her owner. Then, too, it was illegal to teach slaves to read and write, and a slave could not own property without his master's consent. Slaves were forbidden to travel together without a white escort or to congregate at night except in the presence of a member of the dominant race. In some states the laws were revolting in their severity, as in Mississippi, where it was provided that when a black was guilty of perjury, he should be nailed to the pillory by his ears, and that his ears should then be cut off. It must be stated, however, that a number of these stringent regulations, a large percentage of which were enacted between 1830 and 1860, were enforced only at spasmodic intervals. Immediately following a slave insurrection the authorities were apt to be unusually vigilant, but for the greater part of the time many of the repressive statutes were ignored by both races.

Hostile critics have frequently emphasized that the planter who paid his overseer in crop shares thereby offered him a strong inducement to overwork the slaves committed to his charge. In so far as the eighteenth century is concerned, this is undoubtedly a valid argument. In the nineteenth century, however, the planters saw the potentialities of such an arrangement, and substituted quite generally a system of fixed salary payments to overseers. It should also be noted that whereas there were not a few unduly severe regulations and statutes governing the movements of slaves, and a number of grossly repressive laws affecting their civil capacities, the killing or maiming of a slave by a white man was almost everywhere held to be a crime of exactly the same magnitude as the killing or maiming of a white man by a slave.

As for the feudal magnificence in which the planters of the old régime are widely supposed to have lived, it was largely mythical, except in a relatively small area. In the lower Mississippi Valley and the lowlands of South Carolina, in Tidewater Virginia and a few scattered upland regions there was, it is true, a mode of life not wholly unlike that traditionally ascribed to the entire South. But in the remainder of the vast territory below the Mason and Dixon Line evidences of baronial manor houses are almost non-existent. In each of the Southern states the overwhelming majority of the whites owned no slaves, and of those who did own them, only a small percentage had as many as twenty. It is a lamentable fact, too, that the abode of the average planter was architecturally undistinguished, while the grounds, as a consequence of the slave system, which everywhere made for indolence and inefficiency, were ordinarily in a sad state of disarray. On the other hand, there is nothing apocryphal about the far-famed "Southern hospitality." It was genuine, open-handed, and well nigh universal.

In the Old South the family was the unit about which much of the life of the section revolved. Since most planters lived in comparative isolation, often miles from the nearest habitation and usually a great distance from anything remotely resembling a city, the family circle occupied a place which it could not have occupied under different conditions. In summer the head of the household and his wife and children whiled away many a long hour together on the verandah or under the trees which almost invariably surrounded the home, while during the winter months they gathered in close communion about the family fireside. Unfortunately, however, this idyllic picture was in many instances seriously marred by the fact that while the planter was rearing a large brood of children in the "big house," he was rearing another brood of mulattoes in the slave quarters.

Northern abolitionists frequently adverted to the clandestine relationships on Southern plantations between white men and black women. If these relationships were not as widespread as unfriendly critics contended, there was a firmer basis for charges of miscegenation than for the accusations of cruelty which were hurled at the heads of the planters with such regularity by the Garrisonians. Cruelty existed, of course, more of it, indeed, than many Southerners care to admit, but a majority of modern scholars agree that it was the exception rather than the rule. Such competent and conscientious students as John Fiske, U. B. Phillips, and F. P. Gaines concur in the dictum that the average master treated his slaves with kindness and consideration, while A. B. Hart avers that "on good plantations there was indeed little suffering and much enjoyment." There was, in fact, in many instances a feeling of profound attachment between master and slave in the Old South, a feeling which transcended racial barriers and frequently lasted until death intervened. This is beautifully exemplified in the following inscription, placed over the grave of a faithful Negro by the Southern family he had served:

JOHN:
A FAITHFUL SERVANT
AND TRUE FRIEND:
KINDLY AND CONSIDERATE:
LOYAL AND AFFECTIONATE:
THE FAMILY HE SERVED
HONORS HIM IN DEATH:
BUT IN LIFE, THEY GAVE HIM LOVE:
FOR HE WAS ONE OF THEM

CHAPTER V

AUTHORS AND EDITORS

THE HALF century which followed the outbreak of the Revolution is peculiarly unimportant in the history of American letters. During this early epoch in the life of the republic few literary productions of consequence emerged above the welter of lachrymose and stilted fiction, bombastic and flatulent poetry, and ranting and grandiloquent historical writing which afflicted the period. In both manner and matter the literary output of the years which followed the War for American Independence descended almost uniformly to bathos.

The exceptions to this generalization are few in number. Several notable commentaries on the science of government were produced in the late eighteenth century. The political writings of Thomas Jefferson retain their vitality despite the passage of the years, while those of John Taylor of Caroline deserve to be rescued from the virtual oblivion into which they have fallen. Madison's contributions to *The Federalist*, like those of Hamilton and Jay, merit the immortality which is theirs, and a few other writers on political and governmental themes, North and South, achieved freshness of treatment and distinction of style. On the whole, however, the literary output of the era is singularly dreary. This is particularly true of the South. Above the Potomac the appearance of "Thanatopsis" in 1817 fixed an important milestone in the history of American poetry, while the publication of Cooper's *The Spy* in 1821 was equally significant in the realm of the novel. But no contribution to *belles-lettres* of anything like comparable magnitude came from Dixie during these years. Emerson said of Massachusetts for the period from 1790 to 1820 that "there was not a book, a speech, a conversation, or a thought in the state." He was speaking hyperbolically, of course, and his strictures were not to be taken literally. Yet his sweeping indictment of Massachusetts is applicable in large measure to the South as a whole during the late eighteenth and early nineteenth centuries in so far as its fiction and its poetry are concerned.

But while Emerson hurled at his native state the imputation that its people were for thirty years without aptitude for private conversation or public speech, this charge, at least, cannot be sustained against the men of the Old South. The ante-bellum Southerner, it is generally conceded, could hold his own vocally, whether in public or private, against any rival. In fact his intense desire to master the spoken word was one of the factors in his neglect of the profession of letters. The cherished ambition of almost every young Southerner was for a public rather than a literary career. Not only so, but a desire for distinction in the field of prose or poetry, rather than in that of politics, was frequently looked upon as a species of eccentricity hardly compatible with the finer instincts of a properly reared Southern gentleman. William Wirt, one of the better known essayists and biographers of the period, employed a pseudonym for many years, lest an open avowal of his auctorial activities be held against him by his colleagues in the legal profession. "Why do you waste your time on a damned thing like poetry? A man of your position might be a useful man," a friend of Philip Pendleton Cooke, author of *Florence Vane*, demanded of him one day. Other contemporary Southrons suffering from *cacoëthes scribendi* underwent similar experiences.

There are a number of additional reasons why the region which gave to the nation so amazingly brilliant a coterie of statesmen should have produced so vapid a group of literary men. For example, the South was sadly lacking in a literary center where writers could enjoy the stimulus of a congenial society. New England had such a center in Boston, while the middle states looked to New York and Philadelphia. In the vast region to the southward, however, there was no literary clearing house of consequence during the entire ante-bellum period. It is true that there was at times a sporadic literary activity centering in Charleston and having to do mainly with the editing and publishing of periodicals. On the other hand, the important book-publishing houses were all in the North.

Thus Southern society was not only rural, but there were at the same time no urban foci about which its literary activities might properly revolve. Seldom in the history of the world has a social order composed entirely of country gentlemen made any noteworthy contribution to literature or art, and the planter civilization of the Southern states was no exception. But there is still another factor which must be taken into consideration in any adequate treatment of the reasons for the South's failure in the literary field. This is the lack of intellectual virility in the Southern churches. Whereas the churches elsewhere, particularly in New England, produced original thinkers and writers over a long period, "the concern of the Southern churches," to quote an eminent critic, "has been more with morality than thought, more with the beauty of holiness than with the holiness of beauty."

Consequently the ambitious young Southern writer, isolated on his ante-bellum plantation, found many obstacles blocking the road to literary achievement. His family usually desired him to seek a public career, and discouraged his literary endeavors. His friends, many of whom felt that no gentleman would so degrade himself as to earn his living with his pen, were of like mind. Besides, as time went on and the cleavage between the sections became increasingly acute, patriotic Southerners felt that duty required their presence in the arena of public affairs. And if, by some miracle, an aspiring young writer overcame these manifold discouragements and produced a competent and workmanlike piece of prose or a poem of imaginative beauty, he found to his dismay that his fellow-Southerners were unappreciative, and that although the more successful planters had well stocked libraries, these libraries contained few books by native authors.

There is little doubt that the average Southerner of culture neglected the works of American writers for those from European sources. Indisputably many of the planters were book-buyers. A history of the

Harper publishing firm declares that before the Civil War "the South was a great buyer of books," while a similar history of the house of Putnam speaks of the heavy shipments of standard classics to the South, particularly New Orleans. Another New York publisher wrote that his most expensive invoices for editions of the European classics went before the war to "the old mansions on the banks of the James and the Savannah and the bluffs of the Mississippi."

Southern readers of fiction were especially strong in their preference for the novels of Sir Walter Scott. The reason is not far to seek. Scott wrote of the Middle Ages, with its feudalistic social structure; not only so, but he managed to invest this dull and dismal epoch with a romantic glamor and a spurious glitter which in actual fact it did not possess. The glowing pictures he painted of the aristocratic order which prevailed universally in the Middle Ages naturally appealed to the Southern slaveholders, themselves the leaders in a society similarly constructed. As the planters became more and more united in the defense of the slave system, they found the novels of Sir Walter Scott increasingly to their liking. "Beyond doubt," says Dr. H. J. Eckenrode, "Scott gave the South its social ideal." And if the planters derived inordinate satisfaction in reading of the noble lords, the lovely ladies, and the chivalrous knights who trip gaily through the pages of Scott, they exhibited a corresponding lack of interest in the more realistic and more democratic literary creations of Charles Dickens. Not until after the Civil War, when slavery was a thing of the past, did the works of Dickens attain their fullest measure of popularity in the region below the Potomac. We have seen that the amount of enduring literature produced in the South during the half century following the Revolution was almost negligible, and have noted that this can be partially explained by the fact that Southerners of talent generally elected to enter public life rather than to pursue polite letters as a profession. Certainly the explanation of the South's literary hysteresis is not to be found in any lack of mental endowment on the part of the average planter. The Southerner held his own too well in legislative halls and on the hustings for anyone to question seriously his cerebral capacity. Joseph Le Conte, the distinguished Southern scientist, recounts in his autobiography that he was greatly impressed by the intellectual attainments of the ante-bellum planters, and at the same time suggests a rationale for the paucity of tangible present-day evidence of those attainments.

"Nothing could be more remarkable," he wrote of the planters, "than the wide reading, the deep reflection, the refined culture, or the originality of thought and observation characteristic of them, and yet the idea of publication never even entered their minds."

Le Conte illustrated his thesis by describing a conversation he had some years prior to the Civil War with Langdon Cheves of South Carolina. Long before Darwin published his *Origin of Species* Cheves, in this conversation with Le Conte, enunciated the theory which afterward brought Darwin worldwide fame. Yet it never occured to Cheves to give publication to his views, Le Conte said.

It should be noted, however, that during the three decades immediately preceding the Civil War the atmosphere in the South was not conducive to the free play of ideas. The intense preoccupation of the section with the slave question made it so morbidly sensitive to criticism and so intolerant of the views of those who found fault with its peculiar institution that free speech was stifled. This consideration doubtless did not enter into the failure of Cheves to publish his evolutionary hypothesis, since there are no grounds for believing that such publication would have interfered in any way with the cherished theories and opinions of the slaveholders. It seems clear, on the other hand, that the almost complete cutting off of free discussion in the South had a strongly repressive effect upon the intellectual development of the region.

Reference has been made to the publication of various periodicals in Charleston during the antebellum era. The first of these, in fact the first magazine to make its appearance in the Southern states, was the *South Carolina Weekly Museum*, which was launched in 1797 and suspended the following year. Another early and equally short-lived periodical was the *National Magazine*, published in Richmond in 1799 and a part of 1800. The initial venture of this sort west of the Alleghanies was the *Medley*, which made its début in Lexington, Kentucky, in 1803. These and other magazines appeared suddenly in the South during these early years and as suddenly vanished. They are unimportant except as pioneer efforts in the direction of an autochthonous periodical literature in the area, efforts which later were to achieve a fair measure of success.

It was not until the establishment of the *Southern Review* at Charleston in 1828 that a magazine commanding any sort of national audience appeared in Dixie. In point of fact, the audience of the *Southern Review* can be described as "national" only in a very limited sense, for its contents were so ponderously academic and so heavily pedantic as to frighten away all but the most stout-hearted. The *North American Review*, founded at Boston in 1815 and for long the country's most esteemed periodical, was heavy enough, in all conscience, but its Charlestonian rival went even further in the direction of undiluted classicism. The most prolific contributor to the *Southern Review* was the immensely learned Hugh Swinton Legaré, who also served as editor during two of the four years that the magazine was able to continue publication. At the end of that time it quite naturally collapsed for want of a clientèle.

Other periodicals of larger circulations and wider influence were to appear in the South after 1830, but examination of these will be deferred until a later chapter. For the present let us consider journalism as practiced in the Southern states during the post-revolutionary period.

Owing to the sparsity of population and the almost complete absence of cities, there were few newspapers of consequence in the South until the turn of the century. In fact there were only thirty-seven papers in all the thirteen colonies in 1775, of which Charleston, South Carolina, had three, Williamsburg, Virginia, two, and Newbern and Wilmington, North Carolina, and Savannah, Georgia, one each. The remaining twenty-nine were in the North.

In the late eighteenth century the party organs at the national capital set the pace for the newspapers of the country. These organs were Philip Freneau's *National Gazette*, staunch supporter of the Jeffersonian program, and the *Gazette of the United States*, of which John Fenno was editor and in which Hamiltonian policies were promulgated and defended. Freneau and Fenno were Northern men, and their influence upon Southern journalism is important only to the extent that newspapers everywhere felt the impact of the vigorous and virulent crusade they conducted. Both sheets were appalling in their scurrility, yet Jefferson evidently approved the one and Hamilton the other. B. F. Bache and William Duane were other strong Jeffersonian editors at the seat of government, while William Cobbett wielded a vitriolic pen in behalf of Federalist principles.

Perhaps the first genuinely powerful editorial voice to be heard in the South was that of Joseph Gales, who founded the Raleigh *Register* in 1799 as a Jeffersonian journal, with the coöperation of Nathaniel Macon and others. Gales immediately made his influence felt by helping to carry North Carolina for Jefferson in the presidential election of 1800, and three years later was instrumental in securing the defeat of four influential Federalist congressmen. During his thirty-three years as editor of the *Register* he was a steadfast supporter of liberal causes, an ardent advocate of democratic principles, and a vigorous foe of slavery. Before coming to this country in 1795 from his native England, he had been known as a journalistic crusader for liberalism, and his editorial career on this side of the water was in the same tradition. Dr. William E. Dodd has called the *Register* "the first and greatest partisan newspaper" in North Carolina history.

Another paper of wide influence was the Charleston *Courier*, founded as a Federalist gazette in the South Carolina city by two New Englanders in 1803. One of them died two years later, and the other, Aaron S. Willington of Massachusetts, took control. Willington remained as publisher of the *Courier* until his death in 1862. Under his leadership the paper not only established itself as the most enterprising journal in South Carolina, but at the same time it pursued a policy of printing both sides of controversial questions, a decided rarity at the period. From the outset it was a staunch advocate of public schools. In 1832 the *Courier* fought the nullificationists with all the power it could command, but in subsequent years it came to terms with its environment to a large extent, and by the time the Civil War began was a thorough-going organ of the Charleston secessionists.

The other great Charleston daily was the *Mercury*. One of the most widely read journals in the country during the ante-bellum period, it was the leading exponent of the extreme Southern viewpoint on all controversial questions. The *Mercury* was the organ of the nullifiers in 1832, and it became more and more violently pro-Southern and secessionist as the "irrepressible conflict" neared. Editorial direction of the paper

seems to have been placed successively in a number
of different hands, but the policy of the *Mercury* appears
to have been fairly constant. It was read carefully in
many editorial sanctums throughout the nation and
by politicians everywhere, for it was recognized as
reflecting the opinions of the more bellicose Southern
fire-eaters. A partial antidote to the doctrines advocated by this crusading daily was provided by the
Greenville *Mountaineer*, established at Greenville, in
upstate South Carolina, in the late 1820's. The
Mountaineer, always edited with intelligence and particularly so under the régime of Benjamin F. Perry,
was an able advocate of democratic doctrines and
popular sovereignty, as well as a determined foe of
the nullifiers and disunionists.

One of the most capable and powerful editors of
the nineteenth century was Thomas Ritchie of the
Richmond *Enquirer*. Ritchie assumed editorial direction of the paper immediately upon its establishment
in 1804, and from that time until he relinquished control in 1845, his influence was tremendous. Whether
or not one agrees with the statement of Ritchie's biographer that he did more than any other man to keep both
Clay and Calhoun from the presidency, it is indisputable that the *Enquirer* was a controlling force in the
councils of the Democratic party in Virginia and the
nation for many years. The paper was, on the whole,
a distinctly liberal influence, although its editor
wobbled on the slavery question and ended by becoming a forthright defender of human servitude. He was,
on the other hand, an ardent champion of better educational facilities for the masses and more adequate

representation for the western half of the state, as well as extension of the franchise to all freeholders. At the same time he was startlingly ahead of his generation in his advocacy of women's rights, and he even tolerated the idea of woman suffrage.

The *Enquirer's* chief journalistic rival in the Old Dominion in these years was the Richmond *Whig*, founded by John Hampden Pleasants in 1824 as an organ of the party whose name it bore. Although the two papers were naturally in frequent disagreement over matters relating to politics, Pleasants joined Ritchie in urging upon the constitutional convention of 1829-30 a more equitable apportionment of representation and less stringent suffrage requirements. The papers were also a unit in importuning the state legislature of 1831-32 to provide for the gradual abolition of slavery in Virginia. Pleasants' career was abruptly terminated when he was killed in a duel in 1846 by Thomas Ritchie, Jr. The younger Ritchie had published in the *Enquirer* an anonymous communication which charged that Pleasants was planning to found an abolitionist journal. Although the editor of the *Whig* had openly urged gradual abolition fifteen years before, sentiment on the slavery issue had changed markedly by 1846 and a heated altercation ensued. Pleasants finally challenged Ritchie when the latter called him a coward, and was mortally wounded in the duel which followed.

Such a thing as an abolitionist newspaper in Virginia or any other Southern state in the forties would have been almost out of the question. A journal of that nature probably would not have lasted a week.

Quite possibly the editor would have been driven beyond the Mason and Dixon Line, and his presses dumped into the nearest river. But in the twenties there were a number of abolitionist papers in the South.

There is considerable disagreement among authorities as to which was the first publication of the kind in the United States. According to McMaster, Charles Osborn's *Philanthropist*, published at Mt. Pleasant, Ohio, in 1817, preceded all others in the advocacy of immediate emancipation. Osborn also is said to have published the *Manumission Intelligencer* at Jonesboro, Tennessee, in 1819-20, while Elihu Embree's *Emancipator* was established at Jonesboro in 1820. Two years afterward John Finley Crowe set up his *Abolition Intelligencer* at Shelbyville, Kentucky, and as late as 1828 the *Liberalist* was founded in far-Southern New Orleans. But the real temper of the people of New Orleans at this period was indicated a few years later by the action of the vigilance committee of East Feliciana Parish, Louisiana, in offering $50,000 reward for the delivery into its hands of the prominent abolitionist, Arthur Tappan, of New York.

In North Carolina, William Swaim established the Greensboro *Patriot* in the twenties, and agitated courageously for the wholesale manumission of slaves, despite torrents of abuse from various directions. Swaim, president of the Manumission Society of North Carolina, declared in 1826 that no newspaper in the state was earnestly engaged in defending slavery. Before many years were past, as we shall see, the situation was to be reversed, and every North Carolina editor was either to lapse into a studied silence on the question or to take up the cudgels in active defense of the institution. The shift in sentiment in this commonwealth was typical of what was happening throughout the South. The reaction against the egalitarianism of the revolutionary period was setting in. During the succeeding decades it was to sweep everything before it in the Southern states, choking off free discussion and putting the section completely on the defensive until the bloody arbitrament of the sixties.

CHAPTER VI

DIVISION AND REACTION

THE NEGRO problem occupies a place of such paramount importance in the history of the Old South that many are prone to overlook the fact that there was an even older race problem confronting the planters—namely that which concerned the relationships between the whites and the Indians.

The great majority of the Indians belonged to one of four tribes—the Cherokees, the Creeks, the Choctaws, and the Chickasaws. They had been driven back gradually from the coast as the white settlers moved into the interior, and at about the period of the Revolution were holding their ground as firmly as might be in the lower end of the Appalachian range.

Many solutions of the Indian problem were suggested after the War for American Independence, but the only program which met with general favor was comparatively simple. It called for the expulsion or extermination of the Indians. In the South, as in the North, the policy of the whites toward the redskins was coldly selfish and brutally cruel. The story of the relationships between the races is one of callous indifference on the part of the whites to the legitimate claims of the aborigines, and of reckless disregard for the solemn treaties which guaranteed those claims. There is no more disgraceful chapter in American history than that which tells of the relations between the United States government and various state governments on the one hand and the Indians on the other.

Perhaps the most flagrant of the injustices perpetrated upon the Indians in the Southern states were inflicted upon the Cherokees. This tribe had been on terms of extreme friendliness with Governor James Oglethorpe, founder of the colony of Georgia, and more than once had saved the colony for England. In 1785 a Federal treaty was signed with the Cherokees, which treaty was immediately violated in the grossest manner by the white inhabitants of the frontier State of Franklin. In 1791 the United States government signed another treaty guaranteeing to the Cherokee nation "all their lands not hereby ceded." This document also was violated with the utmost impunity by the whites. As time went on, continued pressure was brought to bear on the tribe to make further cessions. The Indians refused in 1801 to submit, but soon found the Federal government was too strong to be successfully resisted. They accordingly relinquished all their lands in South Carolina in 1816. The following year the United States government signed a treaty guaranteeing 640 acres to every Cherokee head of a family living east of the Mississippi River who would signify his desire to become a citizen, such land to revert in fee simple to his children. But these Indian treaties were apparently made for the sole purpose of being broken, for it was only a short time before the Cherokees were being urged to make further concessions. They thereupon refused flatly to sell or relinquish another foot of land. This remonstrance brought from the Federal authorities statements of regret at their inability to protect the redskins in their rights, coupled with renewed offers of money for the desired concessions. The Cherokees valued the lands of their forefathers far above any mere cash consideration, and they repeatedly implored the national government to keep its promises to them.

This action on their part was characterized by the Governor of Georgia as "tricks of vulgar cunning" and "insults from the polluted lips of outcasts and vagabonds"! The Georgia legislature shortly thereafter passed an act outlawing the Cherokee nation, annulling all its laws and ordinances and branding all Cherokees and Creeks as incompetent to testify in any court action to which a white person was a party. The Indians filed suit against the State of Georgia, and the case was carried to the United States Supreme Court, but they failed to get relief. The Court held that an Indian tribe was not a foreign nation, and that it therefore could not bring suit. This decision completely blasted the hopes of the Cherokees. In 1835 they bowed to the inevitable and signed a treaty with the Federal government by which they relinquished all their lands east of the Mississippi. With bitter memories of broken pledges and violated agreements, the Cherokee nation abandoned its ancestral hunting grounds and removed beyond the Father of Waters.

It should not be inferred from what has been said

here that the redskins were never guilty of perfidy in their dealings with the whites. On the contrary, they were at times chargeable with bad faith. It was because Osceola, leader of the Seminoles, a branch of the Creeks, refused to abide by the agreement of his tribal chieftains to remove the tribe from Florida to Arkansas that the Seminole War, longest of all the Indian wars, was fought. This conflict began in 1835, following several bloody butcheries of whites, and was pursued with considerable barbarity on both sides. Not until more than 20,000 volunteers from many states had participated were the Seminoles finally subdued in 1842 and driven beyond the Mississippi. By that year the Creeks, the Choctaws, and the Chickasaws had all gone to join the Cherokees in the West. The South had solved its Indian problem—by driving out the Indians.

But while the South was arriving at what seemed to it a satisfactory solution of this question, its Negro problem was becoming increasingly acute. Despite half a century of post-revolutionary agitation against slavery, many Southerners in the early 1830's were gradually reaching the conclusion that the "peculiar institution" was not so dreadful after all. They were doubtless aided in arriving at this judgment by the fact that cotton culture with slave labor had become more profitable since the invention of the cotton gin. Another factor which helped to develop this attitude of mind was the activity of the Northern abolitionists, led by the voluble William Lloyd Garrison, who, at the age of twenty-five, without money or friends, had launched his *Liberator* in Boston on January 1, 1831.

DIVISION AND REACTION 97

The tirades of Garrison and his *confrères* angered the slaveholders and placed them on the defensive. Not a few Southerners who disapproved of slavery, and who would have been receptive to arguments against it from other sources, felt that they must reply to the denunciatory harangues of the abolitionists. They accordingly became apologists for the system.

Another event which had an important bearing upon the slavery controversy occurred during the same year that the *Liberator* began thundering against the South. This was Nat Turner's insurrection. Fifty-five whites, mostly women and children, were massacred in cold blood in this slave revolt, which took place in Southampton County, Virginia, in August, 1831. Word of the uprising traveled swiftly to all parts of the South, and consternation reigned in many localities, especially those in which the blacks outnumbered the whites. The fact that Turner was a Negro preacher of some education and that one of his lieutenants in the revolt was a free Negro seemed particularly significant to the slaveholders. It convinced many of them that the slaves ought not to be educated and that the free blacks were a menace. As in the case of the Denmark Vesey conspiracy in Charleston nine years before, the Nat Turner insurrection brought forth considerable repressive legislation in the slave States.

The reaction of the Virginians to the insurrection differed, however, in certain respects from that of the South Carolinians to the Vesey plot. Whereas no discernible movement in the direction of abolition had been launched in Charleston after the discovery of that conspiracy, in Virginia numerous memorials to

7

the state legislature urged the elimination of the slave system and the removal of all the blacks beyond the borders of the commonwealth. So widespread was the popular interest in this movement that the assembly which convened in December, 1831, devoted a major share of its attention to the various proposals. With Thomas Jefferson Randolph leading the movement for gradual emancipation of all the slaves in the Old Dominion the entire question of slavery was debated at great length. Many legislators of prominence denounced the slave system in unsparing terms and urged that some plan be devised for ridding Virginia of its blighting influence. A bill setting up a comprehensive system for the deportation and colonization of the free Negroes of the state and such as might become free thereafter, finally passed the House by the substantial margin of 79 to 41. But when the measure reached the Senate it was defeated by a vote of 18 to 14, after important changes had been made in its provisions. The theory behind this bill was that it would not only set up machinery for the removal of all free blacks from Virginia, but that at the same time it would greatly reduce the number of slaves, since many owners would free their Negroes if the state would bear the expense of their transportation to Africa or elsewhere. Elaborate plans for the gradual emancipation and deportation of the slaves also were proposed, but they too were defeated.

The failure of this legislation was tragic in its consequences. Adoption by the Virginia assembly of a nicely articulated program for gradual emancipation might have had a far-reaching effect in the slave states. But nothing of this sort was accomplished, and the assembly ended by passing various repressive measures designed to lessen the dangers of slave insurrections. The liberals were so thoroughly disheartened by the collapse of their program that they made no further efforts in its behalf. Slaveholders throughout the South concluded that there was no feasible plan for getting rid of the chattel system and began emphasizing its good points and minimizing its defects. The Tennessee constitutional convention of 1834 considered proposals for emancipating the blacks, but concluded that it would be unwise to disturb the status quo.

One of the reasons for the failure of the border states to move definitely for the abolition of the slave system at this period was the practice in those states of breeding slaves for the expanding market. Participants in the debates in the Virginia legislature of 1831-32, during which the slave question was discussed at such length, agreed that the Old Dominion was rearing slaves for sale in the cotton states, and that thousands were being disposed of annually in this way. Not only so, but leading Virginians, such as Governor William B. Giles and Thomas R. Dew of the William and Mary College faculty, felt that slave-breeding for such purposes should be encouraged.

Undoubtedly one of the most potent influences exerted at the period on behalf of a reactionary policy in the Southern states was the philosophical defense of slavery promulgated by Dew in 1832. Repudiating utterly the doctrines of human brotherhood and equality enunciated in the Declaration of Independence,

and substituting a paternalistic and benevolent system patterned after the Positivist social order of Auguste Comte, Dew boldly came to the defense of the slave system.

The argument of Dew came at a time when Southerners of anti-slavery proclivities were smarting under the attacks of the Northern abolitionists, and, despairing of finding any practicable plan for getting rid of the slave system, were groping for an adequate defense of the institution. Although Dew was only thirty years old, his statement of the case for slavery was regarded as the ablest yet presented, and was highly effective in hastening the pro-slavery reaction. In South Carolina, where the doctrines of Cooper were familiar, a whole school of apologists for human servitude came forward to champion the Southern social order.

Already in South Carolina events disturbing in their implications were serving to intensify the economic and social cleavage between the sections. Henry Clay's desire for the presidency had led him to bid for the support of the Eastern manufacturers through the enactment of his tariff bill of 1824. This legislation was strongly opposed by the planters, and its passage was the signal for indignant outbursts from below the Potomac. Then in 1828 came the "tariff of abominations," by which the duties were hoisted to a point far higher than ever before. The legislatures of five Southern states united in impassioned protest, but it was only in South Carolina that the sectional antagonisms engendered by the tariff were transmuted into overt resistance. In that commonwealth a convention called for the purpose adopted an Ordinance of Nullification, hurling defiance at the Federal government, pronouncing the tariff laws void in South Carolina, and threatening withdrawal from the Union if any efforts were made to coerce the people of the state into obedience. The tariff was reduced shortly thereafter and the ordinance was rescinded.

The nullification movement was led by a small but exceedingly powerful coterie of lowland planters. What manner of men were these audacious Carolinians who had so intransigently defied the Federal authority? They were the scions of a proud and fiery race, quick to draw and quick to forgive, equally at home on the dueling ground or on the rostrum, in the ball room or following to hounds. In their veins flowed the blood of fine old English stock, frequently tempered by Scotch-Irish and Huguenot strains. Sterner and more dignified than the Virginians, more punctilious in matters of dress and conduct, they could nevertheless unbend on occasion and enjoy a glass of Rhenish wine or a graceful minuet. Many of them had been educated at the best European universities and were widely read in the classics, well versed in the histories of ancient and modern civilizations. With few exceptions they were distinctly aristocratic in outlook, distinctly conscious of their patrician lineage.

The social life of these landed gentry centered in Charleston, a city of architectural refinement and cultural distinction, of wistful charm and romantic loveliness. For those who belonged to or were *personæ grata* to its ruling caste, Charleston during the antebellum period was the most engaging spot in the

South, if not in America. Less cosmopolitan than New Orleans, with its strong intermixture of Spanish and Gallic elements, less easy-going than Richmond, with its julep-drinking tobacco planters, Charleston possessed an atmosphere of gayety tempered with dignity which was unique. During the "season," which lasted for several weeks each winter, the city was festive with balls, dinners, and races, but for the remainder of the year it was relatively quiet. In spring, summer, and autumn the gentry engaged one another in conversation on their spacious verandahs; strolled along the battery, with Fort Sumter looming ominously in the distance across the miles of shimmering water; or sat in their gardens in the languorous Southern air, amid the perfume of roses, jessamines, and azaleas.

But this Carolinian city was important in the life of the Old South not only for its delightful picturesqueness but also for the tremendous influence which the political and social theories of its ruling class exerted upon the minds of the governing element throughout the slave states. With a population never exceeding 43,000, less than half of whom were white, Charleston played a larger and more significant rôle in shaping the national destiny during the period from 1830 to 1860 than any other city in America.

After the nullificationist controversy of 1832, the slave states were to look more and more to South Carolina for leadership in the increasingly acrimonious conflict between the sections, and the extreme secessionist and pro-slavery doctrines with which the leaders of the Charlestonian aristocracy were identified, were to find favor with an ever-widening circle of slaveholders. Slowly but surely John C. Calhoun was to lead the South into the position of pronouncing chattel servitude a blessing rather than a curse. To be sure, the planters were never anything like unanimous in the adoption of this view, publicly expressed by Calhoun on the Senate floor in 1839, but as the years went by more and more of them came to hold with the great Carolinian that slavery, as practised in the South, was a "positive good." Although the reasoning which led Calhoun to this conclusion seems highly fantastic in the light of the universal detestation of slavery by enlightened peoples in the twentieth century, the integrity of his mental processes is not open to question. Even his bitterest enemies conceded that his character was unimpeachable and his motives above reproach.

As heretofore indicated, the gradual shift in the Southern attitude on the slave question was hastened by the assaults of the Northern abolitionists. In 1833, two years after the redoubtable Garrison founded the *Liberator*, the American Anti-Slavery Society was organized, and the issue was joined in earnest. The Garrisonian attacks on the South, its institutions, and its civilization became increasingly clamorous. It is not surprising that these indiscriminate tirades against the Southern people as a whole were resented on both sides of the Potomac. For while the humanitarian impulses which motivated the onslaughts of the abolitionists are beyond all praise, and the indomitable courage with which they carried on their crusade in the face of mob violence and threats of death is equally admirable, it is not to be denied that the language of a number of these anti-slavery agitators was abusive and intemperate.

Slavery had been abolished in every state north of Mason and Dixon's Line by the time the abolitionists launched their jehad, so that their strictures were directed in large measure toward the region where human servitude still held sway. Yet the opposition they encountered in the North was in some respects more implacable than that which they met in the South. Garrison had the following to say on this subject in 1831:

"During my recent tour for the purpose of exciting the minds of the people by a series of discourses on the subject of slavery, every place that I visited gave fresh evidence that a greater revolution was to be effected in the free states—and particularly in New England—than at the South. I found contempt more bitter, opposition more active, detraction more relentless, prejudice more stubborn, and apathy more frozen, than among the slaveowners themselves."

The fact that New England was originally more active in the slave trade than any other section of the republic, and the further fact that it did not abolish slavery within its bounds until slave labor was revealed as unprofitable in Northern climes, is convincing evidence that the moral sense of the average New Englander had never been aroused by the spectacle of human bondage. And not only was this true of New England as a whole, but Thomas Nelson Page has written that "Massachusetts has the honor of being the first community in America to legalize the slave trade and slavery by legislative act; the first to send out a slave ship, and the first to secure a fugitive slave law."

It is not surprising, therefore, that when the Garrisonians began their attacks on the South, the people of New England were indifferent to the agitation, if not actually hostile. Not only did they exhibit small concern for the disestablishment of slavery in those states where it still existed, but they felt that the abolitionist diatribes would injure New England's business relationships with the trans-Potomac region. There was much bitterness of feeling against Garrison, and he was frequently threatened with death. But neither threats nor persuasion could move this iron-willed reformer. The consequence was that in 1835 he was set upon by a Boston mob, described as including "many gentlemen of property and influence," dragged through the streets by a rope, and saved from hanging by the intervention of the police. Similar mobs attacked other anti-slavery agitators in the North. One of the latter, the Rev. Samuel May, was assaulted in this manner on six separate occasions in Vermont and Massachusetts. In almost all the Northern states abolitionists were roughly handled and furiously denounced.

If such was the reaction of the free states to the movement, it is not to be wondered at that the slave states received the abolitionist attacks with rage and terror—rage at the violence of the abuse and terror lest the inflammatory literature of the Garrisonians foment servile insurrections. Congressman J. H. Hammond of South Carolina spoke for a substantial group of Southerners when he said in 1836: "I warn the abolitionists, ignorant and infatuated barbarians as they are, that if chance shall throw any of them into our hands, they may expect a felon's death." The Georgia legislature posted a reward of $5,000 for anyone who would kidnap Garrison and bring him to that state to stand trial on charges of inciting slaves to revolt. A few influential Southerners, Governor A. B. Roman of Louisiana among them, urged the adoption of a more conciliatory attitude toward the Northern agitators, but their voices were drowned out in the general tumult. A mob sacked the Charleston postoffice in 1835 and made a bonfire of the abolitionist literature it found there. Shortly thereafter a determined effort was made by the slaveocracy to secure the enactment of Federal legislation forbidding the circulation of "incendiary" material through the mails, but the effort failed. In its frantic desire to stifle all public discussion of Negro servitude, the Slave Power then succeeded in pushing through Congress a "gag resolution." This measure, enacted in 1836 and maintained in effect until 1844, made it mandatory that all petitions for the abolition of slavery be "laid on the table" without being discussed or read. This flagrant violation of the historic "right of petition" was excoriated fiercely by John Quincy Adams, as congressman from Massachusetts. After years of effort, he succeeded in bringing about its repeal.

It should not be imagined, however, from what has been said of the Garrisonian school of abolitionists that it was the only school of abolitionists. On the contrary, a large majority of the Northern foes of slavery were strongly hostile to Garrison. Taking the view that his indiscriminate attacks were hurtful to the very cause they were intended to promote, these men and women advocated more conservative tactics. The leader of the moderates for a good many years was James G. Birney of Kentucky. Birney, as was pointed out in an earlier chapter, was constrained by the intolerance of the slaveholders to leave his native state. After publishing an anti-slavery journal in Ohio for a year, he removed to New York, and by 1840 was recognized as the ablest and most influential of the anti-Garrisonian abolitionists. In 1844, as presidential candidate of the Liberty party, he polled enough votes to defeat Clay, who was "pussyfooting" on the slavery issue, and to elect Polk, a devoted ally of the slaveocracy.

The abolitionist group which acknowledged Birney as its spokesman advocated reform through political action, whereas Garrison specifically repudiated such a course and denounced the Constitution as a "covenant with death and an agreement with hell." In addition, Birney was too well aware of the practical difficulties in the way of abolition to hold any fellowship with Garrison in his impatient demand for immediate and unconditional emancipation. This capable Kentuckian was a man of liberal habits of mind who confronted the immensely complex question of emancipation without rancor or acrimony, and with arguments which were thoroughly rationalized and competently presented. A Southern slaveholder who had at first contented himself with efforts to ameliorate the condition of the slaves, Birney gradually became an uncompromising advocate of abolition. He died in

1857, too early to witness the triumph of the cause to which he had devoted the best years of his life.

Feeling was becoming increasingly tense in the forties as the debates in Congress grew more and more vitriolic and the economic divergence between the sections grew ever wider. In 1836 R. Barnwell Rhett of Charleston had proposed to a gathering of Southern congressmen in Washington that a committee be appointed to consider the best method of dissolving the Union, and in 1844, when the Massachusetts legislature passed a resolution declaring that the annexation of Texas "tended to drive the states into a dissolution of the Union," leaders throughout the slave states urged their representatives in the national legislature to draw the issue once and for all between the North and the South.

Articulate anti-slavery sentiment in Dixie was now almost non-existent. All of the 106 anti-slavery societies which Lundy counted in the region in 1827, had disappeared. In earlier years manumissions had been encouraged and free Negroes had enjoyed considerable liberty of movement. In Georgia, indeed, Negro veterans of the Revolutionary war had been received as guests in the homes of prominent citizens, and in North Carolina the Rev. John Chavis, a full-blooded Negro who had been born free in that state, had conducted one of the best classical schools in that part of the South, with many planters' sons among his pupils. But by the middle of the nineteenth century the free blacks found their movements severely circumscribed. No free Negro was permitted to enter a slave state, and every such Negro who was already a resident was required to register and procure a license. Manumissions were forbidden unless provision was made for the removal of the manumitted person or persons.

If these regulations appear harsh, it should be borne in mind that free Negroes were roughly handled in the North at the period, although there was no serious race problem there. Race riots in Northern cities were not unknown, and Negroes on occasion did not receive even elementary justice in the courts. Practically all the Northern states denied the franchise to free blacks, whereas several Southern states had permitted them to vote prior to 1831. And while it was contrary to law to educate Negroes in the South, it must not be forgotten that a school for blacks at New Haven, Connecticut, was suppressed in 1831; that Prudence Crandall was subjected to unspeakable indignities and driven out of the state for opening a school for Negro girls at Canterbury, Connecticut, in 1833, and that the teacher of an academy at Canaan, New Hampshire, which was open to both races, was given one month to get out of town with his colored pupils in 1835.

In the deep South hostile criticism of the chattel system had been completely silenced by 1840. In the upper tier of slave states, however, a handful of intrepid men still ventured to speak adversely of the "peculiar institution." Among these was Cassius M. Clay of Kentucky, the son of slaveholding parents, and a distant kinsman of Henry Clay. His severe attacks on the slave system led to his defeat for the Kentucky legislature in 1841. He resolved at once to make war on the Slave Power with all his resources.

Despite floods of abuse and repeated threats, Clay published an anti-slavery paper at Lexington and another a few years later at Louisville. In 1849 he ran for governor on an emancipationist platform and polled over 3,600 votes, enough to defeat the Whig candidate.

Another Kentuckian who was often, although not always, an outspoken critic of slavery was Henry Clay. He lacked the crusading fire of his relative, but was at times remarkably frank in his public expressions, even as late as 1851, the year preceding his death. And yet despite Clay's open hostility to human bondage, the Kentucky legislature, which was strongly pro-slavery, prevailed upon him in 1849 to return to the Senate for another term, although he had announced his retirement from public life.

George Tucker, first chairman of the University of Virginia faculty, regarded slavery as a "social, economic and political" evil. In 1843 he wrote that the institution tended to make the slaveholder "idle, indolent, proud, luxurious and improvident." Dr. Henry Ruffner, president of Washington College, published a pamphlet in 1847 advocating the gradual abolition of slavery on economic grounds. The following year R. R. Howison, Virginia historian, asserted that a majority of Virginians regarded the institution as an "enormous evil," while in 1856 Robert E. Lee declared that few would deny that it was "a moral and political evil in any country." These statements contrast with that of John S. Carlisle in the Virginia Convention of 1861 that slavery was "a social, political and religious blessing."

Daniel R. Goodloe of North Carolina was another Southerner who did his own thinking and was not content to parrot the pro-slavery arguments of Calhoun and Dew. He went to Washington in the forties and joined the editorial staff of the *National Era*, prominent anti-slavery weekly. Goodloe subsequently became editor-in-chief and remained in that position until the paper suspended on the eve of the war.

But while there was less intolerance in the upper South than in the regions nearer the Gulf, the atmosphere, even in the tobacco states, was heavily charged with bigotry. Several professors in this territory lost their positions because they opposed slavery, the most flagrant case of this kind being that of Professor B. S. Hedrick of the University of North Carolina. This young man was so thoughtless as to state, in response to a question, that he expected to vote for Frémont for president in 1856. His reason for preferring Frémont, he said, was that Fremont was on the right side of the slavery question—the same side, he was at pains to point out, as Jefferson, Henry, and Madison. But the Raleigh *Standard*, edited by W. W. Holden, demanded his expulsion from the university faculty solely because of his admiration for Frémont, and the board of trustees obligingly complied shortly thereafter, despite the fact that Hedrick had not tried to convert any of the students to his views. Ridiculed in the press of the state, which refused in most instances to publish his statements, except in garbled form, he departed for the North, after narrowly escaping severe injury at the hands of a mob.

Another young North Carolinian who was strongly

hostile to slavery was Hinton R. Helper. Like Goodloe and Hedrick, Helper came from a middle class family —that is, his parents were not affiliated either with the powerful guild of the great slaveholders or with the large group known as "poor whites." His parents owned four slaves. When only twenty-six years old, Helper completed *The Impending Crisis*, a slashing attack on the Slave Power, in which he denounced the intolerance of the South and showed that slavery was slowly impoverishing the Southern people. All the leading New York publishers rejected the manuscript for fear of alienating their Southern clientèle, and Helper finally had to turn it over to an obscure book agent for publication. This man brought the volume out in 1857, and it was an instantaneous success. While intemperate in spots, the book presents a devastating picture of the terrible economic effects of the slave system. It should not be imagined, however, that Helper was moved to write *The Impending Crisis* by any humanitarian desire to liberate the blacks. After the Civil War he wrote a book violently attacking the Negro race and seriously urging the whites to expel as many Negroes from the country as possible and to massacre the rest!

On the other hand, the humanitarian motive was uppermost with the Grimké sisters of Charleston, who, as already noted, had chosen exile from their native state in preference to life "amid the horrors of the Southern prisonhouse," as one of them expressed it. By the middle of the century they had become leaders in the American Anti-Slavery Society, and Angelina had developed astounding powers of oratory. Throngs

came to hear her flaming denunciations of the slaveocracy. If she was guilty at times of unpardonable absurdities, as in her affirmation at Philadelphia that she
had never seen "a happy slave," some of the statements
of the opposition were equally fantastic. Consider, for
example the assertion of Governor M. S. Perry of
Florida that slavery was "that institution which lies
at the basis of Southern prosperity, power, civilization and happiness," or that of Congressman Albert
G. Brown of Mississippi that slavery was "a great
moral, social, political and religious blessing—a blessing to the slave and a blessing to the master."

It was inevitable, with the growing antagonism
between the sections, that the various churches should
have been drawn into the whirling vortex of controversy. Few intradenominational discussions of doctrinal questions arose between 1830 and 1861 to
distract attention from the one all-absorbing topic.
It is true that differences over theological matters,
combined with divergencies on the slavery issue, split
the Presbyterian church in the late thirties into Old
School and New School Presbyterians. The vast majority of the former group were in the Southern states
and were predominantly Fundamentalist in faith and
pro-slavery in attitude, while an overwhelming percentage of the latter lived above Mason and Dixon's
Line, adhered to more Modernistic theological concepts and were, on the whole, opposed to slavery.
There was also a lively and highly diverting clash
between Baptists and Methodists in the fifties. J. R.
Graves, editor of the *Tennessee Baptist*, took umbrage
at what he regarded as unwarranted slurs cast by the

8

Methodists at other denominations, particularly his own. Graves was especially incensed by the statement of Methodists that immersion, as practised by Baptists, was "superstituous, indecent, disgusting and sinful," and the further declaration that "there is not a female, perhaps, who submits to it, who has not a great previous struggle with her delicacy." In a series of articles in the *Tennessee Baptist*, subsequently sold widely in book form under the title of *The Great Iron Wheel*, Graves unsheathed his snickersnee and laid about him in vigorous fashion. Methodism, he declared, is a "clerical despotism—and yet Americans tolerate and support it." It is "the Popery of Protestantism—as absolute and all-controlling as Jesuitism," he went on, while its local preachers· are "degraded" and its band-meetings differ only slightly from "the Romish confessional."

This amusing controversy must have helped to take the mind of the South from the feverish discussion of the slave question in which the churches of both sections were then engaged. The Episcopalians managed to avoid the subject almost completely in their sermons and public gatherings throughout the antebellum period, but the pulpits of the other principal denominations rang with contentious debate. The Presbyterian split over slavery and doctrinal matters was followed a few years later by divisions in the ranks of the Methodists and Baptists. The Southern members of the former denomination seceded in 1845, following differences over slavery at the general conference of the preceding year, while the controversy over human servitude had an equally shattering effect upon the Baptists. In the same year that the slave-holding Methodists broke away from their Northern brethren, the slaveholding Baptists did likewise. In 1858 there was another break in the Presbyterian ranks over slavery. The schisms thus created have not been healed to this day.

In the border states relations between the Northern and Southern branches of the disrupted denominations were frequently characterized by an acrimony and a bitterness scarcely consonant with the exalted professions of religious bodies. Guards with shotguns were stationed at the entrances to some of the churches in this region, and there was mutilation of Bibles and destruction of other church property. Grand juries in border territory sought to prevent the circulation there of such anti-slavery publications as the *Christian Advocate and Journal* of Baltimore and the *Western Christian Advocate* of Cincinnati, on the ground that they tended to incite the slaves to rebellion. On the far-flung frontier of Texas conditions were not unlike those prevailing in the border states of the Old South. Following the split in the Methodist Church, the *Texas Advocate* urged "the thorough and immediate eradication of the Methodist Church, North, in Texas with whatever force may be necessary."

It should not be imagined from the foregoing, however, that the Northern churches were all solidly aligned against the South's peculiar institution. Very much to the contrary, some of slavery's strongest defenders were to be found among the New England clergy, and the Northern churches in general were hostile to the abolitionists when they began their activities in earnest in the thirties. Such openly avowed anti-slavery ecclesiastics as were to be found were almost invariably affiliated with Northern denominations, but those denominations were generally silent on the issue during the years immediately preceding the outbreak of the war.

A mere handful of Southern clergymen managed, after 1835, to express strong aversion to chattel slavery without suffering ejection from their churches and forcible removal to the North.

One of these was Dr. Robert J. Breckinridge of Kentucky, an ardent and impetuous zealot who was amazingly liberal in some respects and distressingly narrow in others. Dr. Breckinridge did not hesitate to speak out courageously in denunciation of slavery. Upon being asked on one occasion if he would "sacrifice his political principles to carry emancipation," he replied "I can and I will." Just prior to the opening of the Kentucky constitutional convention of 1849 he urged upon a public meeting in Lexington the adoption of resolutions strongly criticising slavery on political, economic, and moral grounds, and asking the approaching convention to take practical steps to ameliorate this condition. Breckinridge made a brave fight against insuperable odds. The resolutions were adopted but no action was taken by the convention. Yet this man who was capable of such large-minded humanitarianism frequently delivered violent attacks on the Roman Catholic church, so violent, in fact, that his friends at one time feared for his life.

Another abolitionist cleric who fought on with indomitable resolution despite the abuse and threats of the slaveholders was the Rev. John G. Fee, also a Kentuckian. Fee, like Breckinridge, was the son of slaveholding parents, and when he announced to his father that his conscience bade him preach against slavery, the latter ordered him out of the house, never to return. He never did. Although mobbed twenty-two times and left for dead twice, Fee refused to keep quiet and he also refused to leave Kentucky. He continued his crusade within the borders of his native state until the outbreak of the war.

Breckinridge and Fee were almost the only preachers in the entire South during the two decades preceding the opening of armed hostilities who were vigorously outspoken in their opposition to slavery, and who at the same time were able to avoid being driven beyond the Potomac or the Ohio. Moncure D. Conway of Virginia expressed strong anti-slavery sentiments as pastor of a Unitarian church in Washington, D. C., in the fifties, and lost his charge as a result. Subsequently he edited an abolitionist paper in Boston. Daniel Worth returned to North Carolina from Indiana shortly before the war and spent the winter of 1859-60 in jail on a charge of circulating Helper's *Impending Crisis*.

But if adverse discussion of slavery from the pulpit was virtually impossible in the upper South, it was doubly so in the lower South. There the churches were practically a unit in defense of the system. The attitude of the vast majority of Southern ministers and laymen was stated by the eminent Dr. J. H. Thornwell of Columbia in 1850, the year before his election to the presidency of South Carolina College, when he said: "The parties in this conflict are not merely abolitionists and slaveholders—they are atheists, socialists, communists, red republicans, jacobins on the one side, and the friends of order and regulated freedom on the other. In one word, the world is the battleground—Christianity and atheism the combatants; and the progress of humanity the stake." Dr. Benjamin M. Palmer of New Orleans, probably the most prominent and influential clergyman in the Southern states, gave it as his considered judgment in 1860 that it was the "providential trust" of the Southern people "to conserve and perpetuate the institution of domestic slavery as now existing," and added: "The position of the South is at this moment sublime." Two years later the Southern Presbyterian church expressed its "deep conviction of the divine appointment of domestic servitude" and emphasized the "peculiar mission of the Southern church to conserve the institution of slavery."

Such being the attitude of the religious denominations in the slave states toward the chattel system it is not surprising that the two principal political parties in the South, the Democrats and the Whigs, should have become equally reactionary. The Democrats, who at the turn of the century had with justice laid claim to the liberal leadership of the republic, had now rejected the principles of their founder and had become hidebound in their conservatism. Following the death of Calhoun in 1850, Jefferson Davis of Mississippi became the party spokesman. While it is difficult to believe that anyone could have been more reactionary on the slavery issue than Calhoun, Davis accomplished that seemingly impossible feat. Upon the death of Clay in 1852, thousands of the Whigs followed Alexander H. Stephens and Robert Toombs of Georgia into the Democratic party, which was coming to be universally recognized as the party of slavery. Thousands of other Whigs affiliated with the Know-Nothing movement, which sought to rouse the citizenry against the chimerical Roman Catholic menace, much in the manner of the twentieth century Ku Klux Klan. The Know-Nothings received their death blow, however, in 1855 when Henry A. Wise, from several points of view one of the most liberal and enlightened men in the ante-bellum South, defeated their candidate for governor of Virginia in a whirlwind campaign.

It was at this period that a movement to reopen the African slave trade was launched in the deep South. Although the proposal never mustered anything like a majority in any state, it was hospitably received by a considerable number of planters in South Carolina, Georgia, Alabama, Mississippi, Louisiana, and Texas. A formal suggestion that the trade be reopened came from Governor J. H. Adams of South Carolina. Congressman Emerson Etheridge of Tennessee accordingly introduced a blistering resolution in the House of Representatives in 1856, severely scoring the plan. The resolution declared that any suggestion that the trade be revived was "shocking to the moral sentiments of the enlightened portion of mankind," and that if this proposal were carried out by Congress, it would "justly subject the United States to the reproach and execration of all civilized and Christian people." Only twelve Southern congressmen, in addition to Etheridge, voted for this resolution, and eleven of these were from the upper South. William R. Smith of Alabama was the lone supporter from the Gulf states. The others were Leander M. Cox, Samuel F. Swope, Warner L. Underwood, Alexander K. Marshall, and Humphrey Marshall of Kentucky; Charles Ready, Thomas Rivers, and Felix K. Zollicoffer of Tennessee; Robert T. Paine and Richard C. Puryear of North Carolina, and Justin F. Morrill of Virginia.

The year 1856 also witnessed the ruffianly caning of Senator Charles Sumner of Massachusetts by Representative Preston Brooks of South Carolina. Sumner, it is true, had delivered a vituperative speech in the Senate denouncing Brooks's uncle, Senator A. P. Butler, who was absent at the time, but one cannot excuse Brooks for beating the Massachusetts abolitionist into insensibility with a cane while he was seated defenseless at his desk. Yet sectional feeling was so intense at the period that the South Carolinian's action was widely applauded throughout the slave states, and he was presented with a number of handsome canes, including one from the students and officers of the University of Virginia and another from the students of Franklin College, later the University of Georgia.

The caning of Sumner served to widen still further the breach between the sections and to sharpen antagonisms on both sides of the Potomac. But the situation was aggravated to an even greater degree by two legislative enactments which rankled in the breasts of thousands upon thousands of Northerners.

The first of these was the Fugitive Slave Law, while the second was the Kansas-Nebraska bill, with its attendant repeal of the Missouri Compromise. The Fugitive Slave Law, embodying *ex post facto* provisions and other objectionable features, was widely regarded as a barbarous piece of legislation, and was openly nullified in many parts of the North. In addition, the feeling was general in the free states that the Missouri Compromise had been repealed in flat violation of a solemn pledge. When on top of all this the Dred Scott decision carried the process a step further, pronounced the compromise void in law, even before its revocation, and declared that neither Congress nor any territorial legislature could forbid slavery in a territory, the wrath of the North knew no bounds.

The situation was aggravated further by the verbal onslaughts of the Southern fire-eaters, notably William L. Yancey of Alabama. Yancey was even dissatisfied with the Kansas-Nebraska Act, although its passage represented the greatest of all the triumphs of the Slave Power. He felt that the act permitted future settlers in the territories to decide for themselves whether those territories were to be free or not, and he was unwilling to concede them that right. The blazing oratory of this passionate defender of slavery did much to fan the flames of animosity between the sections. So powerful, indeed, was his influence with the extreme secessionists that a competent historian has advanced the thesis that Yancey is one of half a dozen men who did most to shape American history in the nineteenth century.

Events were moving rapidly to a climax and there

was an atmosphere of febrile suspense as the political parties prepared for their national conventions in the spring and summer of 1860. The newly formed Republican party had espoused many of the principles of the old Jeffersonian party of that name, whereas the Democratic party had identified itself with the cause of reaction.

The Democrats convened at Charleston in April. A contest developed over a suggested declaration in the platform, favored by Southern pro-slavery radicals, that Congress must defend slavery in the territories. The plank was voted down, but under the spell of Yancey's burning eloquence, the irreconcilables from the far South withdrew from the hall. All efforts to heal the breach in the ranks of the Democracy were ineffectual. The more conservative wing of the party nominated Stephen A. Douglas of Illinois as its standard bearer, while the extremists chose John C. Breckinridge of Kentucky. The Constitutional Union party, composed largely of remnants of the old Whigs and Know-Nothings, named John Bell of Tennessee on a platform which tried to say nothing as impressively as possible. The Republicans selected Abraham Lincoln of Illinois, a man who resented the institution of slavery and declared that it should not be extended to the territories. The platform on which he stood excoriated the Dred Scott decision.

There had been threats from the deep South that secession would follow the election of a president on such a platform, and when the returns in November showed that Lincoln was victorious, South Carolina prepared at once to leave the Union. A convention called in the Palmetto State voted without a dissenting voice in favor of secession, and by February 1 Georgia, Alabama, Florida, Mississippi, Louisiana, and Texas had all followed South Carolina's lead. When in April President Lincoln announced that he would replenish the supplies of the Federal garrison at Fort Sumter, the heavily charged atmosphere around Charleston burst into flame. Interpreting the President's statement as a declaration of war, the Carolinians opened fire on the garrison and forced the fort's capitulation. Lincoln instantly galvanized both the North and the South into action with his call for 75,000 volunteers. Virginia, North Carolina, Tennessee, and Arkansas were thus compelled to choose at once between the Union and the Confederacy. Refusing absolutely to have any part in the coercion of South Carolina, they promptly determined upon secession. The war had begun.

What was the South fighting for? Had it plunged into this sanguinary conflict "to perpetuate the institution of slavery"?

While a large element in the South undoubtedly desired the preservation of the slave system—as witness the declaration of the Southern Presbyterian church in 1862, to which reference already has been made, together with statements of a similar nature from various prominent individuals below Mason and Dixon's Line over a period of at least twenty years— and while slavery would have been preserved in the Confederacy, at least for a time, if the South had achieved its independence, the thesis that the South went to war to perpetuate the chattel system is scarcely tenable. It is of course true that there would have been no war, except for the rancors and hates engendered between the sections in the controversies over slavery. But it is difficult, if not impossible, to rationalize the theory that the North was fighting for the primary purpose of abolishing slavery, while the South was fighting for the primary purpose of preserving it.

Consider, for example, the statement of President Lincoln in his inaugural address in March, 1861, on the very eve of the conflict, which statement was in complete harmony with the platform of his party: "I have no purpose directly or indirectly to interfere with the institution of slavery in the states where it now exists. I believe I have no lawful right to do so, and I have no inclination to do so." Consider also the declaration of President Jefferson Davis, made three years later: "We are not fighting for slavery. We are fighting for independence." And finally, consider the assertion of that knightliest of men, the commander of the Southern armies, General Robert E. Lee, who expressed indignation after the war that anyone should charge the South with having fought to perpetuate slavery. Lee, like many of the other Southern generals, and like the great majority of the men in the ranks, was not a slave-owner, for he had emancipated all his Negroes long before the outbreak of hostilities. After Appomattox he rejoiced that the slave system had been abolished in the following words: "I would cheerfully have lost all I have lost by the war and have suffered all I have suffered, to have this object attained."

Why, then, were Lee and the men who followed

him with such courage and devotion willing to plunge a nation into the red maw of war, and to rend asunder the governmental fabric builded by the fathers? They were willing to do so chiefly because the political, economic, and social systems in the North and the South were becoming increasingly divergent, under the stress and strain of the mounting hostility between the sections, and because the South had come to feel that its right to local self-government, its desire to preserve its own institutions and to order its own life after its own fashion, was gravely menaced by a people who seemed to grow more unsympathetic and antagonistic toward it year by year. Although it had at times been guilty of inconsistencies, the South had exhibited a far more constant devotion to the cause of state rights than the North had ever done. Its people felt more deeply attached to their respective states than to the Federal government. Consequently when they became convinced that the integrity of state rights was threatened by a tyrannical authority at Washington under the domination of Northerners largely out of sympathy with Southern modes of thought, it seemed to them that life under such conditions was no longer tolerable. The only alternative, they felt, was secession and war, and from that alternative they did not shrink. Oblivious of the frightful odds, unmindful of the fearful cost, they rushed headlong into the bloody fray and cast the issue upon the lap of the gods.

CHAPTER VII

WRITERS IN THE STORMY PRE-WAR YEARS

THE ROMANTICISM, didacticism, and sentimentality which distinguished American literature during the middle years of the nineteenth century were especially conspicuous in the poetry and prose of the South. John Esten Cooke's characterization of Virginia letters for the first eighty-odd years of the century may be applied, with almost no exceptions, to the literature of Dixie for the three decades preceding the Civil War:

"If no great original genius has arisen to put the lion's paw on Virginia letters," Cooke wrote, "many writers of admirable attainments and solid merit have produced works which have instructed and improved their generation; and to instruct and improve is better than to amuse. Whatever may be the true rank of the literature, it possesses a distinct character. It may be said of it with truth that it is notable for its respect for good morals and manners; that it is nowhere offensive to delicacy or piety; or endeavors to instil a belief in what ought not to be believed. It is a very great deal to say of the literature of any country in the nineteenth century."

Those who would have an explanation for the barrenness of the Southern literary landscape during the ante-bellum era will find it unnecessary to look far beyond the above-quoted deliverance of the excellent Mr. Cooke. His fears that the reading public below the Potomac might suddenly and without warning be exposed to a new idea, or might encounter a novel or a poem from which uplifting thoughts and Messianic motives had been carefully excluded, were unfortunately shared by a majority of Southern *littérateurs* and their clients. The consequence was that the South's contribution to literature, particularly in the decades immediately prior to the [war, was, with a handful of honorable exceptions, quite negligible.

One of the first of the writers to strike a new note in Southern fiction was A. B. Longstreet of Georgia, who began newspaper publication of his *Georgia Scenes* in 1833 and collected them in book form two years later. In 1832 John Pendleton Kennedy had published *Swallow Barn*, a work accepted by critics as inaugurating what has been termed the "nightingale and 'yes massa' " type of novel, but *Georgia Scenes* was in an entirely different tradition. Its author concerned himself with the homely and unpretentious lives of the common people of his native state, rather than with the affairs of the great slaveholders. He told of the brawls, the gander pullings, and the cock-fights of the Georgians of a hundred years ago in a realistic and humorous vein which excited the admiration of Poe and many other contemporary critics.

Longstreet's career touched the Old South at many points. In addition to his work as a writer, he was a jurist, a newspaper editor and a musician, and in 1838 he entered the Methodist ministry. He later served as president of Emory College in Georgia, Centenary College in Louisiana, the University of Mississippi, and South Carolina College. His career as an educator does not appear to have been particularly noteworthy, however. Joseph Le Conte, in fact, pronounced him "utterly unfit for the presidency of a college." Longstreet was liberal in his attitude toward Catholics, much more so, indeed, than the average member of his church, but he was reactionary in his theology and a strong apologist for slavery. Despite his great versatility, his fame today rests upon his authorship of *Georgia Scenes*.

A Southern writer whose name is now practically forgotten, but whose influence was exerted in behalf of better relations between the sections and in opposition to slavery was William Alexander Carruthers of Virginia. His *Kentuckian in New York*, published in 1834, is especially worthy of remembrance.

A man of a different type was Nathaniel Beverley Tucker of Virginia, whose *George Balcome* Poe regarded as the best novel by an American. Tucker was the antithesis of Carruthers in his attitude toward the North. In *The Partisan Leader*, which appeared in 1836, he painted a highly unfavorable portrait of what he conceived to be the typical Yankee, and at the same time came stoutly to the defense of the slave system.

Although he was not a native, Poe is widely regarded as in other respects a typical Southerner. Indisputably the greatest literary figure in the antebellum South, if not in the history of America, he set new standards in the fields of criticism and the short story. Poe first attracted attention in 1833, when he was awarded a prize by a Baltimore magazine for his *MS. Found in a Bottle.* Two years later he became editor of the *Southern Literary Messenger* and his career began in earnest.

Poe's influence as a critical force was decidedly liberal, despite the fact that he made some silly and ill-natured attacks on Longfellow and others. James Russell Lowell declared that he "lifted literary criticism from the abasement of sniveling imbecility into which it had sunk." He pleaded for more honest criticism of books by native writers, and urged an end of "indiscriminate puffing of good, bad and indifferent." While the authorities are in disagreement as to whether he followed his own advice at all times in this matter, particularly where Southern authors were concerned, few will dispute that the theory of criticism which he developed was a liberalizing influence not only upon the American literature of his day but to an even greater degree upon that of the late nineteenth and early twentieth centuries.

In his attitude toward his art, Poe exhibited one of the requisite characteristics of the true liberal, namely, a receptiveness to new ideas. Not only so, but his creative genius was so extraordinary that he himself formulated new theories of criticism and the short story which have endured to the present day, while his poetry was highly original and wholly unlike anything that had gone before. With respect to his views in regard to chattel servitude, however, he did not rise above his environment. "Poe is the only poet, so far as I know," the late Professor G. E.

9

Woodberry once wrote, "who is on the record as the defender of human slavery."

A still more ardent defender of the slave system was William Gilmore Simms, second only to Poe in the Old South's gallery of literary men. Simms was a native of South Carolina, but he was not born into its ruling caste, and it was a good many years before he was accepted by Charlestonian society. The fact that he supported himself with his pen handicapped him in the best circles until he finally achieved such fame as to force his recognition by the patricians.

The tragedy of Simms' career is to be found in the fact that he squandered his manifold talents and dissipated his immense energy "in trumpery fields that belong to the literary dray horse." He produced almost a hundred books of prose and poetry, more than enough for an ordinary man, but in addition he was active in a number of other directions. He founded and edited several magazines, dabbled in politics, delivered numerous lectures, gave generous advice and assistance to promising young writers, and sought by every possible means to create a creditable Southern literature. Books, articles, monographs poured from his pen in a veritable Niagara, and some of his romances are inferior only to those of Cooper on this side of the Atlantic. Had he confined himself to the writing of novels he might have achieved a place beside America's literary immortals, but he elected not to do so. Toward the end of his life, when he had lost his fortune, his wife, and nine of his fifteen children, he composed for his tomb the following poignant epitaph: "Here lies one who, after a reasonably long life, distinguished chiefly by unceasing labors, has left all his better works undone."

The activities of Simms and various other Southern literary men as apologists for slavery were redoubled after the appearance of *Uncle Tom's Cabin* in 1852. The instantaneous success of this book, which enjoyed a tremendous sale in this country and Europe, served to place the slave States more than ever on the defensive. This despite the fact that Mrs. Stowe expected the reaction against the novel to be more severe in the North than in the South, the principal villain being a New Englander. But the book was a ringing philippic against slavery, and while it presented a distorted picture of the institution, it had the effect of rousing thousands of Northerners to a realization of the evils of Negro servitude.

Southern partisans immediately launched a counter-offensive, and within a comparatively short time, fourteen pro-slavery novels were on the market. But *Uncle Tom's Cabin* easily outsold all fourteen of them combined. Within less than a year after publication, 300,000 copies had been disposed of in this country, while 1,500,000 more were snapped up in Great Britain in six months. The book was soon translated into more than a score of languages. It has been called with truth "the most influential novel ever published."

Southern counterblasts to the anti-slavery propaganda of Mrs. Stowe and others did not appear wholly in fictional form. True, William J. Grayson of South Carolina contributed a 1,600-line poem, "The Hireling and the Slave," with a view to supplementing the fourteen novels which had already achieved publication. But there were also several serious philosophical and sociological studies having as their object the refutation of arguments that human bondage had no place in a democracy. Albert T. Bledsoe, a professor in the University of Virginia, essayed a philosophical defense of the chattel system in his *Liberty and Slavery*, while George Fitzhugh of Virginia did likewise in his *Sociology for the South* and *Cannibals All, or Slaves Without Masters*.

Such was the prevailing attitude of Southern authors toward the "peculiar institution" from 1830 until the war. It was also the prevailing attitude of the principal periodicals during these years. A partial exception is to be found in the case of the *Southern Literary Messenger*, established at Richmond in 1834. James E. Heath, the first editor, was severely critical of the slave system on both moral and economic grounds, and pronounced it a "great evil." In the forties, however, the magazine joined the other leading publications of its type below the Potomac in espousing the cause of reaction. On the other hand it catered less to sectional prejudices than most of its rivals, which partially explains the fact that it was able to continue publication until 1864, a longer period than any other Southern magazine of the ante-bellum era. It was most widely read during the years when the work of Edgar Allan Poe was appearing in its columns. Poe also occupied the *Messenger's* editorial chair from 1835 until 1837, and succeeded in raising its circulation from 700 to 5,500, a rather substantial figure for a literary journal of the period.

Charleston was the birthplace and also the graveyard of a number of ambitious ventures into the periodical field. The *Southern Quarterly Review* first appeared in New Orleans in 1842, but it was transferred to Charleston almost immediately, and remained there until its demise in the late fifties. William Gilmore Simms edited this magazine for the last seven years of its existence and made it a mouthpiece of the pro-slavery secessionists. The last number contained half a dozen articles strongly defending the slave system or expressing other views which harmonized with those of the Southern fire-eaters. The *Southern Quarterly Review* was the only literary journal below the Mason and Dixon Line which seriously disputed the supremacy of the *Southern Literary Messenger*.

A magazine of a somewhat different type was *DeBow's Review*, established by J. D. B. DeBow in New Orleans in 1846. DeBow, who was then only twenty-five years of age, enlisted the aid of a friend and launched the magazine with such a complete lack of funds that the two lived at first on nothing but bread, with sometimes a little butter. Their sole piece of furniture was a mattress. Yet their magazine, which was designed to promote the commercial prosperity of the slave states, not only managed to survive, but soon boasted the largest circulation in the South. While *DeBow's Review* announced at the outset that it would refrain from discussing questions concerning which there was a serious divergence of opinion between the sections, it abandoned this policy and became more and more partisan. When the air grew electric with the controversy over human bondage, DeBow became violently sectional. The fantastic

scheme for the acquisition of additional slave territory through the annexation of Cuba appealed to him
strongly, and he also urged the reopening of the
African slave trade. In addition to such grotesqueries,
he advocated a Southern boycott of Northern colleges
and Northern manufacturers. *DeBow's Review* had been
metamorphosed from a non-partisan journal into a
radical organ of the pro-slavery extremists.

While it is easy to criticise DeBow, Simms, and the
other Southern magazine editors who championed
the cause of slavery with such ardor, one may be permitted to inquire whether the attitude of these men
was any less admirable than that of Northern editors
who were afraid to publish articles bearing in any
way upon the question of slavery, for fear of losing
subscribers. The editor of *Graham's* declared in 1842
that no Philadelphia periodical permitted the word
"slavery" to appear in its pages; the *Knickerbocker*
magazine published only the most innocuous statements on the subject, while during the fifties the *North
American Review* pursued the pusillanimous policy of
declining all articles of a controversial nature.

But if Southern magazines reflected public sentiment in the regions where they were published during
the thirty years preceding the Civil War, this was
equally true of Southern newspapers. The press from
the Potomac to the Rio Grande was almost solidly
united in defense of slavery and except in Louisville
and Wheeling, on the very edge of slave territory, no
resounding editorial voice seems to have been raised in
opposition. Even in Louisville freedom of utterance
on the question appears, strangely enough, to have

been largely confined to the years immediately prior to and immediately following the state constitutional convention of 1849.

Southern journalism for the period under examination was considerably less scurrilous than it had been at the turn of the century. This was due in large measure to the influence of Thomas Ritchie, who prevailed upon many newspapermen in Dixie to "abandon the infamous practice of pampering the vilest of appetites by violating the sanctity of private life, and indulging in gross personalities and indecorous language." The code duello prevailed universally, however, and every editor realized that he was subject to challenge for his journalistic utterances. The consequence was that it was highly desirable for him to be able to handle a derringer and a quill with equal competence. An idea of the terrific mortality among ante-bellum journalists may be obtained from the fact that five editors of a Vicksburg paper met violent deaths within a period of thirteen years.

Francis Preston Blair, a native Virginian who came to Washington from Frankfort, Kentucky, in 1832 to take over the editorial direction of the *Globe*, may be mentioned as a prominent newspaperman whose judgments on the slavery issue not infrequently ran counter to prevailing Southern prejudices. Blair assumed charge of the *Globe* at the request of President Jackson, and during his editorship the paper was the organ of the Jackson-Van Buren Democrats. An able polemical writer who made the opposition squirm under the thrusts from his vigorous pen, his influence was enhanced by virtue of the fact that he occupied a seat

in the "Kitchen Cabinet." Blair strongly opposed
the annexation of Texas, and when President Polk
ousted him in 1845 for Thomas Ritchie, who had
been persuaded to come to Washington, his journalistic career came to a close. Soon afterward he appeared
as an advocate of Free Soilism and he later denounced
the Kansas-Nebraska Act as a violation of the Missouri
Compromise. He supported Lincoln in 1860, and was
one of the president's most trusted advisers during
the war. After Lincoln's assassination, the vindictive-
ness of the radicals drove him back into the Democratic party.

Probably the most powerful of all the ante-bellum
editors in the Southern states, with the possible exception of Ritchie, was George D. Prentice of Louisville,
who came to that city from Connecticut in 1830 and
founded the Louisville *Journal*. Henry Watterson once
wrote that "from 1830 to 1861 the influence of Prentice was perhaps greater than the influence of any
political writer who ever lived." Watterson added
that this Connecticut Yankee made his paper well
known on both sides of the Atlantic. Prentice was
undoubtedly the most influential Whig editor in his
part of the South, and he is credited with having
prevented the secession of Kentucky. In addition he
was the first of the newspaper "paragraphers," his
pungent paragraphs winning for him quite a reputation as a humorist, while he also achieved more than
local fame as a poet. The *Journal* under his management was a staunch supporter of the Union, both
before and during the Civil War. Prentice was no
abolitionist, but he frequently expressed the belief that

slavery would disappear gradually. More uncompromising hostility to slavery was voiced by the Louisville *Examiner* and Louisville *Courier*, which waged an intensive but futile emancipationist campaign at the time of the state constitutional convention of 1849.

Another native of Connecticut who was an important factor in the journalism of the ante-bellum South was Thaddeus Sanford, who bought the Mobile *Register* in 1828 and retained it for twenty-six years. Sanford expressed vigorous opposition to the nullificationist doctrines enunciated by South Carolina, but at the same time defended slavery and denounced abolitionism. His place on the *Register* was more than filled by John Forsyth of Georgia, who came to Mobile in 1853, and soon made his influence felt throughout the Gulf states. Under Forsyth the *Register* was recognized as the leading Douglas paper in the South. It counseled moderation at a time when few Southerners were willing to listen to such doctrine, but when war finally came, its editor cast his lot unreservedly with his section. John Forsyth was not only a man of brilliant intellectual powers and great journalistic ability, but he had a mind free from pettiness and prejudice. After Appomattox he accepted the inevitable gracefully and urged a like course upon his compatriots. His was one of the most commanding voices in the South pleading for a united nation, and as editor of the *Register* until his death in 1877, he did much to allay the enmities engendered by four years of civil strife. The breadth of his sympathy is further evidenced by his abhorrence of religious bigotry in any form.

At least two editors of conspicuous prestige operated in Tennessee during the decades just prior to the war. One of these was Jeremiah George Harris of Connecticut, who came to Nashville as editor of the Nashville *Union* in 1839 at the invitation of James K. Polk. The latter was a candidate for governor that year and was anxious to "redeem" the state for Jackson. He succeeded, thanks in part to the journalistic support accorded him by Harris. This accomplished newspaperman was especially adept with the twin weapons of ridicule and abuse, and he engaged in many controversies during his years on the *Union*. Like almost all the other New Englanders who assumed charge of Southern papers during the ante-bellum era, Harris abandoned whatever anti-slavery opinions he had entertained in his native habitat and adjusted himself to his new environment. Although as editor of a New Bedford, Massachusetts, paper he had expressed views "strongly squinting toward abolitionism," there was no hint of any such heresy in the columns of his Nashville journal. In fact he demonstrated his complete orthodoxy by taunting John Bell editorially with being an abolitionist, "the basest opprobrium that could be heaped upon a Southerner."

Another Tennessee journalist whose paper enjoyed a wide audience was William G. Brownlow. His Knoxville *Whig* was the strongest newspaper in the eastern half of the state, and he himself was always a storm center, because of his openly expressed Union views. "Parson" Brownlow did not oppose slavery prior to the war, but he was ruthless in his attacks on the secessionists. After the commencement of hostilities, his paper was suppressed and he crossed over inside the Federal lines. From that point of vantage he applauded Lincoln's emancipation proclamation. In 1865 Brownlow was elected governor of Tennessee by acclamation, and he exerted his influence to achieve the disfranchisement of all who had taken up arms against the Federal government. He edited the *Whig* for several years after the war, and used it as a vehicle for his radical views.

The most important Whig paper in North Carolina before the war was Edward J. Hale's Fayetteville *Observer*. Hale, whom Roger A. Pryor pronounced "the ablest editor of his time," took over the *Observer* in 1825 and did not relinquish it until the destruction of its plant by the Union army forty years later. Although offered the editorial direction of the New York *World* in 1858, the sectional controversy was then so acute that he elected to remain in his native state. Hale was the spokesman for the conservative forces in North Carolina during the fifties. He counseled moderation, and sought to hold in check the violent bellicosity of the Southern extremists. Until Lincoln issued his call for troops to put down South Carolina, Hale strongly opposed secession, but as soon as the presidential summons went out, the Fayetteville editor recognized that war was inevitable and cast his lot wholeheartedly with his own people.

A journalist of a wholly different stamp was W. W. Holden, who took charge of the Raleigh *Standard*, the leading Democratic paper of the state, in 1843 after six years as editor of a rival Whig daily. He soon made the *Standard* known and feared throughout North

Carolina. Whereas Hale's Fayetteville *Observer* spoke for the moderates, Holden's paper was the organ of the fierce pro-slavery radicals. Holden seems to have been thoroughly unscrupulous. His early shift from Whiggery to Democracy indicated that his principles contained a liberal infusion of india rubber, and by the time the war was well under way, he had completely forfeited the confidence of his followers. Although he had led in demanding secession a few years before, in 1865 he reversed his position and urged the severe punishment of the "rebels." He also advocated unlimited Negro suffrage. Elected governor, his administration was characterized by wholesale corruption. He was impeached for abuse of power and disqualified from ever holding office again.

With the passing of Thomas Ritchie and John Hampden Pleasants in the forties, the Richmond *Examiner* came forward as the most influential and widely read newspaper in Virginia. This journal is said to have been unique in the policy it pursued of publishing the utterances of Theodore Parker and other abolitionists with regard to slavery. It did this although its own view was that the slave system was not properly subject to criticism, since Negroes could not rightly be regarded as human beings. John M. Daniel, a brilliant and slashing writer, was in editorial charge of the *Examiner* from 1847 until 1853. Although he was only twenty-two when chosen to the position, during the next six years he stamped his name indelibly upon the journalism of his time. Daniel resigned to accept an appointment as United States representative at the Court of Sardinia, which post he retained until the secession of South Carolina. He hurried back to Virginia immediately thereafter and became co-editor of the *Examiner*, with Edward A. Pollard. Both men were as zealous in their devotion to the Confederacy as they were distrustful of President Jefferson Davis. As the war progressed they became increasingly bitter in their criticism of him. It is noteworthy, however, that no effort was made by the authorities to suppress the *Examiner*, although numerous Northern newspapers were compelled to suspend operations for similar offenses. "Parson" Brownlow's Knoxville *Whig* seems to have been the only Southern paper of consequence which was suppressed during the four years of war.

When the Southern press raised a chorus of praise for Representative Brooks of South Carolina upon his caning of Charles Sumner, the *Examiner* remarked: "Far from blaming Mr. Brooks, we are disposed to regard him as a conservative gentleman seeking to restore its lost dignity to the Senate." The Richmond *Enquirer*, which was clamoring for the annexation of Cuba in order that the slave territory might be enlarged, also endorsed the caning. "In the main the press of the South applaud the conduct of Mr. Brooks without condition or limitation," the *Enquirer* declared. "Our approbation, at least, is entire and unreserved. . . . It was a proper act, done at the proper time and in the proper place."

Newspaper opinion in the upper South was strongly antagonistic to the proposed reopening of the African slave trade, but in the cotton states, and especially in New Orleans, sentiment was more evenly divided. As early as 1839 the New Orleans *Courier* had suggested such a step, and the New Orleans *Delta* and New Orleans *Picayune* adopted a similar view some years later. The Charleston *Courier*, while celebrating the virtues of slavery, asserted its unequivocal opposition to the resuscitation of the traffic with Africa.

Events were swirling to a climax in the late fifties, and wild suggestions for the annexation not only of Cuba, but of Santo Domingo, Mexico, and Nicaragua filled the air. The Southern firebrands, spurred on by such papers as the Savannah *Republican*, the Atlanta *Southern Confederacy*, the Natchez *Free Trader*, and, most important of all, the Charleston *Mercury*, edited by R. Barnwell Rhett, were calling loudly for secession. It is a surprising fact, however, that the Southern press was on the whole rather conservative in its attitude toward the question of separation. Secessionist papers were especially numerous and powerful in South Carolina and Mississippi, but in most states there was a strong sprinkling of editors who fought staunchly against disunion.

This was the situation until the eve of the war, but when actual secession began, the Southerner's intense loyalty to his native heath asserted itself. The average Southern journalist felt that as long as his state was wavering, he was free to advocate or to oppose secession, but he also felt that once his state had determined finally and unequivocally upon separation, he must abide its verdict. The consequence was that when the storm finally broke, the press of the Confederate states spoke almost with one voice.

On both sides of the Potomac editorial pens were

dipped in vitriol as the clangor of war resounded through the land. No more striking illustration of the rampant sectionalism which pervaded both Northern and Southern newspapers upon the commencement of hostilities is to be found than appears in an editorial from the Charleston *Courier*. The *Courier* had been distinguished three decades before for the judicial detachment with which it viewed controversial issues and for a noticeable absence of malignity in its public utterances. Its publisher then had been Aaron S. Willington of Massachusetts, and he was still its publisher. But fifty-eight years of residence in Charleston had changed Willington's attitudes and altered his mental processes. As the North and the South girded for war, the once restrained *Courier* struck out savagely. In an editorial which received the attention of the country it sounded a note of rancorous bitterness:

"The sword must cut asunder the last tie that bound us to a people, whom, in spite of wrongs and injustice wantonly inflicted through a long series of years, we had not yet utterly hated and despised. The last expiring spark of affection must be quenched in blood. Some of the most splendid pages in our glorious history must be blurred. A blow must be struck that would make the ears of every Republican fanatic tingle, and whose dreadful effects will be felt by generations yet to come. We must transmit a heritage of rankling and undying hate to our children."

CHAPTER VIII

ANTE-BELLUM EDUCATION

THE IMPRESSION was widespread in the North after the Civil War that the Old South had been wholly lacking in educational facilities for the masses, and that this condition had helped materially to bring on the intersectional conflict. At the meeting of the National Teachers' Association at Harrisburg, Pennsylvania, in August, 1865, for example, the war was termed one "of education and patriotism against ignorance and barbarism."

It is true, as was noted in an earlier chapter, that the public schools in the ante-bellum South were much inferior to those now functioning in the area, but this criticism may be applied with an almost equal degree of truth to the Northern schools. It should be borne in mind, too, that other countries were even less advanced in this respect than the United States. In England, for instance, it was not until the nineties of the last century that free elementary public schooling was available to any except the children of persons who were willing to take the humiliating oath of poverty.

But those who contend that the Southern states before the Civil War were entirely without public schools are simply ignorant of the facts. Professor

Edgar W. Knight declares that whereas the school systems in the South were not quite so fully developed as those in the North, "in origin, organization and comparative results, there is a striking likeness between schools in North Carolina, Virginia or Alabama and those of the more advanced States of New York, Pennsylvania or Connecticut." He says further that "one does not have to hunt far to discover conditions in the New England States a decade or two prior to the outbreak of the war much like those in certain Southern States in the forties and fifties."

Various factors combined, however, to prevent such school systems as were in operation in the South before the war from achieving anything like the degree of usefulness attained by the systems subsequently established there. Outstanding among these may be mentioned the fact that the schools were operated primarily for the benefit of indigent families. They were usually known as "poor schools" or "free schools" and an aura of penury often hovered about persons attending them. This feeling, it is true, died out almost entirely in some localities. Even in aristocratic Charleston, wealthy families sent their children to the public schools in the late fifties. On the other hand, a rather slow process of education was necessary in most states before the prejudice against this type of schooling could be overcome.

While the Old South did not produce any pioneers in this field whose influence equalled that of Horace Mann or Henry Barnard, there were leaders in almost every Southern state who exhibited a lively appreciation of the value of public education and a broad

10

grasp of the problems involved. Chief among these were Calvin H. Wiley of North Carolina and Dr. Robert J. Breckinridge of Kentucky, who were successful in bringing the public school systems in their respective states to a higher degree of development than any other school superintendents in Dixie.

John C. Calhoun, who seems after 1830 to have espoused the reactionary side of every public question, was opposed to the education of the "poor whites" on the ground that it would "do nothing for them," but many other pro-slavery men took the opposite view. As far as the South's "peculiar institution" was concerned, they were orthodox, but on matters relating to the education of the whites, they were liberal.

Early efforts looking toward the establishment of systems of secondary education in the four original Southern states already have been outlined. In the Southwest, the Republic of Texas showed that it was not unaware of the desirability of an educational system when it inserted in its Declaration of Independence in 1836 the charge against the Mexican government that that government had "failed to establish any public system of education," and added: "It is an axiom in political science that unless a people are educated and enlightened, it is idle to expect the continuance of civil liberty or the capacity of self-government." Mirabeau B. Lamar, president of Texas for three years, beginning in 1838, was its foremost educational statesman. In response to his recommendation, the Texan Congress passed legislation in 1839 setting aside three leagues of land in each county for the support of an academy, and fifty leagues for the establishment and endowment of two universities. While it is true that little else was done in Texas to promote the cause of education until after the Civil War, Lamar helped to prepare the ground for the subsequent fruition of his plans. Another frontier leader who appreciated the need for better educational facilities for the people was James S. Conway, first governor of Arkansas after its admission to the Union. In his inaugural address in 1836 he declared that Arkansas should "insure universal education," and he stressed the need again the following year. Little came of his efforts, however, until after Appomattox.

Charleston, like New Orleans, Savannah, and other large Southern cities, had fairly adequate public schools before the war, but the State of South Carolina made little progress in this direction during the period. This despite the fact that such prominent leaders as George McDuffie and Colonel R. F. W. Allston favored an improved system of secondary education and increased appropriations. In the fifties Dr. J. H. Thornwell, who urged the superiority of state schools over sectarian schools, although he himself was a minister, led a movement for better methods of educating the masses. He accomplished little of a definite nature.

Virginia, like South Carolina, was conservative in its traditions, and while similar efforts were made there, they were foredoomed to failure. Dr. Henry Ruffner, Thomas Ritchie, and James M. Garnett joined hands in the early forties in a crusade which had as its object the setting up of sufficient schools for the masses and the reduction of the illiteracy rate, which had been revealed shortly before as disgracefully high. But the movement was thwarted by the wealthy planters. Henry A. Wise, himself a leading slaveholder, afterwards pleaded without appreciable effect for increased taxes for the support of a statewide system of common schools.

Down in Mississippi Governor Albert G. Brown, who was mainly instrumental in founding the University of Mississippi, began an active agitation in the forties for the "establishment of free schools in which every poor white child in the country may secure, free of charge, the advantages of a liberal education." After several appeals to the legislature, he obtained the passage of "the first statute in Mississippi contemplating a uniform and general system of common schools." This legislation was inadequate, however, and after Brown went out of office his program was forgotten amid the tumult of the slavery controversy.

In the neighboring commonwealth of Alabama, Dr. Basil Manly, president of the state university, and William L. Yancey were staunch advocates of an adequate common school system, and in the fifties, when Alexander Beaufort Meek, widely known versifier, was elected to the legislature, he sponsored a bill establishing the Alabama public schools. While the system did not begin to function properly until after the war, Meek is customarily termed its "father."

Dr. Robert J. Breckinridge was elected superintendent of the Kentucky public schools in 1847, and it was due to his efforts that the school fund created some years previously was saved to the Blue Grass

State. Hostile influences had combined for the purpose of scrapping the entire Kentucky common school system, but this indomitable man not only thwarted the scheme, but during the six years of his incumbency as superintendent he increased the total school enrollment from 20,000 to 201,000. He also secured the establishment of a state normal school. When he resigned his office, the public school system was no longer in danger of extermination, but on the contrary, was highly regarded by a majority of the electorate.

In North Carolina Calvin H. Wiley was even more successful than Breckinridge in arousing interest in popular education, and it was due to his efforts that North Carolina was able to boast of the most highly-developed state system of public schools in the Old South. Wiley's work has been described by competent authorities as not unworthy of comparison with that of Mann and Barnard. Chosen State Superintendent of Public Instruction in 1852, he held the post until its abolition in 1866. During his administration the school system developed in an extraordinary manner. Thanks to his popularity, his energy, and his ability, Wiley was able to achieve remarkable progress. He toured the state from end to end, sometimes spending as much as half his modest salary for traveling expenses. He managed to obtain the largest free school appropriations in the South, and he published a journal of education. Even in 1863, despite the demoralization induced by the war, Wiley sought to put into operation a grade school system and to provide facilities for the training of teachers.

While the progress made in North Carolina, Kentucky, and other states led, in general, to improved methods of secondary education in the Old South, the region always lagged behind the North in this respect. Its native white illiteracy rate was considerably higher, and its appropriations smaller. One Southern white child in seven was in school for at least part of the session in the South in 1860, as against one Northern white child in every five or five and a half.

During these years, when the Southern states were strengthening their public school systems, there were also a few significant developments in the realm of the higher learning. These developments were particularly significant at the University of Alabama, the University of Mississippi, and the University of Virginia. It is also worth recording that the enrollment in a number of Southern colleges and universities increased markedly in the fifties, under the stimulus of sectional appeals made by commercial conventions to Southern parents not to send their sons to Northern institutions, where heretical ideas as to slavery and other matters might be inculcated. This campaign had the effect of sending the attendance at the University of Virginia skyrocketing within a decade to by far the largest in Dixie. Whereas it had less than 200 students in 1848, this total had risen to almost 700 ten years later. It is a noteworthy fact, too, that only eight students on the rolls of this institution in 1859 came from the free states.

Jefferson's university at this period had come under the influence of Gessner Harrison, professor of ancient languages there for thirty-one years, beginning in 1828, and his efforts in behalf of more thorough methods of instruction had a most salutary effect upon the institution he served, as well as upon higher education in the South as a whole.

Another vigorous impetus was given the cause of higher learning below the Potomac by the work of Frederick A. P. Barnard at the state universities of Alabama and Mississippi. Barnard was on the faculty of the University of Alabama for seventeen years, beginning in 1837, and the soundness of his scholarship and the breadth of his learning, combined with the excellent work of Basil Manly as president of the institution, gave this university a period of unprecedented prosperity. Barnard went to the University of Mississippi in 1854 as professor and subsequently was made president and chancellor. During his administration the university's position with the people of the state was greatly strengthened, and it rose to a commanding position among the educational institutions of the lower South. Barnard, who afterward went to Columbia College in New York City, as president, has been termed by President Nicholas Murray Butler "one of the greatest figures, in many ways the greatest figure, in the whole history of our American education." He was a native of Massachusetts.

The University of Georgia, still known as Franklin College, went into something of a decline a few years before the war, owing to the state legislature's refusal to set aside adequate sums for its operation and maintenance. Wilson Lumpkin led a fruitless drive

for legislative relief. Governor Joseph E. Brown then
renewed the fight on the eve of the war, when the
enrollment had fallen below one hundred students,
but he also failed.

At the College of South Carolina a liberalizing
influence for more than two decades was Francis
Lieber, German-born professor. He was "our first
academic political philosopher," and he formulated
"a philosophy of freedom in the land of slavery." In
view of the serious conflict between his opinions and
those of the leading citizens of the Palmetto State,
it is not surprising that he was unsuccessful in obtaining the presidency of the college when a vacancy
occurred in 1855. The following year he departed
for the North, to remain until his death.

We have seen that the ante-bellum public school
systems below Mason and Dixon's Line were inferior
to those on the upper side of that line. The Southern
colleges and universities, on the other hand, challenged the supremacy of those in the North to a considerably greater degree at that time than they have
done since the war. Vastly superior financial resources
enabled Northern institutions to forge far ahead in
the late nineteenth century, but this condition did
not obtain in earlier years.

During the first half of the century the Southern
colleges had a larger total enrollment in proportion
to population than the Northern colleges. In 1840 the

South had one student for every 376 inhabitants, as
against one for every 550 in the rest of the United
States. Not only so, but in 1860 the discrepancy in
favor of the South was still larger. It is also a striking

fact that in 1860 the South had more colleges than the North, these colleges had nearly as many students in them as the Northern colleges, although the South's white population was less than half that of the North, and more money was spent on them than was spent on the Northern colleges.

Some authorities feel that the quality of the instruction furnished in the Southern institutions was, on the whole, inferior to that provided elsewhere. This is probably true. Certainly in the years immediately preceding the war there was a regimentation of opinion in the Southland as to slavery and related topics which extended to all the colleges and universities and left little or no room for freedom of thought or expression. On the other hand, where matters not intimately bound up with the controversy between the sections were concerned, Southern institutions afforded opportunities for sound learning and broad scholarship which were not often surpassed beyond the Potomac or the Ohio.

CHAPTER IX

RECONSTRUCTION AND RACE RELATIONS

CONFRONTED on every hand by desolation and decay, the Southern people in the summer of 1865 wearily began the task of salvaging what was left of their once proud civilization. Their wealth had been swept away, their plantations and farms laid waste, many of their cities and towns reduced to cinders, and a quarter of a million of their sons sacrificed to the god of war. The assassination of President Lincoln had removed from the political scene the only man capable of holding the Northern radicals in check, and Charles Sumner, Ben Wade, and Thad Stevens were laying plans for the introduction of universal Negro suffrage into the Southern states. In the North, where the number of Negroes was inconsequential, only six states allowed them to vote, but Sumner, Wade, Stevens, and their fellow-statesmen felt, none the less, that justice required the immediate enfranchisement of the millions of freedmen in the South. Thus began the nightmare of Reconstruction, a carnival of pillage and corruption, of bribery and debauchery, with the leading whites deprived of the ballot in many states and the ignorant and illiterate Negroes, led by unscrupulous carpetbaggers and scalawags, in control. In Florida, Alabama, Louisiana, Arkansas, and the Carolinas the Negroes and their allies were absolute masters of the situation. In Georgia, Mississippi, and Tennessee their grip was somewhat less firm, while in Texas and Virginia they accomplished comparatively little.

During the war Lincoln had suspended the writ of habeas corpus without authority, and had thrown citizens into jail on what James Ford Rhodes describes as "orders as arbitrary as the *lettres-de-cachet* of Louis XIV." Jefferson Davis also had suspended the writ of habeas corpus in the Confederacy, but on the whole there had been less interference with the constitutional rights of the people under Davis than under Lincoln.

Now that the South was prostrate in the dust, the North once more played fast and loose with civil liberties—but this time it was with the civil liberties of the ex-Confederates. President Andrew Johnson, himself a Southerner, sought to curb the radicals, but he was not equal to the task. Immediately following the war, Johnson had been highly intemperate in his references to the secessionists. His devotion to the Union had led him to call the Confederates "traitors," and he had urged the hanging of Lee and Davis. But although this Union Democrat from Tennessee was at one time considerably more abusive of the Southern leaders than Lincoln had ever been, he subsequently modified his position and sought to prevent the imposition of universal Negro suffrage upon his native section.

While he was mistaken in some of his policies, Johnson was a man of the highest character, possessing a rugged integrity and fearless honesty which placed him far above most of his detractors. After due reflection, he concluded that the radicals ought not to be permitted to exploit and humiliate the Southern people, and from that position he refused to retreat. Realizing that Johnson could not be bullied, and infuriated by his various veto messages, Stevens and his cohorts had the Tennessean impeached in the House. After a dramatic battle, they failed by one vote to obtain the necessary majority for conviction in the Senate.

Meanwhile the South, in poverty and despair, was struggling to bring a semblance of order out of the chaos which enveloped it. General Robert E. Lee, even greater in defeat than in victory, now assumed the leadership of the liberal forces which were seeking to allay sectional bitterness and to build up a united nation. Declining the offer of an estate in England, to which an annuity of £3,000 was attached, Lee said he preferred to remain in his native state, to share in its burdens, and to help in rebuilding its shattered civilization. Offered the presidency of little Washington College, he demurred for fear that his association with the institution might injure its standing, but feeling that he would like to "set the young an example of submission to authority," he finally accepted. Thus as a college president in the quiet town of Lexington, Virginia, Lee spent the few years which remained to him. Putting aside all futile repining and setting his face resolutely to the future, the former commander of the Confederate armies counseled his old soldiers and the Southern people as a whole to "abandon all these local animosities and make your sons Americans."

Lee was by no means alone in urging such a policy upon the South. In South Carolina, General Wade Hampton helped to put an end to intersectional enmities, although his own fortune was gone and his splendid mansion near Columbia was in ashes, by advising the Southern citizenry to accept defeat with good grace. Generals Johnston, Beauregard, and Longstreet also urged the people to submit promptly and without undue repining.

Southern women responded here and there to these appeals by placing flowers upon the graves of both Union and Confederate dead when Memorial Day or other similar anniversaries were observed. And in addition to the exhortations from leading military commanders for an end to sectionalism, others equally eloquent came from such men as Benjamin H. Hill and Alexander H. Stephens of Georgia.

Standing six feet six, with a heart and brain proportionate to his immense stature, Ben Hill was a powerful influence for liberalism in the post-bellum South. Although he had thrown himself into the Civil War on the side of his own people with all the ardor of which he was capable, when defeat came he bowed to the inevitable. Unlike the "unreconstructed" Toombs, whose acrimonious diatribes helped to fan the flames of hostility between the North and the South after the war, Hill immediately set to work with a view to reducing to the lowest possible minimum the heats and rancors engendered by the conflict.

"There was a South of slavery and secession," he proclaimed in a famous address before Tammany Hall the year following Appomattox. "That South is dead. There is a South of Union and freedom; that South, thank God, is living, breathing, growing every hour!"

Equally celebrated was his address at the University of Georgia in 1871. He urged his hearers not to "waste time and strength in defense of theories and systems, however valued in their day, which have been swept down by the moving avalanche of actual events," and pointed out that "we can live neither in nor by the defeated past." Venturing into the realm of prophecy, he closed with the stirring climax:

"Shall we rise, or shall we fall yet lower? Shall we live, or shall we die? We shall live! We shall rise! We shall command!"

Liberals in the North were coöperating with those in the South for the purpose of healing the wounds left by the war and promoting intersectional understanding. Among them was John Quincy Adams II of Massachusetts, whose tolerant attitude toward the conquered section attracted much favorable attention below the Potomac and led Wade Hampton to invite him to speak in South Carolina. Adams accepted in 1868. In Charleston he declared that if Hampton was a "rebel," he himself was one also, and that the Southern people were just as loyal as the Northern. The North was not yet ready for such doctrine, however, and the Adams speeches were published there without appreciable effect.

Four years later, Michael Patrick O'Connor, an

eminent Charlestonian lawyer, delivered a speech in historic Faneuil Hall, Boston, in which he called for a "homogeneous and united people, under a common flag and a common country. . . .

"When I say that it is high time that the animosities of the sections were buried, and political antipathies and social jealousies assuaged and reconciled," said O'Connor, "I utter a sentiment which should find response in the bosom of every true American."

Then in 1874 came Lamar's eulogy of Sumner in the House of Representatives, one of the greatest ora tions of its kind ever delivered on this side of the Atlantic. It electrified the country and brought the sections together as perhaps nothing else had done. Representative Lucius Quintus Cincinnatus Lamar of Mississippi had been chosen to deliver one of the addresses in memory of Charles Sumner of Massachusetts, leading abolitionist and advocate of free Negro suffrage after the war. It was assumed by the throng which packed the House of Representatives that Lamar would merely pay a conventional tribute to Sumner's memory, but the great-souled Mississippian did far more than that. Praising the Massachusetts Senator for his "high culture," "elegant scholarship," and "strongly marked moral traits," Lamar described him as a "great man," and closed with the memorable words:

"It has been the kindness of the sympathy which in these later years he has displayed toward the impoverished and suffering people of the Southern States that has unveiled to me the generous and tender heart which beat beneath the bosom of the zealot. . . .

"Would that the spirit of the illustrious dead whom we lament today could speak from the grave to both parties in this deplorable discord in tones which should reach each and every heart throughout this broad territory: 'My countrymen! Know one another and you will love one another.' "

Many men in the audience were weeping openly as Lamar sat down, amid tremendous applause. His oration made him a national figure, and for a time an improvement was noticeable in the relations between the sections. But in a comparatively short while the professional Yankees and the "unreconstructed" Confederates were back at one another's throats, and the bloody shirt was being waved in Congress as of yore.

Twelve years were to elapse before any other Southerner was to make a comparable contribution to the cause of intersectional peace. It was in 1886 that a young Georgian, Henry W. Grady, sounded a note of amity and friendship in a brilliant address in New York City before the New England Society, an address which rang through the country and made its author famous from coast to coast.

In this celebrated oration, Grady described Abraham Lincoln as "the first typical American, the first who comprehended within himself all the greatness and gentleness, all the majesty and grace of this republic," and added: "He was the sum of Puritan and Cavalier; for in his ardent nature were fused the virtues of both, and in the depths of his great soul the faults of both were lost. He was greater than Puritan, greater than Cavalier, in that he was American." In eloquent phrases, the speaker declared that "the South has nothing for which to apologize . . . nothing to take back." He spoke movingly of his admiration and love for his father, a Confederate soldier who had been killed in action. "But," Grady declared, "I am glad that the omniscient God held the balance of battle in His Almighty hand, and that human slavery was swept forever from American soil—the American Union saved from the wreck of war."

Grady was deluged at once with invitations to deliver addresses in all parts of the United States, and he was finally prevailed upon to speak in Dallas. The train on which he made the journey to Texas was met by large crowds at every station, and Joel Chandler Harris expressed the opinion that "no such tribute as this has ever before been paid, under any circumstances, to any private American citizen." The address at Dallas was followed by others, and Grady's fame spread to the farthest corners of the republic. Recognized as the great apostle of good will between the North and the South, at his untimely death in 1889 there was an outpouring of grief such as the country had seldom seen. The entire population of Atlanta was plunged into a gloom as profound as that which had enveloped Charleston in 1850 when John C. Calhoun went to his long rest in St. Philip's churchyard.

The last address which Grady delivered dealt with the race problem in the South, a problem then more than two and a half centuries old, and particularly acute since the enfranchisement of the blacks. The loyalty of the slaves during the war, when their masters were at the front, had been one of the most striking examples of faithful adherence to a trust in all history, and Southern liberals were anxious to see that the freedmen were treated with justice, not only as a reward for their conduct from 1861 to 1865, but also because they belonged to the weaker race and were entitled to special consideration by virtue of that fact.

But the politicians who were in control in the North postponed a sane solution of the race question for many years when they imposed upon the conquered states a reconstruction policy which not only failed to promote understanding between the races, but which tended, on the contrary, to foment ill feeling. Reconstruction put the Southern people on the defensive, and led them to adopt "black codes" and to organize in bands of night riders, such as the Ku Klux Klan. Struggling under intolerable conditions, they felt that no other methods would be adequate.

The "black codes," which were enacted by the Southern legislatures in 1865 and 1866, were not passed with a view to the reënslavement of the Negroes, although they were widely regarded in the North as having been designed for that purpose. They were born of what the whites of the former Confederacy conceived to be the exigencies of the situation, and they frequently had the direct or implied sanction of the Freedmen's Bureau. Undoubtedly they were open to criticism in some respects, but not to such criticism as came from certain Northern sources. The Chicago *Tribune*, for example, was vitriolic in its condemnation of the Mississippi "black code." It declared that the North would make a "frog pond" of Mississippi unless the objectionable legislation was repealed. Yet at the time that the *Tribune* was bellowing its denunciations, Illinois had on its statute books regulations touching the Negro which were even more severe than those of Mississippi.

From a practical standpoint, the provisions of the "black codes" are comparatively unimportant, since none of them ever actually became effective. But the Ku Klux Klan not only was organized in the South; it functioned actively for a number of years. The Klan was in large measure the South's answer to the unscrupulous carpetbaggers and other thieves and demagogues who preyed upon the region for a decade after the war. Founded in Tennessee as a social club, its members noticed that superstitious Negroes who saw them at night, hooded and sheeted, were frequently transfixed with terror. It occurred to them that since the Negroes were being inflamed against their former masters by Northern incendiaries, and criminal assaults against white women were becoming increasingly numerous, the Klan might serve as an engine for holding the blacks in check. The Klansmen thereupon assumed the task of patrolling the highways at night, robed in ghostly white. Calling to one another along the moonlit roads, they spoke in sepulchral tones of "dead men's bones" and "buckets of blood," frightening the colored population out of its wits, and causing many Negroes to forget, at least temporarily, the evil counsels of unprincipled agitators, and to become once more industrious and law-abiding.

General Nathan Bedford Forrest was the first head of the Ku Klux Klan, and at the outset his lieutenants in the various states were men of standing and substance. The organization was sanctioned by General Lee on condition that it remain purely protective. Unfortunately, but inevitably, scoundrels took advantage of the opportunity which the masks afforded to wreak personal vengeance upon their enemies. "Poor whites," many of whom hated all members of the Negro race, flogged innocent and well-behaved blacks under cover of the Klan's regalia. Such practices were fiercely excoriated by General Forrest, who ordered all Klansmen to unmask in 1869. But many disregarded his instructions, with the result that murders, robberies, whippings, and other crimes were prevalent in the South for years.

While it is highly deplorable that such an organization as the Klan was needed in the South after the war, and while it is easy to argue that no band of hooded men should ever be permitted to force its ideas of right and wrong upon others, or to ride about the countryside terrorizing the ignorant and the credulous, it must be remembered that Southern civilization was fighting for its life during the ten years which followed Appomattox. The desperate situation induced by Thad Stevens's Reconstruction Acts required a desperate remedy. The Klan was the result.

But the fact that this organization devoted much of its attention to frightening the Negroes should not be taken as an indication that its leaders were necessarily antagonistic to them. For example, General John B. Gordon of Georgia was the leader of the Klan in his state not long after the war; yet he ran for public office in 1866 on a platform which included free schools for the colored race.

It is, indeed, rather surprising that so many prominent Southerners espoused the cause of Negro education during the dark years of reconstruction, when everyone was impoverished. J. L. M. Curry introduced resolutions at Marion, Alabama, in 1866 calling for the education of the Negroes by the whites of the South. The following year the Mississippi State Teachers' Association went on record as favoring public schools for the blacks. William D. Bloxham, a prominent Florida planter, voluntarily opened a school for them on his plantation, and such men as Wade Hampton and Benjamin H. Hill urged that they be given decent treatment and adequate schooling. Discussing the newly acquired right of the Negroes to the exercise of the suffrage, Hill declared in 1870:

"It has therefore become our duty, as it is also our interest, not only to permit and assent to its exercise, but also to render every protection, and even assistance to the colored man in its free and unrestricted enjoyment. . . . A black man who cannot be bought is better than a white man who can, and a Republican who cannot be bought is better than a Democrat who can."

The work of many white women in helping to educate the Negroes during this period also is noteworthy. Some of these women were of the best Southern families, while others came down from the North as educational missionaries to the colored race. The lofty humanitarianism which moved the latter group was magnificent, but many of these quixotic Northern ladies were so completely uninformed as to the true state of affairs in Dixie and so incapable of adjusting themselves to their new environment that their use-fulness was greatly impaired.

As the North gradually withdrew its bayonets from the throat of the South, the former Confederate states shook themselves free of the rogues and picaroons who had preyed upon them since 1865. It now became possible for them to formulate such definite programs for educating the Negroes as the state of public opinion within their borders and the condition of their treasuries would allow. It need hardly be said that there was formidable opposition to the establishment of schools for the freedmen. Substantial elements in every state, including thousands of "poor whites," fought bitterly against any such program. Many felt that the dreadful poverty into which the South had been plunged made the education of the blacks impossible, even if it were desirable; and they did not believe it to be desirable. This was especially true of the lower class whites, who now were awakening to the realization that the freedmen were to be their economic competitors.

But despite the relentless opposition of the conservatives and the reactionaries, the plan for educating the Negroes made slow but sure progress. At the same time relations between the races gradually became more cordial. There were, indeed, several extraordinary manifestations of the decline of race prejudice during these years. In Arkansas, for example, J. C. Corbin, a Negro who had been appointed state superintendent of public instruction in 1873, was not ousted when reconstruction was brought to an end by the constitution of 1874, but was permitted to retain his office until the close of the following year. In Louisiana, Francis T. Nicholls, the first governor elected after reconstruction was brought to a close in that state, appointed P. B. S. Pinchback, a Negro, to the state school board. In North Carolina, Governor Zebulon B. Vance urged the legislature in 1877 to appropriate sufficient funds for the establishment of a Negro normal school "the want of which is more deeply felt by the black race even than the white."

A Bostonian who contributed a series of articles on the South to the *Atlantic Monthly* during 1882, declared that after some months in the former Confederacy he had found that "the Republican politicians in the South are much less hopeful regarding the improvement of the Negroes and their capabilities in the direction of the duties of intelligent citizenship, than are the Democrats or 'Bourbons.'" He added that "many of the local Republican politicians with whom I conversed said that it was not desirable to give these Negroes any political education or enlightenment, and that if it were desirable, it would not be possible."

Four men, three of them white and the other colored, may be said to have borne the brunt of the struggle to educate the Negro during the post-war years. They were Samuel Chapman Armstrong, a former Union soldier who had come to the South in 1866 as an agent of the Freedmen's Bureau; J. L. M. Curry of Georgia and Alabama; the Rev. Atticus G. Haygood, who, like many of the other liberal leaders in this era, was a Georgian, and last but not least, Booker T. Washington.

General Armstrong, who was placed in charge of a

large camp of Negroes in the neighborhood of Hampton, Virginia, in 1866, conceived the idea that the blacks would be greatly benefited by industrial education. He managed to interest Northern individuals and organizations in the plan, and the land on which the camp was situated was purchased the following year. By 1868 he was able to open the Hampton Normal and Industrial Institute. This industrial school for Negro teachers was gradually developed by its founder into one of the most important institutions of the kind in America. For a quarter of a century General Armstrong served as its guiding genius, and under him it became a leading force in Negro education.

Booker T. Washington received his early training under Armstrong at Hampton and subsequently established at Tuskegee a school for the education of the Southern Negro which differed from that at Hampton in that it was wholly under colored management. Washington had been born a slave in Virginia. After the war he heard of the Hampton Institute, and burning with a desire to attend it, "beat his way" to the school, a distance of 500 miles from the West Virginia coal mine in which he was working. In 1881 he assumed the task of opening an industrial school for Negroes at Tuskegee, Alabama, modeled along similar lines.

Tremendous obstacles confronted him, but he was undaunted. Operations were begun in a dilapidated shanty and a tumble-down church near by. The roof to his "class-room" was in such a lamentable state of decay that he found it necessary to lecture under an umbrella when it rained. Funds were virtually non-existent. But this indomitable man was spurred on by an inner flame, an ardent, surging desire to do something substantial for his race. He wished to teach his fellow blacks the dignity of work, to impress upon them that work should be looked upon "as a privilege, as something that is placed here for the highest benefit of human beings," rather than as something to be avoided. The establishment of Tuskegee Institute not only enabled him to inculcate this philosophy in the minds of the students there, but at the same time the industrial education which the institute provided made it possible for the students to apply that philosophy in their daily lives following graduation. Tuskegee and its founder gradually became known to the country, and the interest of Northern philanthropists was aroused. Before many years had passed, substantial donations were coming in, and the future of the school was assured.

In his work at Tuskegee, Washington strove to raise the level of intelligence and morality among the Negroes in his section of the South. In the early eighties he found that the colored preachers and rural school teachers were "miserably poor in preparation for their work and poor in moral character."

But Washington not only sought to lift up the black race; he also endeavored by every means in his power to improve its relationships with the whites. His greatest contribution to the cause of interracial understanding is to be found in his famous address at the Atlanta Exposition in 1895.

Another apostle of good will between the races was J. L. M. Curry, who enunciated the doctrine soon after the war that there should be "equal and exact justice in the distribution of State funds in aid of education of both whites and blacks." Dr. Curry, one of the great Southern liberals of the post-war era, became general agent for the three and a half million dollar Peabody Fund in 1881, in which capacity he exercised general supervision over the establishment of public schools and the training of public school teachers for both races in many parts of the former Confederacy. He retained this post for over twenty years, with the exception of a brief period during which he served as minister to Spain. Toward the end of his life he also took over the administration of the Slater Fund, a $1,000,000 trust set up exclusively for the promotion of Negro education. Possessing great powers as an orator, as well as unusual personal magnetism, Curry played a large part in rousing the South to a sense of responsibility for the education of the blacks. His "was perhaps the first voice to declare that there was no place for a helot in our system, and that the Negro must be trained properly for life in this nation." Although a native of Georgia, he spent the greater part of his life in Alabama, and that state has placed his statue in one of the niches reserved for her sons in the capitol at Washington.

Dr. Curry's predecessor as agent for the Slater Fund was the Rev. Atticus G. Haygood. While president of Emory College Haygood had written *Our Brother in Black*, a book describing the progress made by the Negroes since the war and pointing hopefully to the race's future. Although he was moderate enough in his statements, the work was severely criticised below

Mason and Dixon's Line when it appeared in 1881.
Two years later he was placed in charge of the Slater
Fund, which position he retained until he became a
Methodist bishop in 1890. As administrator for the
Slater Fund, which, like the Peabody Fund, had been
provided by Northern philanthropy, Haygood helped
to make possible the training of thousands of Southern
Negroes.

In the early eighties, when the movement for more
adequate schooling for the blacks was gathering momentum, the whites began the enactment of "Jim
Crow" laws separating the races on the railroad trains
and street cars, in the schools and other places of as-
semblage. George W. Cable of New Orleans, already
famous for his faithful portrayal of Creole life in
Louisiana, took vigorous exception to this legislation
in *The Silent South*, a volume which he followed some
years later with *The Negro Question*. While disclaiming
any desire for "social equality," Cable objected to
the setting up of enactments under whose terms the
Negro is "arbitrarily and unlawfully compelled to
hold toward the white man the attitude of an alien,
a menial, and a probable reprobate, by reason of his
race and color." He advocated the repeal of statutes
calling for the separation of the races in public places,
and urged a juster attitude on the part of the stronger
racial group toward the weaker.

Cable was roundly abused for his views on this
question, and Henry Grady took issue with him in a
magazine article.* The Georgian did not indulge in
the billingsgate which had been employed by some of

* "In Plain Black and White," *Century*, April, 1885.

Cable's critics, but he was emphatic in stating that the South would never agree to the "social intermingling of the races." Declaring that both the whites and the Negroes opposed it, he expressed himself as believing that it would lead to racial amalgamation. Grady went on to say, however, that "it is manifestly wrong to make a Negro pay as much for a railroad ticket as a white man pays, and then force him to accept inferior accommodations." He declared that the South stood "on the platform of equal accommodation for each race, but separate." Separate schools, he said, should be maintained, since this was the desire of both whites and blacks, but there should be "perfect equality in grade and efficiency." Grady felt, too, that the Negro should be afforded every opportunity for advancement, every opportunity to fit himself for the responsibilities of citizenship. While thousands of Southerners disagreed with Grady, his views on the race question were much more widely held in Dixie than those of Cable, and they had a profound effect upon Southern thought.

Still more profound, perhaps, was the effect of Booker T. Washington's address at the Atlanta Exposition in 1895, characterized by the Atlanta *Constitution* as "one of the most notable speeches . . . ever delivered to a Southern audience." Washington urged the members of his race to remain in the South and to work out their destinies in the land of their forefathers. He disposed of the idea of "social equality" as being "the extremest folly" and added: "In all things that are purely social we can be as separate as the fingers, yet as the hand in all things essential to

mutual progress." The speaker closed with a plea for
"a blotting out of sectional differences and racial animosities and suspicions, in a willing obedience of all
classes to the mandates of law." "This, this," he
concluded, "coupled with our material prosperity,
will bring into our beloved South a new heaven and
a new earth." The complete address was published
in newspapers in all parts of the country, and the Boston *Transcript* said that the sensation it caused in the
press had "never been equaled."

While the sentiments which Washington expressed
were regarded almost universally in the South as singularly sane, Dr. W. E. B. Du Bois took issue strongly
with the Tuskegee principal's point of view, particularly with his declaration that "in all things that are
purely social we can be as separate as the fingers, yet as
the hand in all things essential to mutual progress."
Du Bois asserted that Washington had asked the black
race to abandon its opportunities for political power
and for the higher education of its youth; had urged
them to cease insisting upon equal civil rights with
the whites, and had counseled them to concentrate
upon industrial education, the accumulation of wealth
and the conciliation of the dominant race in the South.
He felt that the Southern Negro should at least demand "the right to vote, civic equality and the education of youth according to ability," no matter what
the effect upon interracial relationships.

Until his death in 1915, Washington was always far
more conservative than Du Bois, far less belligerent
in his attitude toward the whites, but he was not as
conservative as one might infer from the interpreta-

tion Du Bois placed upon his Atlanta speech. For example, Washington stated in his stirring autobiography, *Up From Slavery*, which appeared in 1901: "I do not believe that any State should make a law that permits an ignorant and poverty-stricken white man to vote, and prevents a black man in the same condition from voting." This sounds very much like Du Bois' demand for the right of franchise.

Washington's view relative to the ballot was shared by not a few Southern whites, among whom was Thomas Nelson Page. "It is not merely the Negro, it is ignorance and venality which we want to disfranchise," Page wrote. "If we can disfranchise these we need not fear the voter, whatever the color." The novelist added that the hope of the black race lay in "the educated Negro."

But such opinions were anathema to the "poor whites." During the nineties these men of the up country laid the lowland aristocrats by the heels in a number of Southern states and took control. With this element in the saddle, relations between the races became markedly worse. Recognizing the Negro as a serious economic competitor, the whites from the hill country resolved to "keep him in his place." All too frequently his "place" turned out to be at the end of a rope which dangled from a roadside tree. The number of lynchings took a jump simultaneously with the rise of the "poor whites" to power, and for the years 1891-94, inclusive, were more numerous than at any time before or since, as far as records show. The banner year was 1892, when 235 lives were taken in this fiendish fashion.

In fairness to Benjamin R. Tillman of South Carolina, who was generally regarded as an enemy of the
blacks, it must be said that he was chiefly responsible
for writing into the constitution of his state in 1895
a provision designed to curb the practice of lynching.
This clause provides for the suspension from office of
any sheriff from whom a prisoner is taken by a mob,
and for his dismissal, in the event that a subsequent
investigation finds him to have been guilty of negli-
gence. It also levies a fine of at least $2,000, subject
to the judgment of the court, on any community
where a lynching takes place, the money to be paid to
the heirs of the person lynched. However, there have
been few prosecutions under this constitutional section during the thirty-seven years that it has been a
part of the organic law of South Carolina.

Governor W. Y. Atkinson of Georgia was another
leader who sought at this period to curb the appalling
number of Southern lynchings. He recommended that
officers of the law who were unable or unwilling to
protect a prisoner from lynchers be required to remove the captive's handcuffs, give him a gun and permit him to defend himself. Atkinson's suggestion did
not meet with favor, however. The temper of the controlling element in Georgia and elsewhere seemed one
of distinct antagonism toward the colored race. In
Texas, Brann the Iconoclast was suggesting "that if
the South is ever to rid itself of the Negro rape fiend,
she must take a day off and kill every member of the
accursed race that declines to leave the country."

Since reconstruction the whites had been disfran-
chising the blacks by means of trickery and subter-

fuge, and now in 1890 the Southern states, with Mississippi in the lead, began drafting constitutions and adopting legislation which made possible the accomplishment of the same result within the law. Several states had carried out this program when the Wilmington, North Carolina, political riots occurred, and these interracial clashes hastened the process elsewhere. Before many years had passed, legislation designed to deprive the great bulk of the Negroes of the ballot had been enacted throughout the South.

While in one sense this wholesale disfranchisement of one race by another is beyond extenuation, the argument advanced by Dr. Edwin A. Alderman at the turn of the century is not to be completely ignored. Alderman asserted that with the Negro no longer "a menacing political factor, disturbing the judgment of men and arousing their passions," the South could at last "think on him righteously and justly as a human being, as a racial problem." He pointed out further that character and intelligence had now been made prerequisites to voting, and that the Negro had thus been provided with an incentive for the development of these qualities. He added that Southern whites were profoundly convinced that having deprived the Negro of the ballot, they must "justify themselves to posterity" by acting toward him "in a spirit of justice and wisdom." The extent to which they have lived up to this self-imposed responsibility will be considered in another chapter.

CHAPTER X

POST-BELLUM EDUCATIONAL LIBERALS

THE CIVIL War almost ruined the South financially and the succeeding orgy of larceny euphemistically termed "reconstruction" completed the process. The poverty which bore down upon the region with crushing weight for years after Appomattox made the initiation of Southern educational movements extremely difficult. Paradoxical as it may seem, however, the leaders in this very reconstruction régime were largely instrumental in rousing the former Confederacy to a realization of the need for a broad educational policy. It was the carpetbaggers, of fragrant memory, who wrote into many of the new state constitutions mandatory provisions for systems of free public education, and it was the carpetbaggers, too, who provided uniform taxation for the support of those systems. Lastly, it was while the carpetbaggers were in control that the policy of free education for the Negroes was adopted.

But if the substitution of mandatory systems bolstered by taxation was a distinct advance over the old pre-war method, which usually had been discretionary and permissive in character, there remained the problem of where the needed funds were to be obtained. Edgar Gardner Murphy stated the case pithily when he wrote that the South "with the gravest problems of our civilization challenging her existence and her peace, was expected to assume the task of the education of two populations [the white and the black] out of the poverty of one."

Establishment of the Peabody Fund after the war, with Dr. Barnas Sears, a Northerner, as general agent, gave the cause of public education below the Potomac a powerful impetus, and by the time of Dr. Sears' death in 1880, each of the former Confederate states had set up a public school system, either in actual fact or on paper.

William Henry Ruffner of Virginia was among the Southern leaders who aided materially during the early post-war years in promoting the establishment of adequate public school systems. Elected the first superintendent of public instruction for the Old Dominion in 1870, he served with marked distinction for more than a decade. Dr. Ruffner was the son of Henry Ruffner, the notable Virginia liberal of before the war, and his habits of mind were not unlike those of his father. Assailed by the Rev. Dr. Robert L. Dabney and other reactionaries, he replied on the platform and in the press, setting forth his conviction that opportunities for schooling should be afforded the masses, both white and black. Professor John B. Minor, the celebrated professor of law at the University of Virginia, was one of Ruffner's most valuable allies in his fight with the conservatives, while the Richmond *Whig* rendered important journalistic support. Following his retirement as superintendent of public instruction in the early eighties, Ruffner served a brief term as first president of the State Female Normal School.

Equally stimulating to the development of public education, not only in his own state but also in others, was the work of Dr. Gustavus J. Orr of Georgia. Orr was the moving spirit both in the preliminary steps leading up to the passage of Georgia's first public school law in 1870 and in the subsequent development of the state school system. George W. Cable paid a warm tribute to Orr, "a man of the Old South" whose post-bellum attitudes served, he said, as "a noble, personal refutation of the superficial notion that the world must look to the young South, only, for progressive ideas of human right among us."

At a somewhat later date, such men as Edward S. Joynes, Henry W. Grady, and Atticus G. Haygood became active in the movement. But the individual who did most to promote the development of public free schools between the Potomac and the Rio Grande in the last two decades of the century was J. L. M. Curry, who succeeded Sears as general agent of the Peabody Fund in 1881. This able and indefatigable man traveled to all parts of the South addressing legislatures and public gatherings, holding conferences, and making surveys. His philosophy was succinctly expressed in an address before a Southern legislature, when he said:

"I am not afraid of the educated masses. I would rather trust the masses than king, priest, aristocracy or established church. No nation can realize its full possibility unless it builds upon the education of the whole people."

Curry's biographer declares that "the vision that appeared to Lee . . . was the same that appeared to Curry. . . . It was a vision of many millions of childhood standing impoverished and untaught amid new duties . . . appealing with outstretched hands."

He found a valuable ally in the Rev. A. D. Mayo, a Unitarian minister from New England, who devoted twelve years to educational work in all parts of the South. This acute observer was well aware of the importance of Curry's activities on behalf of free schools in the region, but he felt, nevertheless, that the greatest single force which contributed to the South's educational advance from 1870 to 1890 was "the direct and indirect influence, especially among the white population, of Southern women." Mayo, who was thoroughly familiar with every aspect of the Southern scene, declared that the one feature of life below the Potomac which had most impressed him was "the push to the front of the better sort of Southern young womanhood, everywhere encouraged by the sympathy, support, sacrifice, toils, and prayers of the superior women of the elder generation."

But in 1890 the great majority of the public schools in the rural districts of the South were still highly inefficient and thoroughly unsatisfactory. Dynamic leaders were arising, however, to carry the message of public education into the remote hinterlands. Charles D. McIver and Edwin A. Alderman, two North Carolina schoolmen who had returned to Chapel Hill for the university commencement, sat up together one night in their hotel room across from the campus, discussing the ignorance and illiteracy of their native state. Seized with an irrepressible desire to make some worthwhile contribution to its educational life, they talked until dawn, and then clasped hands in token that they would lead a state-wide crusade for improved educational facilities for the masses. The agreement was carried out to the letter. McIver and Alderman toured North Carolina from the mountains to the sea, speaking day after day, telling the people that they must tax themselves, preaching the gospel of the free school.

They succeeded in arousing wide popular interest in their scheme, but tangible results were comparatively few until Charles B. Aycock was elected governor. This brave and generous spirit espoused their cause with enthusiasm, and it was largely due to the practical aid he rendered that their efforts were crowned with ultimate success. Another valuable ally was Walter Hines Page, then living in the North, but ever ready to aid in any liberal movement which would promote the welfare of the South. Page had advocated universal primary education and many other progressive reforms while editor of the Raleigh *State Chronicle* some years before, and was in thorough sympathy with the program of McIver, Alderman, and Aycock. His address on "The Forgotten Man" at the North Carolina Normal and Industrial College in 1897 brought down upon him a storm of denunciation, but it was a sound statement of the educational needs of the state, and it jarred many Southerners out of the almost impenetrable fog of smugness and self-satisfaction in which they had been enveloped for decades.

Such a crusade as that carried on in North Carolina could not fail to have a stimulating effect upon other regions in the South. And while the Southern illiteracy rate in 1900 was distressingly high and more than double that for the rest of the country, progress had been made during the preceding decades. True, that progress was not by any means what had been hoped for a quarter of a century before; in some sections, indeed, there had even been retrogression since 1860. But when J. L. M. Curry retired as general agent for the Peabody Fund in 1902, he was able to point out that each of the Southern states had a normal school for both the white and black races, that each had a system of graded schools in the cities and small towns, and that the legislature of each was becoming increasingly sensible of the importance of the rural common school. Unfortunately the South was still comparatively poor, and its country schools could not be adequately financed, even where the legislatures were willing to vote the money. At the same time the roads were such that communication in the rural districts was usually quite difficult. Thus the former Confederacy at the turn of the century was still backward in providing free schooling for boys and girls living outside the cities and towns.

As for the higher learning in the Southern states during the post-bellum era, its proper development was severely retarded at the outset by the fact that such endowments as the colleges and universities had were wiped out in the war. It was only by dint of stupendous exertions that some institutions were kept open at all. The property of Louisiana State University, for example, would have been seized and sold during reconstruction, had it not been for President David French Boyd and a few devoted members of his staff, who hung on without salary and with hardly enough funds to keep body and soul together. Even butter and sugar were beyond their means, but these heroic men struggled grimly on, although for one entire session the average attendance was only four professors and six students. Similar conditions obtained elsewhere. South Carolina College passed into the hands of the Negroes for a time, while the University of North Carolina and the University of Alabama fell beneath the sway of the carpetbaggers and scalawags. This element also managed to get something of a grip on the University of Mississippi.

In Virginia, however, where the reconstruction régime was considerably milder than in the cotton states, it was possible for Robert E. Lee to demonstrate his capacity as an educator without undue hindrance from the radicals. The former military commander infused new life into Washington College during the years of his presidency, transforming it from an old-fashioned institution which emphasized the classics into one more adequate to the needs of the hour.

Another distinctly liberal influence upon higher education in the South after the war was that of Landon Cabell Garland, who had been one of the most distinguished of ante-bellum educators. As early as 1836 Dr. Garland had been elected president of Randolph-Macon College in his native Virginia, and shortly before the war he had accepted a similar post at the University of Alabama. During reconstruction he was on the faculty of the University of Mississippi, and while there he wrote a series of articles for the Nashville *Christian Advocate*, urging the establishment of a central theological seminary for the Southern Methodist Church. Then in 1875 Cornelius Vanderbilt provided the money for the founding of Vanderbilt University, an institution which combined the functions of university and seminary. Garland was made its first chancellor, a post which he held for nearly twenty years. Despite the fact that he was in his middle sixties when he assumed his new duties, this progressive and far-sighted man kept his mind open to new ideas until his death two decades later. Upon one occasion a young member of his faculty protested to him indignantly that certain other professors were teaching the Darwinian theory within the sacred confines of the university, and that such heresy should not be permitted; but the venerable chancellor replied: "Men never amount to much until they outgrow their fathers' notions, sir." Dr. Garland died a few years afterward, hailed as the "grand old man" of Southern education.

By 1885 the colleges and universities in Dixie had recovered in some measure from the effects of the war and its aftermath. If all of them were still in dire need of funds, and if the general average of collegiate instruction was no higher than it had been in 1860, there was encouragement in the fact that the students appeared far more earnest and serious in their work. But the poverty of the Southern institutions of higher learning operated in several ways to their detriment.

It not only made it impossible for them to secure adequate buildings and equipment or to pay sufficient salaries, but it forced many of them to lower their standards for entrance, in order that they might obtain revenue from student tuition fees. Another serious difficulty in the way of the maintenance of proper entrance requirements arose by virtue of the almost complete disappearance of the ante-bellum academies from many parts of the South. In Louisiana, for example, there had been two dozen of them, but twenty years after the war not one was left. The academies were unable to maintain themselves in competition with the rising public schools, but the latter were not yet fully developed. The consequence was that over a period of years the South was without the system of academies it had enjoyed before the war, while at the same time it did not as yet possess a satisfactory substitute for them.

But on top of all this there is still another important factor to be taken into consideration. Dr. Charles Forster Smith, then of the Vanderbilt faculty, contributed two discerning articles to the *Atlantic Monthly* at this period in which he discussed the higher learning in the South and declared that "the greatest evil in Southern education" lay in the fact that there were entirely too many colleges and universities. He pointed out that there were then only seventeen colleges for men in the six New England states, as against sixty-seven in six Southern states, and concluded that "in the United States culture is generally in the inverse ratio to the *number* of colleges." Dr. Smith quoted President R. E. Blackwell of Randolph-Macon College in Virginia as saying in this connection:

"Our Superintendent of Education was boasting, some years ago, that there were proportionately more Virginians pursuing the higher education than any other nationality, not excluding Prussians. This nonsense was repeated all over our state and even in the United States Senate. As long as our people think that a Virginia college is as good as the University of Berlin, why should they be concerned about their educational system?"

Dr. Smith stated that many of the conclusions set forth in his articles were based upon replies to a questionnaire he had sent to a score of prominent Southern educators.

"It is refreshing to note the tone of respect in which all my correspondents refer to the University of Virginia," he said. "It is a tacit acknowledgment of her preëminent position in Southern education. The whole South owes her a debt of gratitude. She first, perhaps, introduced among us the element of real thoroughness in college work. When the war was over . . . . the University of Virginia held aloft, as ever, her high standard of graduation, though it cost her professors money to do so, and she became the one model for all our institutions that aspired to do high and good work. . . . But what might she not have done for . . . higher education, if, while selling her degrees and certificates so dearly, she had been as strict as Harvard in admitting students!"

Curricula of the Southern colleges and universities were liberalized in some particulars during the post-bellum era, notably with respect to the study of English. Thomas R. Price of the Randolph-Macon faculty, who subsequently went to Columbia, is commonly credited with having been the first American schoolman to recognize the importance of a careful and thorough study of the language of the country. He received valuable coöperation in carrying out his program from Edward S. Joynes, one of the most competent of Southern educators, who served as teacher at a number of leading institutions, and who not only sensed the significance of Dr. Price's plan, but likewise was aware of the need for greater thoroughness and more rigid standards of scholarship in the colleges and universities in the region. In addition to the fact that Southern scholars were pioneers in the study of English, they placed especial emphasis after the war upon courses in French, German, and other European languages, as well as upon those having to do with scientific and historical subjects.

The fact that it was not always the men affiliated with the great universities who did most to develop more liberal concepts of higher learning in the South, is well illustrated by the case of Professor Price, who evolved his theory as to the necessity for suitable instruction in English while attached to a small church college. Another man who made a distinct contribution, albeit of a somewhat different kind, to the cause of education below Mason and Dixon's Line, was James H. Carlisle, president of Wofford College in South Carolina, also a small church-supported institution. Dr. Carlisle served as executive head at Wofford for more than a quarter of a century, beginning in 1875. A profound believer in the importance of individual contact between the professor and the student, the significance of his services to the higher learning in the South is to be found in no small measure in the remarkably intimate personal relationship which existed between himself and the men he taught. Dr. Carlisle was a big, broad, tolerant man, ever zealous in the search for truth, and he possessed a personality so astounding that it was commonly said that "merely to be associated with him was in itself a liberal education." At his funeral there were such manifestations of universal sorrow as had seldom been seen in South Carolina. Hundreds of Negroes lined the highway as the bier was borne past, a final tribute of love and respect to one who had done much to open broader vistas of opportunity to their race.

A man who exerted a wider influence upon the educational life of the South than Carlisle was William Preston Johnston, son of General Albert Sidney Johnston. Johnston's greatest contribution was made during his fifteen years of service as the first president of Tulane University. That institution opened its doors in 1884, and under his brilliant executive leadership it soon became a factor of paramount significance in the educational life of the deep South. Although his program was fought relentlessly by ecclesiastics and other reactionaries, he managed to establish the university on the broad and liberal basis of religious freedom and academic liberty. Postulating the desirability of an adequate system of primary and secondary schools throughout Louisiana, President Johnston devoted much of his time and thought to this phase of the state's educational life. For a decade he was a virtual invalid; but despite failing health he fought on with unconquerable determination, until death overtook him in 1899. He had raised Tulane to a place of undisputed leadership in the Gulf states, and to high rank among the universities of America. A. D. Mayo termed him "beyond question, with the exception of his friend, Dr. J. L. M. Curry, the most notable of the new educational leaders of the South."

Thus as the nineteenth century drew to a close, the institutions of higher learning in the former Confederacy were moving out of the shadows which had enveloped them after Appomattox. The increasing prosperity attendant upon the slowly developing industrialism of the region in the nineties not only provided it with badly needed material wealth, but was also of immense benefit in inducing a saner mental attitude on the part of the people. Serious obstacles still barred the way to the highest educational achievement, but foundations had been laid in the South during the post-bellum era for the progress which was to come in the twentieth century in the fields of primary, secondary, and higher education.

CHAPTER XI

EVOLUTION AND THE EVANGELS

FATAL in its implications for scriptural orthodoxy, Darwin's evolutionary hypothesis burst upon a mid-Victorian world with shattering effect in 1859. Emphasizing the mutability of the species, it threw into the discard such time-honored theological bulwarks as the Old Testament stories of the creation and the flood, and relegated Adam and Noah to a place beside Thor, Vulcan and other mythical personages of antiquity.

But while American theologians became aware of the *Origin of Species* soon after its publication, they did not realize for some years that old-fashioned Protestantism was being shaken to its foundations by this newly promulgated theory. When they did awaken to this situation, they met it as churchmen have been wont to meet such issues since the beginning of time, namely, with heresy hunts and other repressive measures. In doing so, they were merely emphasizing that established churches in all lands have almost invariably been identified with the cause of reaction, with the advocates of "class and privilege."

Thus it is not to be wondered at that efforts were made on this side of the water to throttle Darwinism as soon as its implications were grasped by the orthodox. The reaction was particularly severe in the South as a whole and in the rural districts of the North, the strongholds of American Fundamentalism. Of the two, the South was the more conservative. It was there that many of the clerics who led Northern movements in support of the infallibility of the Scriptures received their training. Southern ecclesiastics had long been recognized as more Fundamentalist in their theological concepts than those in other sections, and at the same time they wielded a larger influence among their parishioners. The consequence was that a particularly determined and prolonged fight to save traditional Christianity was waged in the South. Bible schools, revivals, and similar phenomena characterized the Southern scene over a long period of years.

Partly because those who recognized the fallibility of Holy Writ were usually persons of education, the evangelicals became suspicious of the entire educational process. A school of thought accordingly arose which adhered to the view that educational institutions were fundamentally dangerous and diabolical. It was felt that clergymen in particular should hold no fellowship with any college or university, since it was at such places that men's minds became poisoned with the higher criticism.

Bishop Holland N. McTyeire of the Southern Methodist church was among the influential ecclesiastics below the Potomac who refused to countenance such balderdash. It was at his instigation that Landon Cabell Garland wrote his series of articles for the Nashville *Christian Advocate* in 1868 urging a more thoroughly trained ministry. Far different, however, was the feeling of Bishop G. F. Pierce. This pious man was stirred to action by the heterodox notions which were being broadcast by McTyeire and Garland.

"The best preachers I ever heard had never been to college at all—hardly to school," he exclaimed. "It is my opinion that every dollar invested in a theological school will be a damage to Methodism. Had I a million I would not give a dime for such an object."

The position of the saintly Bishop Pierce was not unlike that of another prelate of the same denomination, Bishop W. W. Duncan, who once remarked: "In my time I used to read Shakespeare and Scott and all those writers. But nowadays I read nothing but the Bible, because I know it is the word of my God."

But the brummagem arguments of Pierce and Duncan went down before those of more enlightened men, and Vanderbilt University was set up, with McTyeire as president of its Board of Trust and Garland as chancellor. McTyeire, who left the stamp of his personality ineffaceably upon the infant institution, favored the diffusion of higher education to all elements of the population. At the outset, however, no literary or educational qualifications were deemed requisite for men desiring to enter the biblical department, the "call to preach the gospel" being adjudged all-sufficient. A decade later McTyeire succeeded in bringing about a reorganization of this department, and the requirements for entrance were raised to conform to those of the academic school.

Far less creditable to President McTyeire was his treatment of Professor Alexander Winchell, the accomplished occupant of the chair of geology at the university, who had the temerity in 1878 to express a belief in the pre-Adamitic origin of man. This heresy came as a profound shock to the Vanderbilt Board of Trust. President McTyeire informed Winchell that "our people are of the opinion that such views are contrary to the plan of redemption," and requested his resignation. He refused to submit it, whereupon the board advised him that his chair had been abolished. A few months later the Tennessee Conference of the Southern Methodist church adopted resolutions which said:

"This is an age in which scientific atheism, having divested itself of the habiliments that most adorn and dignify humanity, walks abroad in shameless denudation. The arrogant and impertinent claims of this 'science, falsely so-called,' have been so boisterous and persistent, that the unthinking mass have been sadly deluded; but our university alone has had the courage to lay its young but vigorous hand upon the mane of untamed Speculation and say: 'We will have no more of this.'"

The following year "untamed Speculation" reared its head in the Southern Baptist Theological Seminary at Louisville. Dr. Crawford H. Toy, a young and uncommonly able member of the seminary faculty, began to entertain grave doubts as to the authenticity of certain portions of Holy Writ, and the fact became bruited about. Ere long rumblings were heard in the hinterlands, and officials of the seminary were seized

13

with alarm, lest such heresy be punished with a cutting off of their appropriations. The gravamen of the complaint against Toy was that his views as to the composition of the Old Testament ran strongly counter to prevailing Baptist theology. He was advised to provide the trustees with a written statement of his opinions, accompanied by a letter of resignation. He complied with the suggestion, and the board promptly informed him that it had determined to dispense with his services.

Not to be outdone by the Methodists and Baptists, the Presbyterians seized the banner of orthodoxy in the seventies and issued a resounding appeal to the faithful "to rise in arms against Physical Science as the mortal enemy of all the Christian holds dear, and to take no rest until the infidel and atheistic foe has been utterly destroyed." Dr. James Woodrow, a member of the faculty of the Southern Presbyterian Seminary at Columbia, battled bravely against the tide of obscurantism which threatened to engulf his church. Fully aware that in doing so he was imperiling his future as a Presbyterian minister, he fearlessly championed the cause of science in general and the theory of evolution in particular. His insistence upon the validity of Darwinism finally brought on such a wave of protest that he asked a trial by his presbytery in 1884. That body brought in a verdict of "not guilty," but the attacks upon him became so incessant that he was finally compelled to leave the seminary. The entire matter was investigated by the General Assembly of the Southern Presbyterian church in 1888, and a decision adverse to Dr. Woodrow was rendered.

Meanwhile this greatly beloved and highly respected man was occupying a chair at the College of South Carolina, a short distance away from the Columbia seminary. Many of his former students in the seminary attended his lectures at the college, despite the protests of their ecclesiastical superiors, and in 1891 he was elevated to the presidency of the institution.

Among those who led the assault on Dr. Woodrow while he was a teacher at the seminary was Dr. Robert L. Dabney. This rock-ribbed Fundamentalist had served as chaplain and adjutant on the staff of "Stonewall" Jackson during the Civil War, and was one of the most influential of Southern churchmen. In addition to attacking scientists in violent fashion, Dabney exhibited strongly reactionary tendencies in various other directions. In contrast to General Lee, he remained bitter and irreconcilable to the end, denouncing the North and fighting over, in retrospect, the battles of 1861-65. It was largely because of his aversion to things Northern that he opposed the suggested union of the two branches of Presbyterianism. To this feeling, too, may be partially attributed his antagonism to the public schools, which he regarded as "infidel, disorganizing and Yankeeish."

But if Dabney and his colleagues succeeded in ousting Woodrow from the seminary at Columbia, their victory, like those achieved by the Methodists and Baptists at Nashville and Louisville, was in reality a defeat. Andrew D. White has pointed out that since Winchell returned to the University of Michigan upon his expulsion from Vanderbilt, Toy joined the Harvard faculty following his departure from the Southern

Baptist Seminary, and Woodrow was elected president of the College of South Carolina after he had been adjudged guilty of heresy, each of these men was able to command a larger audience and reach a greater number of persons after his church had sought to stifle him than before. It seemed to White, therefore, that the utter failure of the several efforts to silence Winchell, Toy, and Woodrow served excellently to illustrate the folly of ecclesiastical interference with the search for truth.

It should not be imagined, however, that heresy hunts were carried on exclusively in the Southern states during these years. On the contrary, several were staged beyond the Potomac and the Ohio. One of the most notable of them involved Professor Charles A. Briggs of Union Theological Seminary, New York, who was suspended as a teacher in that institution by the General Assembly of the Northern Presbyterian church during the mauve decade. At about the same time Professor Henry Preserved Smith of Lane Theological Seminary, Cincinnati, was convicted on a similar charge, and a few years later Professor A. C. McGiffert of Union Seminary withdrew from the Presbyterian ministry rather than face an accusation of heresy. It is noteworthy that all three of these men came to grief while professing adherence to the Presbyterian communion. The granite-like conservatism of the disciples of Calvin is further exemplified in a letter written by a Presbyterian clergyman in New York to a colleague in Baltimore when he learned that Huxley had been the principal speaker at the formal opening of Johns Hopkins University, and that the program had not included prayer.

"It was bad enough to invite Huxley," the dominie declared. "It were better to have asked God to be present. It would have been absurd to ask them both."

The effort to stem the rising tide of skepticism in the North took various forms, among them a resuscitation of revivalism. Preëminent among the Northern revivalists was Dwight L. Moody "whose notable campaigns in the early seventies marked a dividing line in methods of religious propaganda." His Southern counterpart, albeit a man of inferior substance and dignity, was Samuel Porter Jones of Alabama, a spiritual forebear of the Billy Sundays and Gypsy Smiths of today. "Sam" Jones came of pioneer Methodist stock, and he boasted that his grandmother "had read the Bible through thirty-seven times on her knees." In his early years he was wont to gaze with undue frequency upon the wine when it was red, but he promised his dying father to reform and kept his promise. Jones then became an itinerant preacher, and soon developed into a pulpit orator of astonishing powers. His fame spread to all corners of the republic and in the eighties he began an evangelistic career which carried him to the principal cities of the country. Jones frequently addressed crowds of 10,000 or more, for his crude and boisterous manner in the pulpit made a strong appeal to the masses. Until the turn of the century he gave a goodly share of his attention to the North and West, but after 1900 the South was the sole beneficiary of his efforts.

Such men as "Sam" Jones, who toured the Southern states delivering the old-fashioned gospel message of a fiery hell for sinners and pearly gates for the righteous, held only slight appeal for the dignified Episcopalians of the region. Members of this small and staid sect were less susceptible to such exhortations and less disturbed over the inroads of science than their more evangelical brethren. Just as in the Old South the Episcopal church had managed to avoid embroilments over the slavery issue, so after the war it was relatively serene in the face of the revolutionary implications of the Darwinian hypothesis. There were no doctrinal controversies within the church comparable in severity to those which exploded in the ranks of the other principal Southern denominations. True, the Virginia Theological Seminary at Alexandria was evangelical and conservative throughout the post-bellum years, despite the liberalizing influence of such men as Dr. William Sparrow, Dr. Hugh Codman Potter, and Bishop A. M. Randolph. Dr. Sparrow's motto, "Seek the truth; come whence it may; cost what it will" was subsequently adopted as that of the seminary, and the institution is now much more liberal than formerly. The theological department of Sewanee University in Tennessee was similarly conservative at the outset, but under the leadership of Dr. William Porcher DuBose, one of the great religious leaders of America, it oriented itself to the higher criticism somewhat earlier than the Virginia Seminary.

In their attitude toward drinking, dancing, card playing, and horse racing the Episcopalians, like the Roman Catholics, have generally been tolerantly libertarian, both North and South. Concentrated largely in thickly populated areas, the members of these denominations have never shared the country-man's instinctive distrust of urban thought-patterns, his intuitive itch for legislative enactments depriving easy-going city dwellers of their pleasant diversions.

Like the Episcopalians, the Catholics in the Southern states managed to adjust themselves to the newer scientific discoveries without any unseemly intradenominational wrangling. A commanding figure in the church at this period was James Gibbons of Maryland, who was placed in charge of the new vicarate apostolic of North Carolina in 1866, and two years later, at the age of thirty-four, was consecrated a bishop, the youngest of the 1,200 Catholic bishops scattered over the world. There were few Catholic congregations in North Carolina, and in his journeys through the state, the future cardinal was invited to preach to his communicants in courthouses, Masonic lodge rooms, and Protestant churches. It was at this stage of his career that he came to appreciate the non-Catholic viewpoint and to lay the foundation for the important rôle he was to play in the history of religious toleration in this country. Catholics and Protestants were perhaps on more cordial terms in North Carolina during the residence of Bishop Gibbons than they have ever been, before or since. In 1872 he was transferred to Richmond as bishop of that diocese, and after serving with distinction for five years, was appointed archbishop coadjutor of Baltimore. He spent the remainder of his long life in that city, fighting for

American ideals of liberty, recognized as the greatest
Catholic liberal in the republic.

CHAPTER XII

THE RISE OF THE COMMON MAN

WHILE the assumption is unwarranted that ante-bellum society was composed wholly of great slaveholders on the one hand and "poor whites" on the other, since such a grouping leaves out of account the highly important middle class of small slave-owners and yeoman farmers, it is none the less true that the "poor whites" occupied a peculiarly unfortunate position in the Old South. Looked down upon by the aristocrats, despised by the slaves, their lot was far from enviable.

With the annihilation of chattel servitude and the consequent demolition of the social structure which had prevailed in the Southern states for centuries, faint stirrings began to be heard among the under-privileged whites during the years immediately following the war. But this element had become so accustomed to playing a minor rôle in governmental affairs, and so habituated to taking its orders from the patricians and the yeomen that its initial efforts in the direction of an improved status and a larger participation in the political life of the area were hesitant and ineffectual.

And although many flagrant inequalities in representation and the franchise had been obliterated before the war; and while the leveling processes in the South incident to the defeat of its armies were ultimately to contribute to the emancipation of the less fortunate whites in a measure almost comparable to the emancipation of the blacks, little more than a beginning was made during reconstruction in opening up wider avenues of opportunity to the poverty-stricken illiterates of the upland regions.

It is true that so long as the former Confederate states were treated as conquered provinces by the Federal authority, no group of Southern whites found it possible to exercise an appreciable influence in public affairs. But with the withdrawal of the Northern troops, control in Dixie reverted to the natives; and since the "poor whites" had not yet asserted themselves to any noticeable degree and were still regarded as more or less negligible factors in the governmental economy of the section, the Bourbon aristocracy and the middle class whites took charge of the situation. Thus began the reign of the "Confederate brigadier," when the South's legislative representatives at the national capital were almost invariably chosen from among the men who had worn the gray from 1861 to 1865, and a reputation for military prowess under the Stars and Bars was apt to be a passport to high political preferment.

By 1880 the same elements of the population that had been in the ascendancy in the Old South were back in the saddle once more, and the lower orders of whites were in their accustomed place at the bottom of the political, economic, and social scale. This large group of ignorant, downtrodden, and virtually destitute citizens, most of whom were tenant farmers ekeing out a bare subsistence on the clay hills and in the pine-barrens, was inarticulate and impotent. Firmly wedded to the one-crop system and to inefficient and antiquated methods of agriculture, these renters and croppers had as yet found no leader capable of welding them into a unified political force.

This was the era when the American plutocracy was perhaps more completely in control than at any time in our history and the poorer classes throughout the republic were exploited with the utmost abandon. The ingenuous Mr. Frederick Townsend Martin, a Northern millionaire, sounded the battle-cry of the moneyed interests when he remarked with guileless candor:

"We are not politicians or public thinkers; we are the rich; we own America; we got it, God knows how, but we intend to keep it if we can by throwing all the tremendous weight of our support, our influence, our money, our political connections, our purchased Senators, our hungry Congressmen, our public-speaking demagogues into the scale against any legislature, any political platform, any presidential campaign that threatens the integrity of our estate."

Among the interests which indulged in the practices so charmingly described by Mr. Martin were the railroads. Steadfastly refusing to make public any information concerning their affairs, these great corporations continued on their predatory way, buying up courts and legislatures, employing almost any methods which seemed expedient. Shortly after the war farmers in various Western states had banded together under the name of Grangers with a view to curbing some of these abuses. The movement spread to the South, and restrictive legislation was adopted here and there. But the railroads wielded such influence that the effectiveness of these laws was largely nullified in the courts.

Then in the middle seventies farmers in the South and Middle West began other movements looking toward their own protection. Agriculturists in Texas, as elsewhere in the former Confederacy, occupied a distinctly unfavorable position at the period, as compared with competing economic groups. The prices they received for their products were low, and lien laws which discriminated against them and in favor of the country merchants were on the books. Texan farmers accordingly combined with a view to remedying this condition. After several years of activity, their organization was incorporated in 1880 under the name of the Farmers' State Alliance.

A few years later the Texas Alliance was threatened with a serious split, but this breach in the ranks was averted by C. W. Macune, a Northerner who had moved to the Lone Star State. Macune was chairman of the Alliance executive committee at the time, and he not only restored harmony but formulated plans for expansion throughout the lower South. His idea was "to organize the cotton belt of America so that the whole world of cotton raisers might be united for self-protection." Union with a similar farmers' organization in Louisiana was the initial step in this ambitious movement. Then in 1887 Macune, who was an able executive as well as a fluent speaker and writer, sent missionaries into the other cotton states. They found the farmers in a highly receptive mood, owing to a steady fall in prices, and by the end of the year were successful in establishing branches of the Alliance in almost every Southern state. During 1888 they also effected a consolidation with the Agricultural Wheel, a similar body founded some years previously in Arkansas, which now had branches in seven other states and claimed a membership of 500,000. Then the following year the Southern Alliance amended its constitution to permit mechanics to become members, thus greatly increasing its influence by identifying itself with the cause of labor as well as with that of agriculture. By 1890 the movement had spread like a prairie fire throughout the cotton kingdom, and the Southern Alliance was estimated to enjoy a total enrollment of from 1,500,000 to 3,000,000.

Here was an organization of enormous potential strength, waiting for dynamic leadership in the various states to enable it to realize its political destiny. That leadership was quick to make itself felt. Several movements designed to curb the more flagrant abuses to which agriculturalists were subject, had been launched before the emergence of the Alliance, and with the arrival of that organization, these movements were given a vigorous impetus.

In South Carolina, where the upstate farmers were in ferment in the middle eighties, they found their avatar in "Pitchfork Ben" Tillman. If Tillman was no aristocrat, he was at least a step higher in the social scale than the "wool hat boys" to whom he directed his rather blatant appeal. After making an unsuccessful attempt in 1886 to elect a governor and legislature friendly to the up country, Tillman roused his followers to such enthusiasm during the succeeding years that their entire state ticket, with himself at the head, was elected in 1890. At the same time they captured the legislature. An important factor in bringing about this result was the Farmers' Alliance, which Tillman had harnessed to his wing of the Democratic party.

The back-country farmers not only took charge of the state government and the assembly, but they proceeded without delay to throw General Wade Hampton out of the United States Senate, in which he had served for the preceding eleven years. J. L. M. Irby, a comparatively obscure and undistinguished politician, was chosen to succeed Hampton, easily the most eminent South Carolinian of his generation. The general had redeemed the state from the carpetbaggers and performed other important services, but he was closely identified with the Charlestonian aristocracy. That was enough for the "wool hat boys," and out he went.

The campaign of 1890 sounded the political knell of the lowland coterie which had been the controlling factor in South Carolina for centuries. The men who had carved for the Palmetto State a place of conspicuous prestige in the annals of the republic and had guided its destinies since its establishment as a British colony, were rudely pushed aside to make way for a raucous band of back-country farmers.

It must be borne in mind, however, that while the ousting of the patricians from their position of dominance was in a sense calculated to make the judicious grieve, it was nevertheless in some respects a change for the better. The lowlanders had disregarded the rights of the up country, they had been instrumental in adopting legislation which discriminated in favor of the merchants and against the agriculturists, and they had maintained a strangle-hold on the Democratic party through the convention system, which enabled the small white population in the Tidewater to outvote the more populous Piedmont. If considerable demagoguery had accompanied the rise of Tillman and his henchmen to power, it can at least be said that they remedied many of the abuses of which the farmers complained. And if "Pitchfork Ben" had serious faults, as he undoubtedly had, he cannot be dismissed as a mere selfish place-hunter. The movement which he led so successfully, and which kept him in the governor's mansion and the United States Senate continuously until his death in 1918, was on the whole a liberalizing movement, even though he was hardly a liberal himself.

The upheaval under Tillman had its counterpart in other Southern commonwealths where similar conditions obtained. True, the aristocracy was nowhere so firmly entrenched as in South Carolina, but there were other conspicuous state-wide contests in 1890 between the underprivileged "one gallus" back-countrymen, and the more well-to-do citizens living in the Tidewater and in the cities.

In North Carolina Colonel Leonidas L. Polk had been organizing the farmers for several years when emissaries of the Farmers' Alliance entered the state.

Polk coöperated in the movement with even greater enthusiasm than Tillman and became one of the outstanding Alliancemen of the country. In 1889 he was chosen president of the Southern Alliance, a position of great authority, and he was already editor of the *Progressive Farmer*, a journal in which for several years he had been setting forth the grievances of the agriculturists. Prominent among these grievances in North Carolina as elsewhere was the convention system of making nominations to political office, a system which prevented the farmers from wielding the influence to which their numerical strength entitled them. Polk lost no time in delivering a frontal assault on the Bourbon element in the Democratic party. In 1888 he had come within an eyelash of obtaining the gubernatorial nomination for a candidate chosen by the agriculturists, and had brought about a marked increase in the number of farmers in the legislature. Then the Alliance made such remarkable strides during the succeeding biennium that it was able to control the state Democratic Convention of 1890, and to secure the adoption of a platform endorsing "the efforts of the farmers to throw off the yoke of Bourbonism." Of the nine Democratic candidates who offered for Congress during the year, four were members of the Alliance and only two found it expedient to criticise that organization.

A still more striking popular revolt was taking place simultaneously in Texas, under the leadership of James Stephen Hogg, a gigantic man whose physique was in keeping with the vastness of his native state. Hogg, who stood six feet two inches in his socks and weighed nearly three hundred pounds, was the son of a Confederate general and the idol of the Texan masses. He was chosen attorney-general in 1886, in response to a demand for enforcement of existing laws against the railroads, then in the heyday of their power. Hogg served in that position for two terms, and at the end of the period his record for curbing rapacious corporations was such that he was nominated for governor in 1890 by the state Democratic Convention, while a "silk banner bearing the picture of a huge hog waved over the hall."

Governor Hogg urged the passage of radical legislation against the railroads and other corporations, abolition of the prison lease system, and revision of the criminal code. He also advocated free schools for at least six months in the year and an endowment for the University of Texas, which had opened its doors in 1883. This unusually liberal program was supported by men of the type of A. W. Terrell, one of the founders of the university, author of the first legislative efforts to improve electoral conditions, and strenuous advocate of economic reforms.

This is not to say, however, that Hogg's program was always fair to the railroads or that he himself was invariably free from demagoguery. On the contrary, some of his assaults on the carriers were inflammatory, and he laid himself open to the accusation of catering to popular prejudices. It must be borne in mind, however, that political campaigns in the Lone Star State at this period were rowdy in the extreme, and that Hogg was by no means alone in his undignified antics. When he sought the renomina-

14

tion in 1892, for example, the Texan Democrats put on one of the most riotous conventions ever heard of. Nearly every delegation was contested. Two chairmen were elected, and they addressed the gathering simultaneously from the same platform, while approximately fifty fights went on in various parts of the hall. The convention split into two factions and one of these named Hogg. In the ensuing campaign, one of the most turbulent on record, Hogg's banner was a huge porker. He was returned to the governorship by a large majority.

The victory of the progressive forces in this contest was due in no small measure to the influence and sagacity of Edward M. House, a young planter who was just beginning to make himself felt as a power in the political life of the state. House had been strongly attracted to Hogg during the latter's first term in the governor's mansion, and when Hogg launched his drive for reëlection, he asked House to direct his campaign. House accepted, and after he had sent Hogg back into the governorship by a 60,000 majority, he became the political arbiter of Texas. Just as in later years he was to wield immense influence behind the scenes at Washington without ever holding office, so at this stage of his career he was a man of mystery, seldom appearing in public, scarcely ever seen in the legislative halls, but the acknowledged leader of the Texan Democracy and the one individual whose support was essential to political achievement in the state. After Hogg had retired from office, House successfully negotiated the election of Governors Culberson, Sayers, and Lanham, each of whom was progressive in his attitude toward the issues of the day. After Lanham's renomination in 1904, Colonel House retired from active participation in state politics, and turned his attention to the national scene, where he was to play so large and important a rôle during the Wilson administration. The cause of liberalism in Texas had prospered in notable fashion under his leadership.

The roll of Southern states which felt the force of the popular uprising which swept over Dixie in the late eighties and early nineties would not be complete without mention of Tennessee, Alabama, Georgia, and Florida.

In Tennessee, the Farmers' Alliance elected J. P. Buchanan governor in 1890 and also secured a majority of the legislature. In Alabama there was a more protracted and bitter struggle which ended in defeat for the uplanders in their revolt against the domination of the black belt. Reuben F. Kolb, commissioner of agriculture, ran for governor in 1890, and received heavy support from the farmers, but was defeated. Two years later he renewed the effort, this time on a radical platform, but he was either beaten again or counted out. Still undismayed, Kolb ran a third time in 1894, only to be declared the loser once more. Undoubtedly the opposition had been guilty of wholesale fraud in the black belt during the contests of 1892 and 1894. Many Negroes were voted, a practice which continued until the constitution of 1901 disfranchised them. Then and only then were the farmers of the Piedmont able to take control of the situation in Alabama.

In Georgia the Farmers' Alliance was supreme almost from the moment of its entry into the State. It elected W. J. Northen governor in 1890 with hardly an effort, and secured a legislature in which Alliancemen were in the vast majority. On top of all this, six congressmen were ousted to make way for spokesmen of the agriculturists. It was thus that the demagogic Thomas E. Watson began his congressional career. With the aid of the farmers he replaced one of the Bourbons at Washington.

Undoubtedly the most notable event in the history of agrarian insurgence in Florida was the Ocala Convention of 1890. This was a joint gathering of the National Farmers' Alliance and the Florida Alliance, which made a series of radical demands, including one for free silver. After adjournment, however, the prestige of the Florida organization declined for various reasons. It began leaning heavily in the direction of the new Populist party, then on the threshold of its rise to prestige and prominence in the West and South, and suffered a fatal reverse when its president was badly defeated as a candidate for governor on the Populist ticket in 1891.

When the Populists of the nation began casting about for a suitable candidate to carry the banner of agrarian discontent in the presidential election the following year, they looked with favor upon the aspirations of Colonel Leonidas L. Polk of North Carolina. Polk, like many other Southern Alliancemen, preferred to remain a Democrat, but believing it was futile to hope for the adoption of the Alliance program by the Democratic party, he concluded that

Populism provided the only way out. But just as his campaign for the nomination appeared to be gathering considerable momentum, death cut him down. Hence when the convention met, the prize went to General James B. Weaver of Iowa, who was named on a platform which called for free silver, adequate regulation of the railroads, a graduated income tax, and popular election of senators, and forbade alien ownership of land. In addition to the fact that most Southerners were strongly opposed to a third-party movement, Weaver was personally obnoxious to many voters in Dixie because of his record as a Union soldier. A cartoon entitled "General Weaver's 'War Record'" and depicting him as a raider of Confederate hen-houses, was widely circulated. When the general carried his campaign into the South in 1892, he was pilloried in the press and bombarded with eggs. One observer declared, indeed, that he "was made a regular walking omelet by the Southern chivalry of Georgia."

The aggressive campaign waged by the Populists forced the Democrats in a number of Southern states to incorporate Populist doctrine in their platforms. This, combined with other factors, such as the general reluctance on the part of Southerners to desert the party which had carried them through reconstruction, prevented the movement from becoming a serious threat, except in one or two states, particularly Alabama, where the farmers' candidate, Reuben F. Kolb, enjoyed Populist backing.

Two years later, however, combinations of Populists and Republicans made heavy inroads into the normal

Democratic vote in a number of Southern states. They actually carried North Carolina by approximately 20,000 majority, owing partly to the great Republican strength there; and they polled over 47 per cent of the total vote in Alabama and over 44 per cent in Georgia. It is probable that in both Alabama and Georgia the Democrats saved the day only by virtue of such heroic measures as wholesale ballot box stuffing and falsification of returns. "We had to do it! " a Georgia patriot acknowledged some years afterward. "Those damned Populists would have ruined the country! "

When William Jennings Bryan made his first and greatest bid for the presidency on a free silver platform, he was the nominee of the Populists as well as the Democrats. In that year the combined Populists and Republicans secured a firmer grip on legislative, county, and state offices in North Carolina than they had enjoyed two years before. They also showed substantial strength in state elections elsewhere below the Potomac and the Ohio. But after 1896 Populism was never again to menace the well-nigh impregnable solidity of the South. For various reasons the party's strength in the region dissipated rapidly. The Southern Farmers' Alliance had gone to pieces because of the unpopularity of its espousal of the Populist cause in 1892; many Populists had joined the Democratic party in 1896 because of Bryan's hospitality to Populist ideas, and the Democrats raised the issue of white supremacy widely in the South when it became manifest that the fusionist victory in North Carolina had led to the appointment of numerous Negro office-holders.

But if this combination of circumstances reduced the third-party movement in the South to impotence by the turn of the century, the ferment of the preceding decade and a half had thrust the back-country farmers and the urban laborers forward into a commanding position, a position which they were apparently destined to retain for an indefinite period. Members of the old Tidewater families who had held the offices and controlled the politics in many of the Southern states, accordingly found themselves shorn of the power they had come to regard as theirs in perpetuity, and forced to make way for a boisterous and pushing group of agrarians and workingmen. In the halls of Congress the dignified and conservative aristocrats who personified the grace and breeding of the Old South were rudely brushed aside, and men who had risen from the ranks were substituted for them. Similarly the newcomers captured most of the state legislatures and the state, county, and city offices.

The results of this social and political cataclysm were salutary in some respects and deplorable in others. It goes without saying that a pronounced improvement in the status of the average man was one consequence of the movement. Not only did the underprivileged whites obtain political rights which had previously been denied them by the aristocracy, but they also exercised their newly acquired authority to secure improved educational opportunities for the masses. At the same time they did much to curb the activities of grasping railroads and other corporations through the passage of regulatory legislation. On the debit side of the ledger must be cast up the cruelty and violence which characterized the treatment of the Negroes by this white element while it was rising to power, together with the unspeakable demagoguery of some of its votaries, and the unsoundness of some of the legislation they sponsored. But despite the fact that the movement produced few individual liberals of consequence, and although it included a good deal that was unwise in principle and shoddy in practice, it can be said that it was, on the whole, a liberalizing force in the South.

CHAPTER XIII

LITTÉRATEURS AND JOURNALISTS

THE YEARS which followed the Civil War were marked by an unusual amount of literary activity below the Potomac. Southerners sought, on the one hand, to earn sufficient money by writing to save themselves from penury; on the other, they rushed into print with a view to defending their section from the virulent attacks which were being made upon it. But while some of the best work of Timrod, Hayne, and Richard Malcolm Johnston appeared during the early period of reconstruction, by far the greater part of the South's literary output at this time was wholly undistinguished. There was an avalanche of pot-boilers, a flood of meretricious journalese and sleazy verse, but little that was of permanent value.

The point of view of many thousands of Southerners was one of extreme bitterness toward the North, and this was reflected in their literary attitudes. Robert E. Lee could advise the citizens of his native state to cease repining and "to work for Virginia—to build her up again, to make her great again"; but a large percentage of the inhabitants of the former Confederacy elected to spend their time in prejudiced and partisan appeals, in opening old wounds and rubbing

old sores, rather than in the kind of constructive
activity which Lee urged upon them. Such poems as
those of Father Abram J. Ryan, particularly "The
Conquered Banner," which strikes a note of hopeless-
ness and despair, were powerful factors in keeping the
eyes of the South turned to the past.

Another exemplar of this tendency was A. T.
Bledsoe, who had served as assistant secretary of war
for the Confederacy. Almost immediately following
the close of hostilities he published a defense of Jefferson Davis, in which he threshed over the old controversies as to slavery and secession. Then he founded
the *Southern Review* at Baltimore, and for the next ten
years he not only devoted much of his time to queru-
lously defending the South, but he set himself sternly
against practically every liberal movement of the era.
Bledsoe viewed all democratic tendencies with alarm,
was inflexible in his opposition to the public schools
and to industrialization in any form, and fought
desperately against the development of modern scientific theory, as tending to undermine traditional
theology.

A quite different point of view was expressed contemporaneously by General D. H. Hill, who established a journal called *The Land We Love* at Charlotte,
North Carolina, shortly after the war. Hill discussed
the Old South in a realistic way in the columns of
this publication, noting its defects as well as its virtues.
He urged a more widely diffused educational system,
and sought to allay animosities between the sections.
Afterward as editor of *The Southern Home* and as
president of the University of Arkansas and the Mili-

tary and Agricultural College at Milledgeville, Georgia, Hill exerted a salutary influence upon the thought of the South.

But while Dixie, as we have noted, was able to make few significant contributions to American letters during the years immediately following Appomattox, a literary renaissance of genuine moment got under way in the region just as reconstruction was drawing to a close. It is highly probable, indeed, that the termination of reconstruction was to some extent responsible for this revival. As long as the carpetbaggers were in control below Mason and Dixon's Line, the inhabitants were mentally so demoralized that they found it almost impossible to view the Southern scene with sufficient detachment to write about it honestly, fearlessly, and without prejudice. At the same time the end of carpetbag rule was the beginning of a period which was to bring a measure of financial prosperity to the South. There was, needless to say, little that could be called prosperity in the Southern states during the late seventies, but conditions were better than they had been ten years before, and they were improving steadily. Since commercial and industrial advancement usually go hand in hand with literary and artistic accomplishment, this was a distinctly favorable circumstance.

About the year 1875 the production of significant poetry and prose in the South began to increase in notable fashion. Much of this material was of a different type from that which had been published during the ante-bellum period. In general it was realistic rather than romantic, and it dealt with actual places,

persons, and conditions, rather than with those which
were imaginary or apocryphal. There were exceptions to this generalization, of course, but the tendency
was in the direction indicated.

This movement was undoubtedly liberal, for it
freed Southern writers from many of the inhibitions
which had hampered them in the past. It not only
enabled them to treat newer, fresher, and more
realistic themes, but it also made it possible for them
to approach their task in a more uncompromising
spirit.

The leading protagonists of the new spirit in South-
ern letters at this period were Sidney Lanier, George
W. Cable, Mary N. Murfree, and Joel Chandler
Harris.

Lanier's importance as a liberalizing force in
Southern literature derives quite as much from his
attitude toward sectional relationships and other
pressing questions of current moment during the
post-war years, and his work in promoting sound
scholarship and thorough criticism, as from his
achievements as an artist. Like his friend Paul Hamilton Hayne, he had suffered intensely during the Civil
War, but like Hayne again, he was glad to put these
sufferings out of his mind after the fighting was over,
and to do everything in his power to restore harmony.
Both men also endeavored to build up more honest
critical standards and to put an end to the practice,
widely-prevalent in the South, of heaping indiscriminate praise upon any literary work which emanated
from a Southern pen.

Lanier's own writing was done in the new realistic

mood, and was influential in inducing a similar attitude on the part of other authors in the South. If he failed to attain true greatness as a poet, largely because of the excessive didacticism of his verse, his work nevertheless deserves high rank. There was inspiration to other writers, too, in Lanier's heroic fight against the consumption which finally carried him off, a prolonged and heart-breaking struggle in which the true nobility of his character made itself apparent. All his important creative work was done while his frame was racked by tuberculosis, and his last poem, "Sunrise," was written when he had a fever of 104 degrees and was too feeble to raise food to his mouth.

George W. Cable burst upon the literary scene almost simultaneously with Lanier, when he began publishing his "Old Creole Days" in *Scribner's Monthly*. These realistic studies of the Louisiana Creoles were soon collected in book form, and their appearance was markedly influential in hastening the revival of letters below the Potomac and directing it into new channels. Cable followed this volume with others dealing with Creole civilization, all done in an admirable spirit of detachment and with a manifest desire to paint a true picture. But the people of New Orleans and the surrounding territory were so in the habit of receiving romantic and glamorous panegyrics from the pens of their native writers that they became greatly incensed at Cable. This, combined with the abuse that greeted *The Silent South*, in which he protested against the South's treatment of the Negro, caused him to remove once and for all to Massachusetts in 1886.

Cable devoted a portion of *The Silent South* to an

impassioned remonstrance against the frightful conditions which then obtained in the state penal institutions below the Mason and Dixon Line. The convict lease system was in operation in every Southern state. According to Cable, this system sprang "primarily from the idea that the possession of a convict's person is an opportunity for the state to make money . . . without regard to moral or mortal consequences." He showed that in several penitentiaries prisoners almost invariably died within ten years after confinement, owing to the horrible conditions under which they were forced to work and the prevalence of disease in the foul and loathsome prisons in which they were incarcerated.

Another writer who succeeded in portraying a segment of Southern life with fidelity and craftsmanship was Mary N. Murfree. Her stories of the mountaineers of east Tennessee appeared under the pen-name of Charles Egbert Craddock, and marked an important milestone in the postwar revival of realism. Although Miss Murfree was herself of aristocratic lineage, she saw the pathos and beauty which underlay the simple lives of the mountain people of her native state, and portrayed it in a long series of novels.

But while Miss Murfree was preëminently the novelist of a particular group of "poor whites," a majority of the important fictive creations of Joel Chandler Harris are Negroes. There is first of all Uncle Remus, whose songs and sayings have become famous around the world. The Uncle Remus series is not only important for its extraordinarily faithful reincarnation of the ante-bellum slave, but it derives further significance from the fact that a Negro is the central figure, whereas theretofore the colored man had customarily been introduced in the rôle of a mere servant or hanger-on to the white man, who held the center of the stage. It is as the author of *Uncle Remus* that Harris is chiefly known today, but he practised much the same artistry in numerous other tales of the Old South and reconstruction—tales which are far from deserving the virtual oblivion into which they have sunk. In these stories and novels he portrayed the plantation of before the war as it actually was, instead of as many romantically inclined Southerners would like it to have been. Dr. F. P. Gaines declares that the plantation is depicted in the works of Harris "with a completeness of understanding not equalled by any other writer." Through the golden haze which enveloped the days of his youth at the old Turner homestead in Georgia, Harris saw the glamour and the romance of life in the ante-bellum South, but his stories showed that he also remembered "the darker aspects of slavery, such as the sufferings of fugitives, the tragedy of mixed blood, the separation of families or the occasional cruelties of overseers."

In this respect he differed radically from his contemporary, Thomas Nelson Page, who seldom permitted such unpleasant considerations as these to intrude themselves upon his literary consciousness. While it is true that his collection of essays entitled *The Old South* contains some rather critical passages, Page's novels and short stories are compounded wholly of the traditional moonlight and magnolias.

So much for the principal writers of short stories

and novels in the former Confederacy during the late nineteenth century. Several of them, as we have seen, found it possible to rise above the welter of prejudice and passion which hemmed them in, and to describe certain aspects of Southern life with forthrightness and candor. In the field of criticism, however, there were fewer manifestations of such a liberal and independent spirit. For more than a quarter of a century after the close of the war there was scarcely anything which might be termed literary criticism below the Potomac. There was an army of defenders of and apologists for the South, who seized every opportunity to rush to the defense of the region and its literature, but there were few indeed who harkened to the plea of Lanier and Hayne for more honest critical standards. Patriotic Southrons were not without provocation at times, as when the *Encyclopædia Britannica* declared in its article on "American Literature" that since the Revolution "the few thinkers of America born south of Mason and Dixon's Line are outnumbered by those belonging to the single state of Massachusetts; nor is it too much to say that mainly by their connection with the North the Carolinas have been saved from sinking to the level of Mexico or the Antilles." This extraordinary assertion brought a lengthy retort from T. K. Oglesby of Alabama. Oglesby exhibited no little erudition, and he was able to marshal a considerable mass of data in refutation of the encyclopædia's contention. But he lost his perspective and descended to banality when he proclaimed that South Carolina boasted "the only woman on record who was the wife of a governor, the sister

of a governor, the niece of a governor, the mother
of a governor, and the aunt and foster-mother of a
governor"; and that North Carolina was the home
of "the biggest man, in mere physical proportions, of
whom there is any mention in the history of the
country."

This tendency on the part of the ex-Confederates
to exalt their civilization above any other in the
history of the world, and to overshoot the mark with
such silly outbursts of braggadocio as that in the foregoing paragraph, was an important factor in prevent-
ing the creation of an appreciable body of sound
critical writing after the war. There was also the unwillingness of many leaders in the region to coöperate
in efforts to build up Southern industry and commerce, or to promote any other movement which
appeared to them to depart from the course of thought
and action pursued in the Old South. Typical of this
school was Charles Colcock Jones, Jr., of Georgia,
whose history of his native state led Bancroft to hail
him as the "Macaulay of the South." Characteristic
of Jones's attitude is the following extract from one
of his addresses delivered in 1891:

"Under the absurd guise of a New South, flaunting
the banners of utilitarianism—lifting the standards of
speculation and expediency—elevating the colors
whereon are emblazoned consolidation of wealth and
centralization of government—lowering the flag of
intellectual, moral and refined supremacy in the
presence of the petty guidons of ignorance, personal
ambition and diabolism—supplanting the iron cross
with the golden calf . . . ; and careless of the land-

15

marks of the fathers, impatient of the restraints of a
calm, enlightened, conservative civilization, viewing
with an indifferent eye the tokens of Confederate
valor, and slighting the graves of Confederate dead,
would counsel no oblation save at the shrine of
mammon. . . ."

Finally in 1892 Dr. William P. Trent published his
biography of William Gilmore Simms. This life of the
most important native writer in the Old South was
not only a study of an outstanding literary figure; it
was also a study of certain aspects of ante-bellum
civilization. The author viewed his subject with complete detachment and made no concessions to current
Southern prejudices. In fact he leaned backward in
some of his statements, as when he declared that "any
tyro in the theory of politics" could see that "secession
was wrong in itself"; or when he averred that the Civil
War was fought "for the preservation of slavery."
Unquestionably, however, the book was scholarly
and valuable, and it marked an epoch in the history
of criticism in the Southern states. But despite the
excellent qualities which Dr. Trent's biography
exhibited, there was fierce resentment in many
quarters, accompanied by demands for the author's
head. It is gratifying to record that Sewanee University, where he was then teaching, refused to heed the
popular outcry.

Two noteworthy historical studies appeared shortly
afterward and gave further impetus to the tendency
toward accuracy and objectivity in Southern scholarship. These were Dr. Philip Alexander Bruce's
Economic History of Virginia in the Seventeenth Century and

Edward McCrady's history of colonial and revolutionary South Carolina.

In the field of periodical literature, the most important development between 1865 and 1900 was the establishment of the *Sewanee Review* in 1892, with Professor Trent as editor. For the next eight years he was the magazine's guiding genius. While its circulation was always limited, the *Sewanee Review* under Trent exerted a liberal influence upon Southern thought. The editor did a good job, not only in his choice of subject matter, but also in the courage with which he presented articles of a critical nature on Southern themes. Benjamin W. Wells for a time was associated with him in the editorial direction of the journal. But with Professor Trent's departure for Columbia University in 1900, much of the vitality and liberalism which had informed his magazine departed with him. The *Review* became increasingly academic and its influence declined. It has never been the significant critical force in the twentieth century that it was in the nineteenth.

It was while Dr. Trent was editing his magazine in Tennessee that W. C. Brann, a Northerner who had removed to Texas, was publishing the *Iconoclast*. Brann was an independent free lance who had a horror of uplifters and reformers, and who delighted to "stir up the animals." If much that he wrote was nonsense, and if his attitude toward the Negro was barbaric in the extreme, he served, nevertheless, as a species of intellectual gadfly to his portion of the South. Brann was a staunch defender of Catholics and Jews and a bitter foe of the evangelical clergy. While his terrific assaults on the latter group may have done more harm than good, he sought to free Texas and the rest of the South from abject obedience to clerical authority. Brann kicked up such a furor that his journal acquired a circulation of 90,000, and was widely read, not only in the Lone Star State but elsewhere. His stormy career came to an end in 1898 when he was shot in the back on the streets of Waco.

Among Southern newspaper men during the postbellum era, Henry Watterson of the Louisville *Courier-Journal* was the most commanding figure, although there were a number of other editors whose work was of the highest calibre and who did yeoman service for liberal causes.

Watterson became affiliated with the *Courier-Journal* in 1868, and he soon made the paper known and feared beyond the borders of Kentucky. For half a century he presided over the editorial page, and for the greater part of that time the *Courier-Journal* was recognized as the most widely-read and most influential paper in Southern journalism. Watterson was not only a great editor; he was in most respects a liberal editor. During the dark days of reconstruction, when it was physically dangerous for him to do so, he championed the cause of the Negro. He was instrumental in having the black laws removed from the Kentucky statute books, and he sent some forty leaders of a bogus branch of the Ku Klux Klan to the penitentiary for their murders of inoffensive freedmen. He also was successful in securing the admission of Negro testimony in the courts. These campaigns for the rights ot the blacks were waged contrary to the advice of George D. Prentice, his predecessor in the editorial chair, who felt that the personal risk was too great. But the young editor had served as aide-de-camp to Forrest and as chief of scouts for Joseph E. Johnston. He seized the first opportunity to announce that he could "shoot with any man in Kentucky across a pocket handkerchief," and when it was seen that he meant business, the opposition became less belligerent.

Watterson also did much to restore amicable relations between the North and the South. He was fierce in his excoriation of Toombs of Georgia, who he said was "moss-grown" and seeking "to continue, in an endless circle of discontent, the passions of bygone social and political conflicts." At the same time he appreciated the greatness of Abraham Lincoln and frequently took occasion to speak of the slain president's magnanimity toward the South.

When William Jennings Bryan was nominated in 1896 on a free silver platform, "Marse Henry" was in Europe. Convinced that the currency was seriously endangered and that Bryan's election would be disastrous, he sent the famous cablegram to his paper:

"Another ticket our only hope. No compromise with dishonor. Stand firm."

The *Courier-Journal* fought Bryan throughout the campaign and almost wrecked itself in the process. Counting the retention of its subscribers and prestige as of less consequence than what it conceived to be the welfare of the country, it risked destruction for a principle. Other leading Southern papers which did likewise were the Montgomery *Advertiser* under Major

W. W. Screws, the Richmond *Times* under Joseph Bryan, the Charlotte *Observer* under Joseph P. Caldwell, and the Chattanooga *Times* under Adolph S. Ochs.

It was particularly hard for Watterson to bolt the Democratic ticket, since such action on his part would inevitably promote the fortunes of McKinley, whose campaign manager, Mark Hanna, was the very incarnation of the predatory plutocracy which the Louisville editor was fond of belaboring as the "Money Devil." Yet he threw his support to the Gold Democrats, Palmer and Buckner, and thereby insured a Republican victory in Kentucky. The *Courier-Journal's* fight on Bryan was conducted by W. H. Haldeman, Watterson's partner, since he himself remained abroad for the time being.

"Marse Henry" was a consistent foe of prohibition and woman suffrage. Prohibitionists were "red-nosed angels" in his editorial columns, and suffragettes were "silly Sallies and crazy Janes." He also was a terrific Hun-hater during the World War. No editor in America was more violent in his denunciation of the Central Powers, and immediately after the sinking of the *Lusitania* he reached the remarkable conclusion that the world was on the threshold of "the most momentous moral crisis since the crucifixion of Christ." Then with the coming of peace, he jeered at all who favored the League of Nations, and in 1919 relinquished his title as editor emeritus of the *Courier-Journal* because the paper announced its support of the league. While his pen retained much of its pungency and power until the end, Henry Watterson's most noteworthy services to the cause of liberalism were rendered prior to 1900.

Another editor who rose to prominence during the reconstruction era was Francis W. Dawson, who had come over from his native England in the sixties to enlist under the Stars and Bars. He received three wounds fighting for the Confederacy, and then after the close of hostilities settled in Charleston. Dawson purchased the *News* with the aid of friends and combined it with the *Courier* under the name of the *News and Courier*. As editor of this paper until his death in 1889, he exercised an influence upon Southern thought which was sane, intelligent, and liberal.

During the carpetbag orgies in South Carolina, Dawson sought to put an end to bitterness. He even advocated the nomination of Negroes on the Democratic municipal ticket in Charleston, and when Governor D. H. Chamberlain, the Radical, turned out astonishingly enough to be a satisfactory executive, the *News and Courier* went so far as to urge his election over Wade Hampton.

Dawson was a tremendous power in promoting the industrial and agricultural development of the state. He also was instrumental in breaking up the widely prevalent practice of dueling in South Carolina. Summoned to "the field of honor," he refused to accept the challenge, and wrote a series of articles against dueling which resulted in the enactment of a statute making it illegal. His crusade was an important factor in putting an end to dueling in this country and led to his decoration by the Pope.

The editor of the *News and Courier* was always a

staunch ally of the Negroes, which may account in some measure for his hostility to the Tillman movement in South Carolina. But in addition to the fact that "Pitchfork Ben" and his followers were not regarded as interested in the welfare of the blacks, they exhibited other characteristics which did not appeal to Dawson. He described Tillman as "the leader of the Adullamites, a people who carry pistols in their hip pockets, who expectorate upon the floor, who have no toothbrushes and comb their hair with their fingers." Apparently he permitted the crude appearance and uncouth behavior of the up-staters to blind him to the fact that they had some genuine grievances.

Dawson suffered the fate of many other Southern editors before him. His career was cut short by a bullet.

Two years later, in 1891, Ambrose E. and N. G. Gonzales founded the Columbia *State*, and in the columns of that daily they also waged ceaseless warfare against Tillman. The Gonzales brothers felt with their murdered colleague that the integrity of the commonwealth was threatened by the hegemony of the back country proletariat. But the *State* did not by any means devote itself exclusively to fighting Tillman and his followers. It demonstrated its inherent liberalism by throwing its resources into the scales in opposition to lynching and child labor and in support of better schools and adequate compulsory education laws. The paper lost the services of N. G. Gonzales in 1903, when he was shot down in broad daylight on the streets of Columbia by Lieutenant Governor James H. Tillman, a nephew of Ben Tillman. James Tillman attributed his defeat for the governorship shortly before to the *State's* opposition, and took this method of obtaining revenge. Ambrose and a third brother, William E. Gonzales, then took charge of the paper. The former died in 1926, and editorial direction has since that time been wholly in the hands of William Gonzales. In the twentieth century, as in the nineteenth, the *State* has been generally recognized as an enlightened and civilized voice in Southern journalism.

While Watterson was building up a great newspaper at Louisville and Dawson was doing likewise at Charleston, Joel Chandler Harris was writing editorials for the Savannah *News* which were recognized as among the ablest and most courageous in his portion of the South. In 1876 he joined the staff of the Atlanta *Constitution*, and when Henry W. Grady bought an interest in the paper four years later and became managing editor, the *Constitution* was able to boast of a pair of liberals who could not be matched on any Southern newspaper. Harris was chief editorial writer almost continuously for the next quarter of a century, and Grady retained the managing editorship until his death.

Even before he joined the Atlanta paper, Harris had deplored the fact that Georgia editors were "harping steadily on the same old prejudices and moving in the worn ruts of a period that was soul-destroying in its narrowness," and he continued to stress this theme in the editorial columns of the *Constitution*. Pleading for a saner attitude on the part of the South toward its own shortcomings, for greater tolerance toward those who were disposed to be critical of Southern institutions and *mores*, he urged an end to wrangling and strife. Always a friend to the Negro, he wrote that "if education of the Negro is not the chief solution of the problem that confronts the white people of the South then there is no other conceivable solution and there is nothing ahead but political chaos and demoralization."

As the author of many faithful portrayals of life in the Old and New South, Harris had no patience with the widely prevalent feeling that Southern authors should confine themselves to rose-tinted eulogiums of the region and its people. "We shall never have any great novel from the South until our writers shake off this Old Man of the Sea, and free themselves from the imaginary pressure under which they labor," he wrote. "Those who would understand what I mean will do well to recall the hot criticism and social ostracism occasioned by George W. Cable's extraordinary studies of Creole life in New Orleans." He expressed similar views in *Uncle Remus's Magazine*, which he founded in 1907 and edited until his death the following year.

Henry W. Grady, his co-worker on the *Constitution* for nearly a decade, shared Harris's opinions on virtually all subjects, and relations between the two men were always harmonious. Grady's dynamic personality and vibrant liberalism, his oratorical ability and journalistic competence made him an ideal associate for the shy and retiring Harris. His zeal for improved intersectional and interracial relations, for better schools for whites and blacks, for the development of

Southern industry and for the upbuilding of a greater South and a greater nation found expression in the columns of the *Constitution.*

Reference has been made in a previous chapter to the brief career of Walter Hines Page as editor of the Raleigh *State Chronicle.* He took over this weekly in 1883 and lost little time in attacking many of the most cherished prejudices and shibboleths of his fellow North Carolinians. Although this was a period when Southerners were especially sensitive to criticism, the youthful editor was not deterred by such consider- ations, and he laid about him in vigorous fashion. North Carolina was "mummified," he proclaimed, and was making obeisance to "ghosts," particularly to "the Ghost of the Confederate dead, the Ghost of religious orthodoxy, the Ghost of Negro domination." For two years he heaped ridicule and invective upon the heads of his readers. Page had many sound ideas, but his methods, naturally enough, made enemies rather than converts. His proposals that the state for- get the past as far as possible and concentrate all its energies upon the development of better schools, roads, farms, and industries, and that it break away from ecclesiastical domination and seek to realize its destiny as a great commonwealth, would have been far more effective if they had been presented in different lan- guage. As it was, his ridicule enraged many members of his audience, who denounced him with vehemence and regularity as a traitor to the South.

Convinced that it would be futile to continue his campaign, Page disposed of the *State Chronicle* and re- moved to New York. There he soon distinguished himself as editor, successively, of the *Forum*, the *Atlantic Monthly* and *World's Work*. He was always eager to give space in the columns of these influential magazines to chronicles setting forth the progress of liberal movements in Dixie. At the same time, despite hostility in certain quarters, he was in demand as a speaker before Southern audiences, and he seized every opportunity to arouse the region to a realization of its needs. As a member of the Southern Education Board and the General Education Board he did much to build more adequate public school systems in the Southern states, he was instrumental in the establishment of the International Health Board which waged such devastating war upon hookworm, and he coöperated to the full extent of his ability with Dr. Seaman A. Knapp in the latter's epochal work in raising Southern standards of agriculture. If Page was at times brutally frank in his criticisms of the land of his forefathers, as for example in his novel, *The Southerner*, his motives are not properly subject to question. Few men have made a more lasting contribution to the development of liberal thinking below Mason and Dixon's Line.

Simultaneously with the commencement of Page's tempestuous career as a newspaper editor at Raleigh, D. A. Tompkins was establishing himself at Charlotte as an engineer and contractor. A few years later he bought the Charlotte *Observer* and placed Joseph P. Caldwell in charge of the editorial page. The duümvirate of Tompkins and Caldwell was well-nigh as notable as that of Harris and Grady on the Atlanta *Constitution*. Tompkins was himself a man of quite uncommon talents, and he gave the gifted Caldwell free rein in his conduct of the *Observer*. The result was one of the great newspapers of the post-bellum South.

The press of North Carolina at the period exhibited scarcely a trace of liberalism and was venomously partisan, but the fact meant less than nothing to Caldwell. He was determined to be honest, intelligent, and fair, and he carried out his design in the face of denunciation which would have dismayed a lesser man. Although the majority of Southern editors were afflicted with intellectual anchylosis, Caldwell kept his mind open to new ideas, and he built up a newspaper which was not only independent in politics, but which came to be recognized as courageously liberal in many other respects as well. He did more than any man of his generation to raise journalistic standards in North Carolina, and it is largely because of his influence that the press of that state today is one of the most enlightened in the South.

CHAPTER XIV

THE NEGRO PROBLEM TODAY

THE SOUTHERN scene at the opening of the twentieth century presented evidences of gratifying progress in various fields. The people were gradually putting the war and its aftermath behind them and were augmenting their material resources, while at the same time they were developing a healthier and saner mental outlook.

There were, however, several discouraging factors in the situation which confronted the South, and not the least of them was the race problem. It was hoped that the wholesale disfranchisement of the Negroes then going forward would remove the blacks from the political picture, but this expectation was not realized. The lower class whites who were now in the saddle virtually throughout the Southern states were too keenly aware of the Negro's potentialities as an economic rival to permit any soft-pedaling of the race issue, either in the realm of politics or in that of business. Lynchings were frequent, race riots were not unknown, and the South was rapidly developing a class of demagogues who were appealing to the "poor whites" of the cities and the upland farms by means of blatant agitation of the race question. Prominent among these panderers to interracial hate were J. K.

Vardaman of Mississippi, Hoke Smith of Georgia, and Ben Tillman of South Carolina.

Vardaman, spokesman for the "hill billies" and "red necks" of Mississippi, was perhaps the most brutal Negrophobe in the South. An idea of his philosophy may be gleaned from his statement that "the way to control the nigger is to whip him when he does not obey without it, and another is never to pay him more wages than is actually necessary to buy food and clothing."

Another thesis promulgated by Vardaman was that "God Almighty created the Negro for a menial." He also contended that there ought to be two sorts of justice in the South, one for white men and another for "niggers," and that nobody ought to expect any law to be enforced in the same way for both races. In his winning campaign for governor in 1903 he advocated giving the Negroes no school funds except such as were raised from taxes they themselves had paid.

This argument that the blacks should receive no money for schools except such funds as they contributed to the treasury was a favorite with the class of politicians of which Vardaman was the outstanding prototype, and it always appealed strongly to the "poor whites." It would, of course, have been just as reasonable to have restricted these same "poor whites" to such school revenues as they raised by taxation, and thus to have cut them off with only a small percentage of what they actually obtained, but this seems never to have occurred to them. They wanted to apply the rule to the Negroes but were not at all interested in applying it to themselves.

Fortunately there were prominent white men in Mississippi who found the Vardaman doctrines abhorrent, and who did what they could to counteract them, just as there were such men in the other states of the South to fight for justice for the Negro. John Sharp Williams defeated Vardaman for the Senate in 1907 in a campaign in which he committed himself to a policy of friendship toward the blacks and protested against "indiscriminate cursing of the whole Negro race." He urged his hearers to remember that "it is not the educated Negro who commits the unspeakable crime . . . it is the brute whose avenues of information are totally cut off." Bishop Charles B. Galloway, a big, broad, generous-hearted man, was another staunch ally of the weaker race, as were Major R. W. Millsaps, founder of Millsaps College, and Walter Clark, president of the Mississippi Cotton Association.

Galloway, Millsaps, and Clark received invaluable coöperation from such men as Edgar Gardner Murphy of Alabama, Chancellor Walter B. Hill of the University of Georgia, Professor Andrew Sledd of Emory Cóllege, Georgia; Professor John Spencer Bassett of Trinity College, North Carolina; and Professor S. C. Mitchell of Richmond College, Virginia. These influential liberals exerted themselves constantly on behalf of justice for the blacks and sought to provide an antidote for the flood of hate which the "poor whites" and their leaders were pouring forth in a steady stream.

It would not be fair, however, to attribute all lack of cordiality between the races to agitation carried on by the underprivileged whites. John Temple Graves, an upper class Southerner, is generally regarded as having been largely responsible for the famous Atlanta race riot of 1906. The Atlanta *Evening News*, of which he was editor, broadcast several extras in one day proclaiming four successive "assaults" on white women by Negro men in the city, whereas no assault had been committed and not more than two of the episodes in question could properly have been called even attempted assaults. The result of these news articles, coupled with an incendiary editorial, was that feeling was raised to a tremendous pitch. A mob of lower class whites formed and began killing Negroes indiscriminately. A lame bootblack who was shining a man's shoes was dragged to the sidewalk and beaten to death. Another young Negro was fatally stabbed with jackknives. Several colored barbers who were peacefully shaving white customers in their shops were killed on the spot. In all, ten Negroes were massacred in cold blood, and not one of them was guilty of any crime other than that of having a black skin. Sixty others were wounded.

Despite his substantial share of responsibility for the riot, Graves continued his editorial policy of cold brutality toward the Negro. Several months after the clash, the *Evening News* said concerning the black man who attacks a white woman:

"No law of God or man can hold back the vengeance of our white men upon such a criminal. If necessary we will double and treble and quadruple the law of Moses, and hang off-hand the criminal, or failing to find that a remedy, we will hang two, three or four of the Negroes nearest to the crime until the crime is

16

242   LIBERALISM IN THE SOUTH

no longer done or feared in all this Southern land we inhabit and love."

About six weeks later the *Evening News* went into the hands of a receiver. Its failure is understood to have been due principally to its policy on the Negro question, particularly before and during the Atlanta race riot.

But with all the rancor and acrimony engendered by this clash between whites and blacks, it had one good result. After the riot a committee of leading Atlantans, appointed to work with public officials in restoring order and confidence, sent for a number of prominent Negroes and conferred with them over the best method of meeting the situation. This is said to have been "the first important occasion in the South upon which an attempt was made to get the two races together for any serious consideration of their differences."

There was urgent need in the Southern states during the early years of the century not only for such conferences between leaders of the two racial groups but also for a more tolerant attitude on the part of whites toward members of their own race who disagreed with them upon some aspects of the Negro problem. This is shown by the fact that when Professor Sledd of Emory College and Professor Bassett of Trinity College ran afoul of prevailing sentiment on this question, they suffered heavily. The former was dismissed by the institution he served and the latter was excoriated in terrific fashion for utterances deemed unorthodox by important elements of the population.* The intensity

* For a fuller discussion of the Sledd and Bassett cases, see Chapter XVIII.

of the feeling on this issue was also well illustrated by the tremendous outburst of indignation below the Potomac when President Roosevelt had Booker T. Washington to dinner at the White House.

The education of the blacks still claimed the attention of thoughtful Southerners as the twentieth century dawned. There was opposition to it from those who felt that funds were inadequate as well as from those who were convinced that education would be harmful. Among the latter group was President Winston of the North Carolina Agricultural College, who asserted that "the Negroes who can read and write are more criminal than the illiterates." This theory was held widely, but it was exploded by Clarence Poe of Raleigh in a magazine article* in which he showed, among other things, that "of our total colored population in 1890, each 100,000 illiterates furnished 489 criminals and each 100,000 literates only 413 criminals." He pointed out, too, that for the preceding two years at the North Carolina State Prison "the proportion of Negro criminals from the illiterate class has been 40 per cent larger than from the class which has had school training.†

Edgar Gardner Murphy, staunch advocate of schooling for the blacks, called attention to the fact that no graduate of Hampton or Tuskegee had ever been charged with rape, a statement which is still true of both of these institutions, and is striking evidence of the salutary effects of education upon the colored race.

* "Lynching: A Southern View," *Atlantic Monthly*, February, 1904.

† For a still more comprehensive treatment of this theme see Gilbert T. Stephenson, "Education and Crime Among Negroes," *South Atlantic Quarterly*, January, 1917.

Murphy also offered the following comment upon the attitude of those who would deny the Negro an opportunity for mental and manual training:

"The poor Negro! The man who would keep him in ignorance and then would disfranchise him because he is ignorant must seem to him a paragon of erect and radiant consistency, when compared with the man who first tells him he must work, and then tells him he must not learn how. He tells the Negro he must make shoes, but that he must not make shoes which people can wear; that he may be a wheelwright, but that he must make neither good wheels nor salable wagons; that he must be a farmer, but that he must not farm well."

It was in 1908 that Dr. James Hardy Dillard of the Tulane faculty took charge of the Jeanes Fund established by Anna T. Jeanes, a Philadelphia Quaker, for the employment of supervising teachers for rural Negro schools in the South. The date is important in the history of the colored race in America, for it marks the year when one of the ablest, bravest, and most tactful of Southern gentlemen determined to devote the remainder of his life to furthering the cause of Negro education. Two years later, Dr. Dillard also became director of the Slater Fund. Since the death of Booker Washington his influence on behalf of better educational facilities for the Southern blacks and better interracial relations has exceeded that of any other man.

One of the secrets of Dr. Dillard's success as an interpreter of racial problems and a spokesman for the liberal element on racial matters is to be found in his emphasis upon the need for justice in the South's treatment of the Negro, as distinguished from an emotionalistic attitude toward the question. He is fond of quoting Booker Washington's assertion that the best Southern speech on race relations he ever heard was made by a certain Governor, who began by saying that he laid no particular claim to a sentiment of love for Negroes, but he believed in justice. Another secret of his success is to be seen in the statement Washington once made of him, that he "speaks to the poorest Negro in Alabama in the same way that he speaks to President Taft."

Teachers representing the Jeanes Fund visit more than 10,000 rural schools for Negroes annually and raise over $500,000 for school improvement, while since 1912 the Slater Fund has aided in the establishment of some four hundred county training schools throughout the South and has rendered other substantial services to Negro education. Dr. Dillard describes Jackson Davis and Virginia E. Randolph of Virginia as "the inventors of the real Jeanes plan," since they were instrumental in having the original Jeanes program for county supervision modified in certain important respects. In 1931, shortly before his seventy-fifth birthday, Dr. Dillard resigned as head of the Jeanes and Slater funds, but he remains on the boards of both foundations.

The South also is indebted to Dr. Dillard for the establishment of the University Commission on Southern Race Questions, forerunner of the Commission on Interracial Coöperation, with which latter organization it has merged in large measure of late. The University Commission was established at the initial meeting of the Southern Sociological Congress at Nashville in 1912, and the following year in Atlanta another forward step was taken by the Congress with the setting up of its Race Section. Dr. Dillard's genuine desire to contribute to the progress of all classes of Southern Negroes is further exemplified by the fact that every summer since 1919 he has held a four-day institute for rural Negro preachers at Trenton in the sandhills of western South Carolina, seven miles from the nearest railroad.

Through the aid of the Jeanes and Slater funds, the Rosenwald Fund, the General Education Board, the Phelps-Stokes Fund, and other similar philanthropies established by Northerners, the public schools for Negroes in the South are gradually being raised to a reasonable degree of efficiency. State appropriations to them are usually much below what the blacks are entitled to on the basis of population, but this situation is improving as the importance of educating the race is gradually coming to be realized.

Tuskegee, which celebrated its fiftieth anniversary in 1931, has been brought to its highest degree of efficiency under Dr. Robert R. Moton, and has expanded in various directions. It now sponsors the National Negro Business League and National Negro Health Week, operates a farm demonstration service in several states and holds the only clinic in the country where Negro doctors can meet and discuss their problems. It is a noteworthy fact, however, that Dr. W. E. B. Du Bois, who was never able during Washington's lifetime to build up a following which could approach that of the Tuskegee founder in numbers and influence, is now easily the outstanding leader of his race in the country. While the Tuskegee faculty is competent and highly trained, it contains only one man of creative genius, Dr. George Carver, whose astounding facility in making rubber, dandruff cure, paper and some two hundred other synthetic products out of the peanut has caught the attention of the nation. Dr. Du Bois, on the other hand, has attracted to himself a large number of men and women of remarkable literary, artistic, and scientific attainments. The fecundity of this group is as extraordinary as the sterility of the faculty of Tuskegee. While the rise of Dr. Du Bois to almost undisputed leadership in recent years could not have taken place without the Negro exodus to the North after the World War, it is rendered none the less significant by virtue of that fact.

Ray Stannard Baker, who made an extended tour of the South and recorded his impressions of the race situation in an excellent series of articles in the *American Magazine* during 1907 and 1908, declared that at that time the South did not believe in a democracy which had a place in it for the Negro; but he added that the attitude of the North was substantially the same.

The unfortunate position of the Negro at the period was shrewdly stated by "Mr. Dooley," the celebrated humorist, as follows:

"I'm not so much throubled about th' naygur whin he lives among his opprissors as I am whin he falls into th' hands iv his liberators. Whin he's in th' South he can make up his mind to be lynched soon or late

an' give his attintion to his other pleasures in com-
posin' rag-time music on a banjo, an' wurrukin' f'r
th' man that used to own him an' now on'y owes him
his wages. But 'tis the divvle's own hardship . . . to
be pursooed by a mob iv abolitionists till he's dhriven
to seek police protection."

The race riots which broke out in many Northern
cities during and after the World War with the influx
of large masses of blacks seemed to indicate that the
whites of the North were no more anxious to treat the
Negro equitably than those of the South. If there was
a terrible riot at Houston, Texas, at this time, there
were a number of such encounters in Northern cities.
Notable among these was that at East St. Louis, Illinois, in which 125 Negro workingmen were killed by
white strikers. *Current Opinion* described this clash as
follows:

"For the greater part of thirty-six hours, Negroes
were hunted through the streets like wild animals. . . .
Man after man, with hands upraised, pleading for
his life, was surrounded by groups of men who had
never seen him before and who knew nothing about
him except that he was black, and stoned to death.
. . . An aged Negro, tottering from weakness, was
seized and hanged to a pole."

There were other severe riots in Chicago, Philadelphia, and Washington, and five separate riots in
New York City.

As for the number of lynchings in the Southern
states of late as compared with other sections, Horace
M. Bond, a leader of the Negro race, declared in a recent article appearing in *Harper's Magazine* that "in

proportion to the number of Negroes in the population, the Middle West of recent years has been as ready to mete out extra-legal justice to the Negroes as has the South."

But while there is encouragement for Southerners in the fact that the annual toll of lives taken in this manner below Mason and Dixon's Line is at present gratifyingly below that of twenty-five or thirty years ago, lynchers in this section during the past decade have been employing atrociously cruel methods. Walter White, whose *Rope and Faggot* is the most thorough study of the question yet published, declares that sadism among Southern lynchers has increased alarmingly, and that burnings at the stake, mutilations, and other manifestations of savagery are more common than formerly. He attributes this to the blood lust engendered by the World War and to the "search of the mob for new thrills," the "inevitable result of many years of lynching."

Georgia, with approximately 465 mob murders to its credit since 1889, is the banner state of the Union in this respect,* followed by Mississippi, Texas, Louisiana, and Alabama, in that order. Thus it is obvious that the lower South is far more proficient than the upper South in the business of putting defenseless and frequently innocent Negroes to death. At the same time it employs more horrible methods to accomplish its designs. A tabulation of the ultra-fiendish lynchings for the ten years which began in 1918 shows Texas in the

---

* It is interesting to note that while Georgia ranks first in number of lynchings since 1889, the state of Wyoming ranks first in number of lynchings per 100,000 population with a rate of 27.47, while Mississippi and Georgia come next with rates of 25.05 and 17.78 respectively.

lead, with sixteen, Georgia second with thirteen, and Florida and Mississippi third with eight each. This tabulation includes only burnings at the stake and cases in which other equally ghastly modes of torture were employed. After the table was drawn up, the Lone Star State further strengthened its claim to its number one rating when a mob fired and dynamited the courthouse at Sherman, "the Athens of Texas," to obtain and burn the body of a Negro who had been placed on trial, and then destroyed three blocks of buildings in the Negro section of the city. The arrival of hundreds of militiamen finally quelled the riot.

The impression is widespread that the vast majority of lynchings are intended as punishment for criminal attacks upon white women by Negro men. This is far from true. The commission headed by George Fort Milton, editor of the Chattanooga *News*, which made a study of lynching in 1931, reported that fewer than one-fourth of the persons lynched since 1890 have even been accused of assaults upon white women. The commission also stated that there is real doubt of the guilt of at least half of the victims of mob violence, and that lynchings are most frequent in rural areas where illiteracy and poverty among whites is most prevalent.

The Association of Southern Women for the Prevention of Lynching reaffirmed at its annual meeting in 1931 that lynching is not a defense of womanhood but "rather a menace to public and private safety," and declared that it "brings contempt upon America as the only country where such crimes occur." In addition to the fact that most Negroes who suffer death in this manner are not accused of rape, latest available statistics show that commitments to prison in the United States for this offense are fewer for Negroes in proportion to population than for Italians, Mexicans, Austrians, Hungarians, Frenchmen, or Russians.

Dr. W. W. Alexander, director of the Commission on Interracial Coöperation, with headquarters in Atlanta, an organization which is doing much to improve relations between the races in the South, pointed out recently that although Negro rapists are almost always feebleminded, there is not a single institution in the former Confederacy for the care of young, delinquent, and feebleminded Negroes. The commission would like to see one or more such institutions established, just as it would like to see many other improvements in the status of the Southern Negro brought to pass. Slowly but surely, through its branches in every part of the South, it is working to build up sentiment for wider opportunities for the weaker race. During the years which have passed since its establishment in 1920, the commission has rendered many valuable services to the Negroes.

For some years the organization was under the direction of Dr. M. Ashby Jones, pastor of the Ponce De Leon Baptist Church of Atlanta. Dr. Jones subsequently relinquished the post upon his removal to St. Louis, but during his incumbency he exercised a powerful influence for a saner and more humane attitude toward the blacks.

Prior to the setting up of the Interracial Commission three men waged a valiant fight in Atlanta for adequate facilities for the higher education of Negroes.

They were the Rev. C. B. Wilmer, a distinguished
Episcopal clergyman now located in Sewanee, Tennessee; the Rev. Plato Durham, deceased, formerly
dean of Emory University, and Joseph C. Logan, deceased, head of the Associated Charities in Atlanta
and subsequently director of the Southern Division of
the American Red Cross. Partly as a result of the agitation they carried on, Governor Hugh M. Dorsey of
Georgia issued a pamphlet *The Negro in Georgia* in
1921. Mr. Dorsey pointed out many flagrant cases of
injustice in the state's treatment of the subject race,
and laid particular stress upon the prevalence of lynching and peonage. "If conditions indicated by these
charges should continue," he wrote, "both God and
man would justly condemn Georgia more severely
than man and God have condemned Belgium and
Leopold for Congo atrocities." This was pretty strong
stuff, and its author was deluged with abuse in consequence.

It is this tendency on the part of many Southerners
to condemn anybody who raises his voice in defense
of the Negro that has made it so difficult for genuine
progress in race relations to be achieved below the
Potomac. A man of the type of Winfield H. Collins,
author of *The Truth About Lynching and the Negro in the
South*, is always sure of an audience in Dixie. Mr. Collins not only is a clamorous defender of mob murder,
when the victim happens to have a black epidermis,
but he almost invariably puts the worst possible interpretation upon the actions of Negroes in their relationships with whites. And in this connection it must
be sorrowfully recorded that the talented John Sharp

Williams, despite his early liberalism on the race question, marred his final term in the Senate irreparably with a defense of lynching.

Although the Constitution of the United States is regularly and systematically circumvented in almost every Southern state by means of enactments which make possible the disfranchisement of the great majority of Negroes, these statutes have been held to be technically in harmony with the organic law. Federal courts have thrown out various laws and regulations excluding Negroes from Democratic primaries, but as yet the blacks have not sought on a large scale to take advantage of their legal right to participate in these primaries, except in Kentucky, where they enjoyed free exercise of the franchise before the Federal decisions referred to were handed down, and in several Tennessee cities, where the situation was similar. Of course one reason why so few Negroes participate in Democratic primaries is that most of them are Republicans.

There is a growing school of thought in the South which holds that any man, no matter what his race, who is qualified to vote ought to be permitted to vote, and that it is wholly unjust for election officials to disqualify thousands of Negroes arbitrarily while permitting other thousands of white illiterates to troop to the polls. It is the view of this element that an educated and respectable Negro is a greater asset to the community and more deserving of the franchise than an unlettered white swineherd from the pine barrens. It cannot be said that this view is held by anything remotely approaching a majority of the Southern whites, but it undoubtedly is gaining in favor. As reconstruction and its atrocities recede further and further into the background, more and more white Southerners are coming to feel that the cry of "white supremacy," raised so often in the past, is in the twentieth century a mere rawhead and bloodybones without substance or meaning.

There is also a growing conviction on the part of a substantial body of Southerners that the Jim Crow laws should be abolished. The argument runs that such laws were desirable twenty or thirty years ago when the great majority of blacks were unclean in person and slovenly in attire, and when the ubiquitous saloon and its readily purchased fire water were conducive to clashes between the lower orders of both races. It is contended that these reasons for separating the races in public gatherings and on public conveyances do not now obtain to anything like the same extent, and that the Negroes should no longer be humilated in this manner.

A much larger element of white Southerners feels, however, that separation of the races should be strictly maintained. Some adhere to this view because of a belief that indiscriminate racial intermingling in theaters and assembly halls, on trains and street cars, "would be the first step in the direction of social equality." Another considerable group is of the opinion that the highest potentialities of the Negro race may best be promoted and developed through the preservation of the Negro's racial identity. They feel that the black man must work out his destiny as a black man—not as a hybrid or an imitation white man—and that although laws providing for the separation of the races are often enforced with cynicism and injustice, it is better for both races to have segregation under such conditions than not to have it at all. The Southern whites who take this view of the matter would greatly prefer to see an even-handed enforcement of the Jim Crow statutes, but they are so convinced of the importance of these statutes to the Negro's future, as well as to that of the white man, and so apprehensive that the integrity of both races would be menaced by unrestricted intermingling in public places, that they are willing to make the best of the present unsatisfactory conditions. There is also a small element which favors colonization of the Negroes in Africa.

Many Southerners insist that whereas the two groups should remain apart, the accommodations provided for Negroes should be identical with those provided for whites. They point out that there is no excuse for a policy which permits a railroad to charge a Negro the maximum fare and then to force him to accept inferior accommodations at the station and on the train. Often on Southern railroads the Negroes are compelled to ride in a wooden coach, the only one on the train. Such a coach is crushed like matchwood between the steel cars, in the event of a collision. Even when this coach is of steel, it is usually immediately behind the engine and hence is filled with smoke and cinders, while half of it often is used for baggage. Although the Negro pays the same fare as the white, he has no separate smoker or diner and sometimes is not allowed to occupy a Pullman berth.

The type of race prejudice which leads to such discrimination as this is also responsible for the frequent failure of Southern blacks to obtain even elementary justice when they fall into the toils of the law. This, it should be said, is due in much larger measure to the attitude of the police than to that of the courts. At times, however, there is a reversal of the ordinary processes, and a white man is heavily penalized for a crime against a Negro.

The most widely discussed case of recent years involving the question whether Southern courts exercise due care in affording Negroes the full protection of the law is the so-called "Scottsboro Case," in which seven young Negroes were condemned to death at Scottsboro, Alabama, on charges of raping two white girls. The assault was said to have taken place in a freight car between Chattanooga, Tennessee, and Paint Rock, Alabama, in the spring of 1931.

The windy tirades of professional agitators who have sought to capitalize on the conviction of these Negro youths should of course be ignored, but a careful survey gives rise, nevertheless, to serious doubts as to the fairness of the trial. This despite the fact that the convictions were upheld by the Alabama Supreme Court with only one justice dissenting.

These Negroes were found guilty and sentenced to death without an opportunity to communicate with their families or their friends. Counsel for the defense was appointed by the court after the trial began, and the appointee conferred with his clients for the first time during a recess allowed by the court for the purpose. And while the authorities are entitled to all praise for the manner in which they called out the militia and prevented a lynching, the temper of the 10,000 visitors who came to town for the trial and the tumultuous applause with which those in and around the courthouse greeted the first conviction must have influenced the jury to a considerable degree.

There are also other factors which cast doubt upon the validity of the jury's findings. The two white girls, who were known to be loose characters, did not give identical testimony at the trial, and the prosecution took one of them off the stand because she was getting so confused that it was feared she would damage the State's case. Although a white boy was in the freight car during the entire time that the girls were supposedly being assaulted by the Negroes, and although he was in the hands of the court while the trial was in progress, he was not put on the stand. There are definite reports that his version of the affair was radically unlike that presented by prosecution witnesses. Another consideration which tends to cast doubt upon the fairness of the trial is the fact that the attorney appointed by the court to defend the Negroes made no argument to the jury, although elaborate argument was presented by the State. These facts, coupled with the youth of the seven defendants, whose ages ranged from sixteen to twenty at the time of the supposed crime, have led thousands of unbiased persons to the belief that they should not go to the electric chair unless a new conviction is obtained under different circumstances.

True, there is evidence on the other side, and this evidence might be convincing, were it not for the vari-

17

ous facts cited above which tend to discredit much of the testimony for the prosecution. Fortunately for the cause of Southern justice an appeal was taken to the United States Supreme Court, and that tribunal agreed to review the case at its term which opens in October, 1932. Thus there is a strong possibility that the convicted Negroes will receive a new trial. Such a dénouement would undoubtedly be to the best interests of Alabama and the South as a whole. No one desires to see these defendants go free if they are guilty, but they should be proved guilty beyond all reasonable likelihood of error. It must not be said that Alabama "railroaded" these Negroes to the chair.

While the Alabama press as a whole has been prone to argue that there is no good reason why any one should question their culpability, a few papers have been outspokenly on the other side. The civilized attitude of the Selma *Times-Journal* is especially praiseworthy. The ordinarily liberal Montgomery *Advertiser*, on the other hand, has been unable to comprehend why so many persons seriously doubt the guilt of the accused blacks and has called loudly for their execution.

So much for the Scottsboro case and its implications. What of the treatment accorded Negro workingmen by Southern labor unions? Dr. Robert R. Moton declares that Negroes are admitted more readily to labor unions in the South than in the North, but even so they are discriminated against in many ways in industry and in various trades. In 1900, for example, the blacks had a virtual monopoly in the field of barbering, but now the white barbers have taken away most of their trade and have succeeded in putting through bills in various Southern states setting up boards of examiners whose function is thought to be the eventual elimination of all colored competition.

Such a movement as this is carried on with the benediction of organizations of the type of the resuscitated Ku Klux Klan, which seek to capitalize upon racial and religious hate. The Klan was called back from the virtual oblivion which had enveloped it since reconstruction days by one William J. Simmons, a former revivalist and traveling salesman and a "jiner" of parts, who seems to have awakened to a keen realization of the commercial possibilities in P. T. Barnum's estimate of the number of suckers born per minute. At any rate, Simmons revived the Klan in 1915, with "white supremacy" as one of its war cries. The going was heavy at first, but when Edward Young Clarke, an able promoter, took charge of the situation in 1920, things began to move at once, and the organization spread like wildfire to all parts of the country. Negroes were the particular objects of the Klan's wrath in the South, while in other sections Catholics, Jews, and aliens were singled out for attack.

The Klan has now declined greatly in strength, and is moribund everywhere, but in the middle twenties its membership was well up in the millions. The reasons for its remarkable growth are analyzed by Frank Tannenbaum in his *Darker Phases of the South*. Mr. Tannenbaum feels that the habits of violence intensified by the war together with the effect of the war upon the Negro were paramount in creating a state of mind receptive to a secret, masked organization

professing devotion to the principles of "white supremacy" and "hundred per cent Americanism." The
South was a particularly lush field of operations for
this Nordic crusade in view of the notions of "social
equality" thought to have been engendered in the
minds of the half a million blacks drafted into the
army and paid the same wages as the white soldiers.
Besides, some two hundred thousand of these Negroes
went to France, where they were often received as
the social equals of the natives, and on their return
many of them left the South for the North. All in
all, the South was ripe for the Klan after the war.

While the organization's membership was well dis-
tributed over the country and was by no means
confined to the South, it seems to have had considerable strength in all the Southern states except Virginia
and the Carolinas. Texas boasted a larger number of
Klansmen than any other commonwealth in Dixie.

The Klan probably would have become practically
extinct by 1928, but the nomination of Governor
Alfred E. Smith of New York for the presidency revived the religious issue in such virulent form that
the organization's complete collapse was postponed.
By 1930, however, the K. K. K. was in such dire
straits that the resourceful Mr. William J. Simmons
recognized the need for a change in nomenclature.
He accordingly announced a "Caucasian Crusade,"
with himself and Congressman Robert Ramspeck of
Georgia among the sponsors, crusaders to be limited to
"real, red-blooded white Americans, inside and out."
This patriotic effort was without appreciable effect.

But there were still other ideas in Georgia. Soon

the American Facist [sic] Association and Order of
Blackshirts arose in Atlanta to assure tremulous
Nordics that it would make the South safe for white
supremacy. Not only so, but it would oust Negroes
from their jobs and install sound Caucasian hundred
per cent Americans in their stead. The Black Shirts
were making headway in Atlanta and had enrolled
twenty-one thousand members, thanks largely to the
craven conduct of the Atlanta newspapers in permitting the order to grow unmolested, when the Macon
Telegraph launched an editorial campaign which soon
put them out of business.

"The best way Macon people can receive the Black
Shirts is to keep their hands on their pocketbooks,"
said the editor of this fearless daily. "It is the custom
of every sucker-tapping organization that ever existed
to have a set of high-sounding principles and ambitious objectives with which to intrigue the man who
has enough money to join, but not sense enough to
stay out. . . . If the kluxing effort [Ku Klux Klan]
had been shown up to start with, thousands of good
Georgians would never have put on a mask or a
nightshirt at $10 for a 35-cent garment and the order
would have died aborning. . . ."

The *Telegraph* published a series of special news
articles on the Black Shirts simultaneously with its
editorial broadside against the order. The movement
was unable to stand a thorough ventilation of its
methods and purposes, and its demise was immediate.*

While such exhibitions of racial bigotry as have

* For a comprehensive discussion of newspaper attacks on the Klan, see
below, Chapter XX.

been given by the Klan and the Black Shirts are profoundly discouraging to Southern liberals, it must be remembered that, after all, both organizations are virtually defunct at the present time. And if the probabilities are that similar societies will arise in the future, it seems reasonable to assume that the "racket" is getting stale, since the Black Shirts were unable in 1931 to rouse the populace at a dollar a head, one-tenth of the initiation fee which millions paid a few years previously to join the Klan.

Over and against the manifestations of intolerance mentioned above may be cited quite extraordinary evidence that race prejudice is on the decline in Dixie. There was the reception given the colored Elks when they held their national convention in Richmond a few years ago, and the City was almost turned over to them. Segregation ordinances were temporarily suspended, Jim Crow regulations in street cars and restaurants were forgotten, private homes made their front porches available to Negroes who wished to see the parade go by, and in general the fifty thousand Negro visitors were made to feel that they were heartily welcome in the former capital of the Confederacy. They showed their appreciation by holding one of the most orderly gatherings Richmond had ever seen.

Nor should the work of the University of North Carolina by any means be overlooked. This institution, undoubtedly the most liberal in the South in this field, has been engaged for a good many years in serious efforts looking toward the betterment of inter-racial relationships. The nationally recognized Institute for Research in Social Science, directed by Dr. Howard W. Odum since 1922, has devoted a large share of its attention to matters pertaining to the Negro. *Social Forces*, from the beginning, featured contributions on the subject. In the Department of Sociology, courses on the Negro and on race problems are given, the University Press has published a number of important studies of the Negro,* the university has heard addresses from several Negro lecturers, and the undergraduate paper has devoted entire issues to the literary productions of Negro writers. At the same time, members of the faculty whose courses deal with race problems are coöperating constantly with the Interracial Commission and with another organization local to North Carolina which pays particular attention to such matters.

At Duke University in the same state, the *Archive*, a student publication, has solicited and printed poetry by Negroes, while the *South Atlantic Quarterly*, which also appears under the ægis of Duke University, has published contributions by leading blacks. The same is true of the *Southwest Review* of Southern Methodist University, Dallas. There is also the fact that Dallas, once a Klan stronghold, has organized a troupe of Negro players which recently produced "a play of race conflict frankly sympathetic to the Negro" before a mixed audience.

These more or less isolated phenomena are not only important in themselves, but at the same time they show the drift of Southern sentiment away from post-

* See below, Chapter XX, for further information concerning Southern writers on the Negro.

bellum attitudes. More significant is the steady improvement in the relationships between the white masses on the one hand and the black masses on the other. This improvement is going forward in the South without any fanfare of trumpets, without any blasts of publicity, but it is none the less real. Despite the disgusting demagoguery of a certain type of Southern politician, despite the kluxery of professional agitators and their followers, there is a growing awareness on the part of the dominant race that the Negro is not a serf or a helot, but a human being with legitimate aspirations for the improvement of his educational, political, and financial status, aspirations which are slowly being realized.

CHAPTER XV

POLITICS AND POLITICIANS

IN VIEW of the fact that even in this third decade of the twentieth century the political complexion of nearly every Southern state is determined almost solely by the race question, it is amusing to read that L. Q. C. Lamar delivered an address at Jackson in 1875, immediately after the overthrow of carpetbag rule in Mississippi, in which he prophesied that the Southern people would now forget about the Negro as an issue and turn their attention to more important matters.

Undaunted by Lamar's melancholy failure as a political soothsayer, B. J. Ramage declared in the *Sewanee Review* in 1896 that "the 'Solid South'—long the fetish of one section of the country and the bugaboo of the other—has at last been shattered to such a degree that all the king's horses and men of the nursery rhyme could not put it together again."

This prognosis proved to be as faulty as that of two decades before. The Solid South had not by any means been smashed. Indeed, in this year of our Lord 1932 it is almost as solid as ever. Kentucky and Tennessee have become doubtful states, but elsewhere the Democratic party reigns supreme, except when the issue of popery becomes paramount and men strike out blindly under some atavistic urge to prevent what seems to them a threat of "foreign religious influence" in the country's temporal affairs.

For some twenty years after the Civil War a Southerner who professed adherence to the Republican party was apt to be ostracized from polite society, but Republicanism had become more respectable by the time the twentieth century dawned. Professor Trent took note of this phenomenon in a magazine article published in 1897, in which he declared that Southerners found it possible in the late nineties to "express almost any political views . . . without running the risk of insult." He went on to say that "one may even be an independent voter and not be too rudely stared at."

But despite this change for the better, there was still political partisanship of a rather malignant type in the region. Acting under the influence of this "reign of passion," as it was termed by John Spencer Bassett, one of the leading Democratic newspapers in the Southern states referred in its news columns to a Republican convention held in 1902 as the "semi-annual gathering of the Federal pie brigade," and described the delegates as "old moss-backs," "revenue doodles," and "bung smellers." Bassett declared that the "reign of passion" had "robbed politics of fair judgment" and added:

"It has accustomed the citizen to party hatred; it has made well intentioned men tolerate and even justify, political fraud; it has helped to preserve the South's provincialism; it has produced a one-sided press; it has made it possible for the South to be 'solid,' and thus has pauperized the intellects of her statesmen."

It should not be assumed from the foregoing, however, that the South was wholly to blame for the lack of cordiality between the sections during these years. There was, even at that time, no little intolerance on the part of the North toward the former Confederacy. In 1910, for example, various posts of the Grand Army of the Republic demanded with vehemence and asperity that the statue of Robert E. Lee be excluded from the Capitol at Washington, and one of them went so far as to rank the Southern generalissimo with Benedict Arnold. This is not difficult to understand when one remembers that a past commander-in-chief of the G. A. R. discovered as recently as 1930 that the United Daughters of the Confederacy are America's "worst enemy."

Such silly outbursts as these, combined with the South's blind allegiance to the shibboleth of "white supremacy," have preserved or, as Walter Hines Page said, have "pickled" the greater part of the region in all its Gibraltar-like conservatism and solidity. This stifling of political initiative has undoubtedly been an important factor in the decline of Southern statesmanship since the Civil War. It is true that, contrary to the well-nigh universal practice in ante-bellum days, a majority of the ablest young Southerners no longer are desirous of public careers; but the fact that almost every present-day inhabitant of the Southland who does aspire to public office must first proclaim and practise undying devotion to the Democratic party, has gone far in reducing nearly to the vanishing point the number of twentieth-century politicians below Mason and Dixon's Line who deserve to be classified as statesmen.

Aside from the fact that unswerving consecration to the cause of a single political party is a bad thing for any state or group of states, the Democratic party in the South is so uncommonly reactionary and has divorced itself to such an extent from the Jeffersonian principles upon which it was established, that the situation is worse than it would otherwise be. The devotion of the early Jeffersonians to the principles of state rights, individual liberty, religious freedom, popular rule and separation of church and state evokes but a feeble response in the breasts of their heirs and assigns today. Southern Democrats invoke state rights when it is to their interest to do so, but not otherwise; they are the most ardent supporters in the Union of the prohibition laws, which have given a death thrust to individual liberty; they turned against their party's presidential candidate by the hundreds of thousands in 1928 because he belonged to the Roman Catholic church; they have hedged the franchise about with so many restrictions that a large percentage of both races are forbidden the privilege of the ballot; and they are almost slavish in their obedience to ecclesiastical authority.

We have seen that the rise of the common man to a dominant place in the councils of the party in the Southern states was the signal for the emergence of a whole school of rabble rousers who usually capitalized upon the race issue and looked to the lower class whites for their support. The most striking feature of the political scene in the South since the turn of the century is to be found in the antics of these demagogues. No other section of the country has produced them in comparable numbers. New York once sent John Morrissey, former heavyweight prizefight champion of the world, and proprietor of a string of gambling houses, to Congress, and Chicago delights to honor "Big Bill" Thompson, whose specialty is "busting King George in the snoot," but the deep South has elevated to high office a whole series of the most incredible and fantastic fellows. This state of affairs is largely attributable to the existence of the race issue on the one hand and the high Southern illiteracy rate on the other. The presence of the Negro in large numbers gives the low-grade Southern office-seeker the political ammunition he needs with which to arouse the unlettered and credulous peasants of the back country.

Ben Tillman set the pattern for this type of Southern politician in the nineties, although it must be said that some of those who came after him far outdid him in buffoonery. One of the first of his more eminent imitators was Thomas E. Watson of Georgia. Watson began his public career in laudable fashion by protesting against the exploitation of white labor in the factories of his state. But when it developed that he was being criticized by persons who feared that white laborers would be replaced by Negroes in consequence of his agitation, he changed his tactics and devoted a goodly share of the years which remained to him to the denunciation of Negroes, Jews, and Catholics.

Anti-Semitic tirades delivered by Watson when excitement over the celebrated Franks case was at its height, are believed to have brought on the lynching of Franks. In addition, his hysterical diatribes against Roman Catholics made him a laughing stock. He is said to have spent $200,000 fighting the Pope. Yet he was in some ways a man of more than ordinary intelligence, the author of an excellent life of Napoleon and a gifted writer.

The salient characteristics of the estimable Vardaman of Mississippi have been noted in an earlier chapter. A man of similar stripe was Jeff Davis of Arkansas, a politician who pandered to ignorance and prejudice and who served three successive terms as governor of his state. At the close of his third term he juggled the finances and made it appear that Arkansas was out of debt. The legislature was taken in by the trick and voted a tax reduction. Davis then rode into the Senate on the popularity which came to him as a result of this slash in levies and left his successor in the gubernatorial chair to worry about the deficit which followed. Once in the Senate, Davis, who was expelled from the Baptist church for excessive drinking, introduced a bill to prohibit the gift or sale of intoxicating liquor in prohibition territory. His other important contribution to statesmanship as a member of the national legislature is to be found in the vast quantities of free seeds which he sent to his hill-billy following in the Arkansas backwoods.

The public services of Cole Blease of South Carolina, heir to the Tillman tradition there, have been equally imposing. As governor of the Palmetto State, he enunciated the thesis for which he is most celebrated: "Whenever the constitution comes between me and the virtue of the white women of the South, I say to hell with the constitution!" In addition to his unblushing advocacy of lynching, Blease has always opposed compulsory education. "I have never yet heard a commonsense argument in favor of it," he once declared. His career in the gubernatorial chair was further distinguished by virtue of the fact that he pardoned or paroled some fifteen hundred convicts. In the Senate he upheld the best traditions of the Southern school of political exhibitionists.

"Jim" and "Ma" Ferguson of Texas are other twentieth-century politicians whose public careers can hardly be said to have added new luster to Southern statesmanship. James E. Ferguson was impeached as governor of Texas in 1917, was found guilty of malfeasance because of gross improprieties in his handling of public funds, and was removed from office. Mrs. Miriam A. Ferguson, his wife, otherwise known as "Ma," became a candidate for governor in 1924 with a view to "vindicating" her spouse. Be it said to the latter's credit that he had always been an outspoken foe of the Ku Klux Klan. Consequently the solid anti-Klan vote went to Mrs. Ferguson in the primary and the election. At the same time she was supported by the "one-gallus" tenant farmers, who have always idolized her husband. The combination was enough to put her over. "Jim" immediately took matters into his own hands and was the real governor of the Lone Star State throughout her term of office. Serious scandals in the highway department led to talk of impeachment proceedings against Mrs. Ferguson, but no such action was taken. "Ma's" gubernatorial career was further distinguished by virtue of her issuance of pardons to some thousands of convicts.

In Mississippi the mantle of J. K. Vardaman has descended upon the diminutive shoulders of Theodore G. Bilbo, a former evangelist who signalized the opening of his political career by admitting the acceptance of a bribe amounting to $645. Bilbo has been a storm center in Mississippi politics since 1908, and has served two terms as governor. The second extended from 1928 to 1932 and was even more notable than the first, for it was during these years that he discharged many professors in the state's institutions of higher education to make way for his political henchmen. A number of the most competent educators in Mississippi, including three college presidents, were summarily dismissed by Governor Bilbo, and political appointees substituted for them. The principal result of this policy was that Mississippi's four major institutions of higher learning lost their accredited standing with five national or Southern educational associations, including the Association of American Medical Colleges, the American Association of University Professors, and the Association of American Law Schools. Bilbo's administration at Jackson was likewise distinguished by an interview he granted newspapermen while sitting in his bathtub, a cake of soap in one hand, a washrag in the other and a cigar between his teeth.

Among the more eminent statesmen from Alabama who have sat in the Senate or held other offices within the gift of the Southern people is J. Thomas Heflin. Heflin began his senatorial career as an amusing but more or less inoffensive inveigher against Wall Street and ended it as an anti-Catholic maniac who spent hours on end raving against the Vatican on the floor of the national legislature. A member of the Ku Klux Klan, his absurd rantings appealed to the members of that organization but were laughed at by persons of more intelligence. He believed or pretended to believe that there was a Jesuit plot to poison him, and spent much of his time ostentatiously peering under his bed or examining his food at hotels as he traveled about. Heflin was for some years the idol of the anti-Catholic press of the country, and as long as the Klan retained its strength, he was able to muster a considerable following. But in 1930, when he ran for reëlection to the Senate, the electorate had grown tired of him, and he was defeated by a large majority.

Blease of South Carolina also was ousted from the Senate in this election, and it appeared that there would be no one in that body from the South to jig around in the cap and bells, when along came Huey P. Long of Louisiana. Huey was chosen to represent his state at Washington after one of the most virulent campaigns on record, a campaign in which billingsgate was hurled in huge quantities, and unprintable epithets were used on every hand. In 1928 he had been chosen governor by the largest majority in Louisiana history, and near the end of his term he had been impeached by the Louisiana House of Representatives on twenty-five counts, including kidnaping, bribery, graft, and moral turpitude. Fifteen

18

of his friends in the Senate formed a solid phalanx, however, and refused to vote for conviction under any conditions, on the ground that the entire proceeding was "illegal." The effort to oust him was therefore a failure. One of the many features of his administration was the reception he gave a German naval commander who paid him the courtesy of a formal call. Huey greeted the visitor clad in green silk pajamas. This is the man the electorate of Louisiana sent to the United States Senate in 1930. The South can rest assured that he will not suffer by comparison with Heflin, Vardaman, Davis, or any others in that noble army of political contortionists who have represented the region at Washington since the closing of the last century.

While it is all too obvious from the foregoing that the deep South has sent to the national capital during the period in question a more gaudy array of sensational misfits than has any other part of the United States, it would not be fair to assume that such men as these are typical of the present political leadership below the Potomac. For every Watson, every Heflin there are a dozen dignified, hard-working Southern senators. It has been Dixie's misfortune during the past thirty or thirty-five years to send a Vardaman or a Long to Congress in almost every election, and to have the public judge the entire Southern delegation by one or two such individuals.

But while the great majority of Congressmen from below the Mason and Dixon Line conduct themselves with reasonable decency and decorum at the national capital, it cannot be said that many of them exhibit palpable traces of liberalism in their attitude toward public questions. This is not surprising, however, for almost all of them are affiliated with the Democratic party, a party which, as heretofore noted, is especially reactionary in the South. As for the Southern Republicans, they are even worse. The Republican party is the antithesis of liberal in the South and everywhere else.

Such a crusading liberal as Governor Aycock of North Carolina, for example, is a rarity among Southern public men. Aycock was one of the most progressive and far-seeing leaders of his generation and the South as a whole owes him a debt of gratitude for his fearless pioneering in the early years of the century. His invaluable services to education have been recited in another chapter. Equally noteworthy was his position on the race question. At a time when no one had ever been punished in North Carolina for participation in a lynching bee, he offered a reward of $400 for every conviction secured in connection with a sadistic orgy of this kind which had taken place shortly before near Salisbury. Aycock was genuinely concerned for the welfare of the masses, whether white or black, and his gubernatorial administration in North Carolina was an important factor in laying the foundation for the state's subsequent progress.

But it was Woodrow Wilson, a man of Southern birth and descent, although not of Southern residence, who crystallized within himself the nation-wide liberal movement of the early 1900's. Wilson was the spokesman in 1912 for the forces of democracy as opposed to those of plutocracy, and his first term was among the most liberal in American annals. Under his leadership Congress enacted income tax laws to equalize the tax burden, made substantial reductions in the tariff for the first time in many years, passed a child labor law, an anti-injunction law, an eight-hour-day law, an anti-trust law, and a rural credits law, and created the Federal Trade Commission, while the Constitution was amended to provide for popular election of senators.

It is true that his first term also witnessed the inauguration of his imperialistic policies in the Caribbean; but it was the manner in which he departed from his earlier principles during his second term which alienated a large percentage of his liberal following. Leaving out of account what many felt to be his failure at the peace conference, there was the enactment of the Espionage Act in 1917 and the still more stringent Sedition Act in 1918. The effect of these statutes was to outlaw all criticism of the Wilson administration, and to loose an army of government spies and snoopers upon the public. Arrests without warrant of wholly innocent persons, arbitrary seizures of property, and use of brutal third degree methods characterized the second term of Woodrow Wilson, and individual freedom became almost a dead letter.

One of the outspoken critics of this Wilsonian massacre of civil liberties was Oscar W. Underwood of Alabama. Underwood's congressional career began in 1895 and continued without interruption until his retirement from the Senate in 1927. In the words of Claude G. Bowers, he was "always a Jeffersonian Democrat, a disciple and interpreter of the Master

of Monticello." At the outset of his career he demonstrated his courage by hurling into the teeth of the
powerful iron and steel interests of Birmingham a
platform which emphasized the need for a "tariff for
revenue only." From that day forward Oscar Underwood was always true to his principles, no matter how
greatly such a course imperiled his political fortunes.
He never permitted the manufacturers to change his
attitude on the tariff. In a Klan-ridden state he was
outspoken in his denunciation of the hooded order.
In a dry state he was vigorous in his condemnation
of prohibition and the Anti-Saloon League. If he was
sometimes found fighting against liberal causes, as
when he sought the defeat of the woman's suffrage
amendment and opposed the labor unions, few ever
doubted his complete sincerity. It was Underwood's
devotion to principle which finally led to his retirement from public life. He preferred not to seek reëlection when success was to be obtained only through
the abandonment of his convictions.

A remarkably liberal record as governor of Virginia
was made a few years ago by Harry F. Byrd. Mr.
Byrd took office as governor of the Old Dominion at
the age of thirty-seven, after a decade of service to
the state Democratic "machine" in the Virginia legislature, and with little to indicate that he would be
more than a conventional politician. But the youthful
executive confounded the skeptics almost immediately
by exhibiting high qualities of leadership. He not only
instituted invaluable reforms in the organization and
administration of his state's governmental affairs, but
he secured the enactment of the Virginia anti-lynching

bill, the first bill of its kind in the United States. This measure makes lynching an offense against the state as a whole, subjects all participants in lynchings to charges of murder, and authorizes the governor to have the attorney-general aid in the prosecution and to spend any sum he (the governor) sees fit in convicting the guilty parties. At the same time, appropriations to education were greatly increased during Byrd's administration, and although he is a wealthy man and many industries were attracted to the state during his term, he made active war on the oil companies and the Virginia subsidiary of the American Telephone and Telegraph Company because he felt that these great interests were seeking to overcharge the public. Incidentally, he won significant victories over both of them.

John Garland Pollard, who succeeded him as governor, has fought machine politicians with considerable regularity for many years. He startled his party by appointing a Republican to the post of state health commissioner. Governor Pollard has long been a staunch friend of the laboring man, and during the legislative session of 1930 he was fearlessly outspoken in criticism of the manufacturing interests which were seeking to defeat important measures introduced for the protection of the workers.

Among the Southern public men who did not tremble before the Ku Klux Klan was Thomas T. Connally of Texas, who won his Senate seat from Earle B. Mayfield, the candidate of the Invisible Empire. Another who refused to truckle to the Klan was Governor Thomas W. Hardwick of Georgia, who ordered the organization to unmask and thereby signed his political death warrant. Curiously enough, Governor Hardwick had gone on record many times in his gubernatorial campaign for rigid enforcement of the Veazey Law, and had urged such amendments to that law as were needed to make it enforceable. This statute, which was drafted by the notorious anti-Catholic, Senator Thomas E. Watson, provided for the inspection of convents and monasteries and was bitterly resented by the Catholics of the state. Over against Mr. Hardwick's order unmasking the Klan must also be placed the fact that on international questions he is a rampant isolationist. It should be added, however, that as governor he abolished the lash in Georgia's prison camps and that until a short while ago he was one of the small number of Southerners on the national committee of the American Civil Liberties Union. Benjamin Meek Miller, the sitting governor of Alabama, should also be mentioned. He was retired from the Alabama Supreme Court by the K. K. K. and was elected to his present office on a platform calling for destruction of "Klan control of the jury box." He has turned a deaf ear to the wails of politicians and has fired numerous jobholders while instituting important governmental reforms.

There are some excellent names in the foregoing paragraphs, but a glance suffices to show that in the aggregate they are not to be compared with the South's galaxy of statesmen of a century or a century and a half ago. Southern political leaders of an earlier era frequently were actuated by principle in their attitude toward matters of public concern. Today, in common with the vast majority of politicians elsewhere, they seem to know few principles save those of expediency. In 1928, for example, when the Democratic party went Republican on the tariff issue because it felt that the votes lay in that direction, Senator Cordell Hull of Tennessee was virtually the only Southern Democrat of consequence who raised his voice in vigorous protest at this abandonment by the party of its historic tariff policy. In 1932 the wholly outrageous tariffs imposed on oil, copper, coal, and lumber could never have been enacted without the aid of the Democrats, including a number from Southern states.

Indeed, one is led sorrowfully to the conclusion that it is in the field of statesmanship that the New South suffers most by comparison with the Old. There are various reasons for this. Few of the most promising young Southerners of today are ambitious for public careers, whereas almost all the better trained young men sought public office in the Old South; the one-party system below the Potomac has served to hamper the development of able political leadership, and last but by no means least, the power of the clergy over Southern politicians in the twentieth century is out of all proportion to what it should be.

The influence of the churches as engines of temporal authority in the South is happily on the decline, but it is still dangerous in most sections for anyone to seek office on a platform which exhibits disrespect for the dicta of the Anti-Saloon League. Adherence to the existing policy of liquor control has been made an absolute *sine qua non* by the great Methodist and Baptist denominations for any office-holder or office-seeker, with the result that many able men who otherwise might be inclined to enter public life have not done do. They regard prohibition as iniquitous and are unwilling to run for office if their only chance of success lies in servile obedience to those who hold the opposite view. Thus the insistence of the evangelical clergy in the South upon the maintenance of the present method of handling the liquor traffic has resulted in excluding or driving from public life a whole class of Southerners, many of them of the highest type.

Not only so, but the attitude of these clergymen is responsible for such absurdities as the law in Alabama which makes it illegal to possess or sell anything which "tastes like, foams like, smells like or looks like beer," or to possess a bottle which in shape bears any resemblance to a beer bottle or a whisky flask. The clerics also are chiefly to blame for the Georgia statute which not only outlaws near-beer but makes it illegal for any citizen of that state to have "any liquor, beverages or drinks made in imitation of or as a substitute for beer, ale, wine or whisky or other alcoholic or spirited vinous or malt liquors," whether alcoholic or not. This same group of clergymen, which includes many Methodists and Baptists with some Presbyterians and Disciples, is likewise responsible for the "blue laws" which have been enacted so widely throughout the South, the Sunday fishing bills, and the anti-evolution bills.*

---

* For a comprehensive discussion of anti-evolution bills, see below, Chapter XVI.

In numerous instances, too, they have aided in the promotion of anti-Catholic movements. For example, the wave of anti-Catholic prejudice which swept the entire country some twenty years ago received considerable impetus from these ministers. The movement culminated in the South in 1916 with the election of Sidney J. Catts, a professional Catholic baiter and bombastic prohibitionist, as governor of Florida, and the enactment by the Georgia legislature of the Veazey Convent Inspection Bill. One result of the passage of the Veazey Bill was the establishment of the Catholic Laymen's Association of Georgia, which has functioned actively since that time and has done much to bring about more amicable relationships between Catholics and Protestants in that state.

When the Klan reached the zenith of its power in the middle twenties, Methodist and Baptist pastors were active in furthering the aims of the organization. This is not to say, of course, that anything like a majority of the ministry of these two denominations held any fellowship with Ku Kluxery. It is a fact, however, that a considerable number took part in the movement. And if no such legislative atrocity as the Oregon school law, forcing all children to attend state-supported schools, was adopted in any Southern state at the instigation of the Klan, the order was tremendously influential in various parts of the South for a number of years.

As indicated above, its membership was declining rapidly when Governor Alfred E. Smith of New York, a Roman Catholic, was nominated for the presidency by the Democratic party in 1928. At once there sprang up in every part of the Southland a campaign of vilification and misrepresentation such as had not been seen since reconstruction, and the moribund Klan was temporarily revived. Like methods were employed throughout the United States by Governor Smith's opponents, but thanks once more to the ecclesiastical racketeers, the flames of religious hate were fanned to a brighter glow below the Potomac than elsewhere.

The clerical crusade against the New Yorker was launched on purely moral grounds, those in charge made plain. Its moral aspect was adequately stressed by Bishop James Cannon, Jr., who assumed charge in the South immediately after Governor Smith's nomination. While the religious faith of the Democratic candidate was not openly emphasized in the first few weeks of the anti-Smith movement, the bars were soon thrown down, and the Protestant press teemed with anti-Catholic broadsides. At the same time, snide fellows went about distributing copies of the bogus Knights of Columbus oath and other scurrilous literature. Mr. Smith, a man of unimpeachable character and extraordinary executive ability, also was made the victim of a "whispering campaign" involving his public and private life which probably surpassed anything in the history of the country. Unpardonable slanders were widely circulated, many of them by wearers of the cloth.

Governor Smith's opposition to prohibition counted against him in the South, but more frequently than not his "wetness" was used as a cloak to screen the real objection to him, namely, his Catholicism. Bishop Cannon, for instance, denied over and over that he

was opposing the Democratic standard-bearer on
religious grounds, but he lost few opportunities to
refer in slurring fashion to Mr. Smith's membership
in the Catholic church. The Bishop's example was
emulated by thousands upon thousands of other Southerners, both clerical and lay. Among these were
Bishop E. D. Mouzon of the Southern Methodist
church, who publicly urged the clergy of that denomination to fight the Democratic candidate because
of his religious affiliations, and Dr. Arthur J. Barton,
prominent Southern Baptist and Anti-Saloon League
official, who stated openly that the religious issue was
more important than the prohibition issue. The
Methodist Preachers' Association of Atlanta adopted
a resolution which asserted: "You cannot nail us to
a Roman cross or submerge us in a sea of rum."
Bishops E. D. Mouzon, H. M. Du Bose, John M. Moore
and W. N. Ainsworth joined with Bishop Cannon in
advocating the entry of the Methodist church into
the fight, while Bishops W. A. Candler and Collins
Denny argued against such a procedure. But when
someone resurrected a statement in which Bishop
Candler had declared fifteen years before that "the
trouble with the Roman Catholic Church is that it
seeks to be both a church and a political party" and
had spoken of "its arrogant claim of being the only
true Christian church," the Bishop expressed himself
as pleased. "I cannot approve the intrusion of any
church—whether Protestant or Romish—into the
arena of party politics," he said. While this dictum
was in a sense consistent with his policy of taking
no part in political contests, one of its chief effects

was to arouse further prejudice against Catholicism.

The consequence of all this was that the entire area from Harper's Ferry to Eagle Pass was in an uproar for months prior to the election. The campaign would have been sufficiently nightmarish in any case, but the regular Democrats made it even more so by beating the tom-toms of "white supremacy" in order to hold the anti-Smith element in line, if possible. It wasn't possible. When the smoke had cleared away on election day, the border states were found to have gone Republican by huge majorities, while Virginia, North Carolina, Florida, and Texas were nestled in the Republican column for the first time since reconstruction. Religious prejudice had smashed the Solid South.

A fitting epilogue to the story of the 1928 campaign lies in the subsequent career of the man who had led the revolt of the "moral forces" in the Southern states. Bishop Cannon was found to have been officially pronounced a flour hoarder during the World War; he was revealed as a customer of bucketshops who traded actively in the market and did not scruple to send cablegrams on Sunday to his broker while touring the foreign mission field; and he was indicted by a Federal grand jury for refusing to tell the authorities how he had spent large sums entrusted to his care for political purposes.* Yet he was widely hailed throughout the South as a martyr to the cause of righteousness—a further illustration of the blind sub-

---

* The indictment was subsequently voided on technical grounds, and the government appealed to a higher court, where the case is now pending (July, 1932).

servience of many thousands of Southerners to ecclesiastical authority, a subservience which they must throw off if the region below the Potomac is ever to regain its place in the sun and be recognized as a thoroughly civilized portion of the republic.

CHAPTER XVI

DARWIN AND THE NEW DEMONOLOGY

WHILE nothing in this or the preceding chapter should be construed as a reflection on the large number of clergymen in the Southern states who possess sagacity, learning, and breadth of view, and who exemplify in their own lives the highest principles of genuine Christianity, it is nevertheless true that Dixie is afflicted to a greater degree than any other section of this country with a type of minister whose influence is far from salutary. This benighted and misguided individual is to be found in all parts of the South in greater or lesser numbers, but his principal habitat is in the country districts, where ignorance and illiteracy are most prevalent. The bucolic denizens of the hinterlands yield readily to his thaumaturgy, and it is due to him that the South at the present time is far more puritanical than New England, the original cis-Atlantic stronghold of zealotry.

George Washington, who might reasonably be regarded as authoritative in his statements as to the origins of the republic, once placed his imprimatur upon the dictum that "the government of the United States is not in any sense founded upon the Christian religion." The truth of this statement should be obvious to anyone who takes note of the fact that so far from setting up Christianity as the country's official creed, the founding fathers specifically provided in the First Amendment to the Constitution for the separation of church and state. Yet for the past decade and more there have been frequent efforts below Mason and Dixon's Line to accomplish a union of the religious and the secular arms through the passage of legislation outlawing the teaching of the evolutionary hypothesis. Not only so, but those efforts have succeeded in Tennessee, Mississippi, and Arkansas.

Many Southerners had imagined that serious agitation over the authenticity of Genesis had been terminated once and for all with the heresy trials of the late nineteenth century, and that the scientist was free in this supposedly enlightened age to expound any theory as to the origin of the universe which seemed good to him. But they reckoned without the rampant Fundamentalists, who suddenly became vocal over a wide area about 1920. In the following year attempts to buttress the historicity of the Bible by legal formulæ were made in Kentucky and South Carolina. In the former state a bill outlawing the evolutionary theory came within one vote of passage in the lower branch of the legislature. In the latter, an anti-evolution rider on the general appropriation bill was stricken out in joint committee, after it had passed the Senate without opposition.

Encouraged by the strength they had exhibited in these two states, the Fundamentalists redoubled their efforts in 1923. They sponsored the introduction of legislation in Georgia, Florida, Alabama, Texas, Oklahoma, and West Virginia. In Florida they managed to get through a joint resolution condemning the teaching of Darwinism in tax-supported schools; in Texas they obtained the passage of an anti-evolution bill in the lower house by a better than two to one majority, but it died on the calendar of the upper house; and in Oklahoma the evolutionary hypothesis was definitely outlawed by a clause in the free textbook bill which passed both branches of the legislature.

The state of mind which led Oklahoma to take this step may be visualized in the pronunciamento of one of her statesmen who bellowed on the floor of the House while the anti-evolution bill was under discussion:

"I promised my people at home that if I had a chance to down this here hellish Darwin I would do it!"

This utterance compares favorably with that of Representative Hal Kimberly, a Fundamentalist member of the Georgia legislature, who proclaimed at the same period that the only books worth reading are the Bible, the hymnal, and the almanac.

"These are enough for anyone," he said. "Read the Bible. It teaches you how to act. Read the hymn-book. It contains the finest poetry ever written. Read the almanac. It shows you how to figure out what the weather will be. There isn't another book that is necessary for anyone to read, and therefore I am opposed to all libraries."

The anti-evolution issue was not clear-cut in Oklahoma in 1923, for the reason that the anti-evolution legislation was incorporated in the bill providing free textbooks in the public schools. Three years later the portion of the statute which related to Darwinism was repealed.

In 1925, two years after the Fundamentalist triumph in Oklahoma, a bill proscribing the theory that "man has descended from a lower order of animals" was introduced in Tennessee. The patron of the measure revealed the extent of his qualifications to deal with the problem by expressing the view that the Bible had been dictated by God in the English of the King James version. The bill passed by the astounding majorities of 71 to 5 in the House and 24 to 6 in the Senate, and was duly signed by Governor Austin Peay. A few months later Tennessee incurred the ridicule of the civilized world by bringing John T. Scopes to trial for teaching the doctrine of evolution in the high school at Dayton. To Europeans the news seemed almost incredible; it savored more of the sixteenth century than the twentieth. After a trial which was the journalistic event of the year and attracted correspondents from all parts of the country, Scopes was convicted and fined $100.

Having won so signal a victory, the Fundamentalists girded up their loins for a drive on other states. Early in 1926 they put an anti-evolution statute on the books of Mississippi. A leading lobbyist for the measure was the Rev. T. T. Martin of the Bible Crusaders of America, author of *Hell and the High Schools* and other works in opposition to the teaching of the evolutionary hypothesis. Only a year before he rendered such valiant service to the cause in Mississippi, he had submitted an essay in a prize contest on the theme: "Why Evolution Should be Taught in Our Schools Instead of the Book of Genesis." Seeking to win $50, he had signed a fictitious name and sent the paper in. Those in charge of the contest recognized his handwriting and forced him to acknowledge his duplicity. Yet the Rev. Mr. Martin was active thereafter in Mississippi and various other states on behalf of Fundamentalist legislation.

Alarmed by the trend of events in Tennessee, Mississippi, and elsewhere, the authorities of Louisiana State University declined to give a course on evolution, although many students requested it. Shortly afterward a measure outlawing the teaching of Darwinism was introduced in the Louisiana legislature. It passed one house but was killed by a parliamentary maneuver in the other.

The movement in opposition to Darwinian doctrine received tremendous impetus below the Potomac when the Southern Baptist Convention, representing the most numerous denomination in the South, formally adopted a statement in 1926 that "this convention accepts Genesis as teaching that man was a special creation of God, and rejects every theory, evolutionary or other, which teaches that man originated or came by way of lower animal ancestry." This affirmation of the Biblical cosmogony was adopted by the Southern Baptist Education Board a few months later, and by the Foreign Mission Board of the same church shortly thereafter. Southwestern Baptist Theological Seminary near Fort Worth hastened to announce that

292 LIBERALISM IN THE SOUTH

the convention's declaration "would be made a test of all officers and teachers of said seminary."

The Southern Methodist church took no action relative to evolution at its quadrennial conferences in 1922, 1926, or 1930. In 1927 its Educational Association, on motion of President W. P. Few of Duke University, went on record as believing that "legislation which would interfere with the proper teaching of science in American schools and colleges is futile and can serve no good." But while the action of this association reflects credit upon its membership, and while the Methodist church as a body did not follow the Baptist church into the Fundamentalist camp, the Methodist denomination furnished more recruits for the war on modern science than any other except the Baptist.

The fact is not without significance, for although there are many learned and cultured members of both the Southern Baptist and the Southern Methodist churches, these denominations also include more illiterates than any other churches below Mason and Dixon's Line, a condition which is readily comprehensible when one considers their altogether praiseworthy efforts to reach the poor as well as the rich. The distressing prevalence of illiteracy among members of these two religious groups has been analyzed thoroughly by Dr. Albert Richmond Bond, a leading Baptist clergyman of Birmingham. * As a result of Dr. Bond's

---

* *Southern Baptists and Illiteracy*, Rev. Albert Richmond Bond, D.D., published by Education Board, Southern Baptist Convention, March 26, 1928, a 31-page pamphlet which discusses the question in exhaustive and convincing fashion.

researches, the Education Board of the Southern Baptist Convention adopted a resolution declaring that "native white illiteracy is a Southern problem and within the South preëminently a Baptist problem." The board might have added another fact that is made equally clear by his investigation, namely, that Southern illiteracy is likewise very much of a Methodist problem.

It was at this period, when Tennessee and Mississippi had both capitulated to the forces of obscurantism and other states seemed on the verge of doing so, that two organizations formed to aid in the crusade against intelligence sprang into being. One of them was the Supreme Kingdom, founded, according to common report, by Edward Young Clarke, who had been separated shortly before from his lucrative job as Imperial Wizard of the Klan and was on the lookout for something equally remunerative elsewhere.

The Supreme Kingdom was established with the benediction of the Rev. John Roach Straton of New York, * William Jennings Bryan, and other staunch believers in Old Testament astronomy, geology, and chronology. Following an announcement in January, 1927, that Straton would lead a nation-wide drive for members and funds, and would deliver sixty lectures for the rather neat fee of $30,000, the Macon *Telegraph* published documents showing the inner workings of the Supreme Kingdom. According to the *Telegraph*, Clarke himself got $8.12½ of every $12.50 initiation fee paid into the organization's coffers, while only

* Straton was reared in the South, and attended Mercer University; W. J. Bryan was a resident of Florida for some years.

$2.37 ½ was set aside for anti-evolutionist activities. When Straton appeared in Macon a short time thereafter as a lecturer for the Supreme Kingdom, the *Telegraph* asked him to examine the documents in its possession, but he refused, with the explanation that he was "not preaching or lecturing for money." Since he had been paid $500 for a previous lecture in Atlanta, his excuse was hardly convincing. At this juncture Straton suddenly discovered that his pastoral duties required his immediate return to New York. That was the last of his lecture tour.

The other important organization which arose at this time to promote the cause of religious orthodoxy was the Bible Crusaders of America. The Crusaders were financed by George F. Washburn, a Northern millionaire who carried on most of his operations from his winter home in Florida, and who proclaimed his desire to "eliminate all teaching of Evolution and Agnosticism from the tax-supported public schools and colleges of America." Mr. Washburn also asserted that the United States is "fundamentally a Christian nation," and announced his intention of asking Congress to remedy the error made by the fathers in not mentioning the name of God in the Constitution. His first act after taking the chairmanship of a committee created to collect $5,000,000 for the establishment of Bryan Memorial University at Dayton, Tennessee, a monument to William Jennings Bryan, who died at Dayton following his exertions in the Scopes trial, was to send questionnaires to the universities, colleges, and seminaries of the United States. Upon receiving their replies, he published a list of fifty-four institutions which young men and women might attend without fear of having their faith in Genesis disturbed. Five-sixths of them were in the South, and half of them were affiliated with the Baptist church.

Meanwhile the war on modern science was going forward on various other fronts. Dr. William B. Riley of Minneapolis and Los Angeles, head of the World's Christian Fundamentals Association, which coöperated closely with the Bible Crusaders of America, announced a plan to force an anti-evolution amendment into the Federal constitution.

The State of North Carolina became a special storm center of anti-evolutionist activity. An anti-evolution bill had been defeated there in 1925 after a bitter battle, thanks in large measure to the efforts of President Harry W. Chase of the state university and President William L. Poteat of Wake Forest College. When it was introduced, the all-important appropriation bill was still undisposed of, but Chase did not permit this fact to deter him. "If this university doesn't stand for anything but appropriations," he said, "I, for one, don't care to be connected with it." He appeared in open and uncompromising opposition to the Fundamentalist legislation and was an important factor in bringing about its defeat.

When the decision was reached to revive the anti-evolutionist crusade there, the Rev. T. T. Martin and other defenders of the faith began an intensive drive with a view to preparing the ground for the 1927 session of the legislature. Martin declared that North Carolina was "pivotal," and that if it could be won, the nation could be won. A "Committee of

One Hundred" was formed to launch the movement, and the city of Charlotte, which boasts that it is the greatest "church-going town" in the world except Edinburgh, was selected as headquarters. The selection was a wise one, for bigotry flourishes there more abundantly, perhaps, than in any community of like size between the Potomac and the Rio Grande. The city enjoys an added advantage as the home of the Charlotte *Observer*, which has become in all probability the most reactionary newspaper of consequence in the South, now that Caldwell no longer directs its policies. But despite everything that the "Committee of One Hundred" could do, despite the *Observer's* efforts to pump life into the campaign, the anti-evolutionists failed to get their bill out of committee at the 1927 session. A factor in bringing about this result was a letter written from England by Professor Frank P. Graham of Chapel Hill and published widely. This failure of the Fundamentalists ended the agitation in North Carolina.

The same year witnessed the opening of a determined drive in Arkansas. That state was a fertile field for anti-evolutionist orators, for in 1924 its Baptist State Convention had adopted resolutions not only opposing all forms of evolution but providing at the same time that no Baptist board or institution in Arkansas could employ anyone, whether college president or janitor, who believed in Darwinism. The convention exempted janitors and other such minor employees the following year, but left the resolutions unchanged in other respects.

When the anti-evolution bill of 1927 was introduced

in the state legislature, it passed the lower house by a narrow margin, but was tabled in the Senate. This result was due in large measure to Dr. Hay Watson Smith, Little Rock Presbyterian, who fearlessly opposed the bill. Dr. Smith published a pamphlet pointing out the absurdity of outlawing a theory to which every prominent living scientist subscribes. But if Arkansas successfully resisted the importunities of those who sought to ban modern scientific inquiry by legislative fiat, it entered the ranks of the "monkey states" in the popular referendum of the following year. In this, "the first anti-evolution initiative measure in history," the upholders of Genesis triumphed by the decisive majority of 45,000. Under the anti-evolution law thus adopted, it is illegal for any state-supported institution in Arkansas to make use of Webster's Dictionary, the *Encyclopædia Britannica*, or any other work which teaches that man is descended from a lower order of animals.

Since the capitulation of Arkansas in 1928, the Fundamentalists have not won any spectacular victories. They made unsuccessful attempts the following year to recapture Oklahoma and to bring Texas into the fold, but that was the extent of their efforts in the direction of state-wide anti-evolution bills. During the decade of the twenties a total of thirty-seven measures of various kinds designed to ban the teaching of evolutionary doctrine on a state-wide scale were introduced, the great majority of them in the South. In the border state of Oklahoma, as we have noted, a bill was passed and subsequently repealed, and in Missouri and West Virginia a fair amount of strength was mustered on behalf of the Old Testament story of the creation. But nowhere else, except in the South, was such legislation given serious consideration.

It should not be imagined, however, that the Fundamentalists have been idle of late. On the contrary, they have been concentrating on "the emasculation of textbooks, the 'purging' of libraries, and above all the continued hounding of teachers," rather than upon the enactment of legislation, and they have been extraordinarily successful, not only in rural areas but also in cities, as witness the action of the Atlanta Board of Education in outlawing the Darwinian hypothesis. This quiet campaign has been carried on in such an effective way that Maynard Shipley, president of the Science League of America and the best-informed man in the United States on the activities of the anti-evolutionists, wrote in 1930 that "nothing can be taught in 70 per cent of the secular schools of the republic today not sanctioned by the hosts of Fundamentalism." He said, however, with regard to the large number of teachers who had been discharged or threatened with such a fate during the previous year because they taught or believed in evolution: "Two of these cases were in California; and most of them were outside the Southern states, which are usually assumed to be the most backward in this regard."

Throughout the agitation against Darwinism in Dixie many brave spirits have stood out in opposition to the forces of ignorance and fanaticism which have threatened to engulf the entire region and drag it down to barbarism. Frequently they have done so at the risk of their jobs, and all too often they have suffered persecution and dismissal.

The individual who is generally credited with having brought about the discharge of the largest number of Southern professors because of their religious beliefs is the Rev. J. Frank Norris of Texas, who is said to have six such scalps in his belt. Norris, incidentally, has twice been indicted on criminal charges, once in 1912 for perjury and arson, when his outgrown church burned down, and again in 1926 for murder, when he shot to death an unarmed man who called on him in his study. Owing to the size of his following, this fire-eating Baptist has been able to keep the Lone Star State in turmoil over a good part of the past two decades. His handiwork may be seen in the ruling of the University of Texas in 1926 that it would not employ any "infidel, atheist or agnostic" or disbeliever "in God as the Supreme Being and Ruler of the Universe." In contrast to the course pursued by the authorities of this institution in the face of Fundamentalist threats was the splendid courage exhibited by the late Dr. S. P. Brooks, president of Baylor University, a Baptist seat of learning. Confronted with the anti-evolutionist manifesto of the Southern Baptist Convention at Houston, Dr. Brooks said: "I would die and rot in my grave before I would sign the Houston resolution."

According to reports regarded by some as authoritative, one of the numerous cases where a university professor was dismissed to satisfy the clamorings of the mob was that of Dr. Jesse W. Sprowls, who was thrown to the lions in 1923 by the University of Tennessee. This was two years before the passage of the anti-evolution bill in that state, but it is contended that President H. A. Morgan and the other authorities of the institution became terror-stricken when they found that Dr. Sprowls was actually planning to use James Harvey Robinson's *Mind in the Making* and other such subversive works as textbooks in his classes. They therefore notified him that his services were being dispensed with. Another version of the affair has it, however, that Dr. Sprowls was not dismissed on account of any beliefs or teachings with reference to evolution; he was ousted because of failure to perform his duties in a manner satisfactory to the university authorities. Such was the finding of those who investigated the case for the American Association of University Professors. But whatever the precise cause of the dismissal, it gave rise to a great uproar in the faculty and five other professors were discharged shortly thereafter in consequence. All had spent many years in the university's service. Among the number was Dr. John R. Neal, who afterward played a highly creditable part in the anti-evolutionist agitation in Tennessee and the labor disorders in North Carolina.

No story of the Fundamentalist attempt to seize the Southern legislatures and thus to control the educational processes of the Southern states would approach completeness without a reference to the magnificent fight waged by Dr. William Louis Poteat in North Carolina to save his state and his church from disgrace. Under fire for years because as a trained biologist he accepted the evolutionary hypothesis as a matter of course, Dr. Poteat refused to alter his position or to resign the presidency of Wake Forest College, a Baptist institution, although a numerous element in the Baptist church was demanding it. Not only so, but when the anti-evolutionist clamor was at its loudest, he proclaimed his faith in the forbidden theory firmly and emphatically. This audacious move brought down a storm of denunciation upon him, but he did not quail before it. Thanks to the loyal support of his faculty and alumni, he was never unhorsed. When at last he relinquished the presidency in 1927 because of his advanced age, after nearly a quarter of a century in office, North Carolina and the nation hailed him as a gallant and a dauntless spirit, liberal in his religious, educational and social attitudes, ever valiant in the search for truth.

Some of the ministers of the Southern Baptist Church who have sought to stem the anti-evolutionist tide are Dr. W. D. Weatherford of Nashville, Dr. M. Ashby Jones, Dr. Edwin M. Poteat of Mercer University, Dr. R. T. Vann of Raleigh, and the late Dr. John E. White of Atlanta and Savannah.

The course followed by the late Dr. E. Y. Mullins, president of the Southern Baptist Theological Seminary at Louisville, during the Fundamentalist furor, was, on the other hand, considerably less admirable. Dr. Mullins wobbled around a great deal, and on the whole gave encouragement to the anti-evolutionists. Charged by the Rev. J. Frank Norris and other extremists with harboring unorthodox views, he drafted the statement adopted by the convention of his church in 1925 which asserted that "man was created by the special act of God, as recorded in Genesis." Whereas

Dr. W. L. Poteat, a biologist, declared that evolution "is taken for granted, just as the Copernican astronomy, or the germ 'theory' of infectious diseases are taken for granted," Dr. Mullins said he did not think evolution "has been or ever will be proved."

While the Southern Methodist church was not torn by dissension over the authenticity of the Biblical account of the creation to anything like the same extent as the Southern Baptist church, certain of its institutions felt the force of the Fundamentalist onslaught. Among them was Southern Methodist University at Dallas, which ousted Dr. John A. Rice for his publication of a sane and intelligent critique of the Old Testament, and for other publications and activities considered unorthodox. But if the authorities of this university failed to take a decisive stand for academic freedom, Dr. J. H. Reynolds, president of Hendrix College in Arkansas, delivered addresses in that state in opposition to statutory interference with scientific research.

Undoubtedly the most powerful Fundamentalist in this great denomination is Bishop Warren A. Candler of Atlanta, one of the foremost exponents of seventeenth-century theology and Scriptural exegesis now living, although it must be said to his credit that he has always been strongly opposed to the passage of anti-evolution bills. Bishop Candler was the leader of the movement which prevented the reunion of the Northern and Southern branches of his church in 1925. One of his principal arguments against the plan was that the Northern church was "rationalistic," and that orthodox Southerners would be contaminated by contact with it. At the same time, the supposedly defunct issue of sectionalism was dusted off by the Bishop or his followers and made to do yeoman service. In like manner, the ancient shibboleth of "white supremacy" was invoked far and wide, for the Northern church admits Negroes to membership, and the idea was disseminated that Negro bishops might somehow obtain control over Southern whites. There were other arguments against the unification plan, but the foregoing were largely responsible for its defeat.

In contrast to Bishop Candler, with his almost medieval theological concepts, is Dr. George B. Winton of the Vanderbilt School of Religion, one of the most liberal and broadminded religious leaders in the South. A man of personal magnetism and unusual capabilities, Dr. Winton paid the penalty for his liberalism in 1926 when he was replaced as editor of the Nashville *Christian Advocate*. Then came the presidential campaign of 1928. An ordinary man would have followed his clerical colleagues into the Hoover camp, particularly a man who shortly before had been driven from the editorship of his church's official organ because of his advanced views. But not Dr. Winton. He felt that "Al" Smith was right on the "paramount issue," the power question, and he voted for him, the attitude of practically all his fellow-churchmen to the contrary notwithstanding.

Among the Disciples of Christ, a sect which is seriously divided over matters relating to the Modernistic interpretation of Holy Writ, an outstanding spokesman for the liberal group in the South has been

Dr. William M. Forrest, professor of Biblical history and literature at the University of Virginia. In his *Do Fundamentalists Play Fair?*, which appeared in 1926, Dr. Forrest charged the Fundamentalists with attempting "to make Christianity and ignorance synonymous terms." He went on to say that "the church has always lost in the battle with science . . . science has always won because theology has always been wrong." His outspoken stand brought him considerable adverse criticism, although practically all of it came from denominations other than his own.

The principal "heretic" in the Southern Presbyterian church at the present time is the able and enlightened Dr. Hay Watson Smith of Little Rock, Arkansas, who is placed on trial at periodic intervals upon complaints filed by reactionary members of that communion, among them Dr. William M. McPheeters, president of Columbia Theological Seminary. To date, however, Dr. Smith has withstood all such assaults successfully. Another evidence of narrowness on the part of the Southern Presbyterians is to be seen in the recent action of their General Assembly in severing relations with the Federal Council of Churches of Christ in America by a vote of more than two to one. This step had been considered and debated by the denomination for years. The final break came in 1931 after a committee of the Federal Council had approved the practice of birth control.

Even the Episcopal church, ordinarily regarded as holding itself aloof from the brawls of theological disputants, has disciplined a number of its priests in recent years. Most of these episodes occurred in the

North, but there was the case of the Rev. Lee W.
Heaton, Modernist rector of a church in Fort Worth,
Texas. Matters in the Heaton case were brought to
a head by the action of Bishop Harry T. Moore, who
proclaimed his determination to proceed against Mr.
Heaton as "the beginning of a concerted movement
to cleanse the Episcopal Church of Modernism."
Bishop Moore found within a period of less than
sixty days, however, that sentiment was strongly on
the side of the defendant and he dropped the matter
forthwith. A few years later, in 1927, the late Lang-
bourne M. Williams of Richmond acquired control
of the *Southern Churchman*, and sought in its columns
to lead an Episcopalian crusade for the revival of
old-fashioned orthodoxy. The movement made only
slight headway. The church as a whole inclines to a
much larger degree to follow the progressive leadership of such men as Dr. W. Cosby Bell of the Virginia
Theological Seminary and Dr. Beverley D. Tucker,
Jr., of Richmond. It should also be noted that in
1931 the Diocesan Council of Virginia took an important step in the direction of improved interracial
relations when it voted almost unanimously to give
the Negro membership of the church representation
on the council on the same basis as the white
membership.

In connection with this reference to the liberal
leadership of the Virginia Episcopalians in racial and
religious matters it is pertinent to call attention to the
liberal leadership of the Virginia Baptists. The Old
Dominion is the only Southern state whose General
Assembly has never had to consider an anti-evolution

20

bill or resolution, and for this the Baptists of the commonwealth deserve the major share of the credit. The rabidly Fundamentalist element in the Virginia branch of the denomination, desirous of emulating similar groups elsewhere in the South through the sponsorship of reactionary legislation, has been held in check by a group of influential leaders which includes Dr. Douglas S. Freeman, editor of the Richmond *News Leader*, and Dr. R. H. Pitt, editor of the *Religious Herald*. When it became apparent that a "Bible bill," making the reading of the Bible compulsory in the public schools, would be introduced in the state legislature, the Baptist General Association of Virginia adopted resolutions drafted by Dr. Pitt which opposed the measure as "an unholy alliance of state and church." The bill was beaten. Yet it must be sorrowfully recorded that their devotion to the separation of church and state did not prevent the members of the Baptist Ministers' Conference of Richmond from protesting to the University of Virginia authorities that Dr. William M. Forrest should be forbidden to disseminate his Modernist views because those views were "contrary to the cherished faith of a great majority of the people of this commonwealth."

Bible bills have been passed by a number of Southern legislatures. Among the states which have not gone in for this sort of thing is Louisiana, where a Bible bill was beaten a few years ago, largely through the efforts of Sidney L. Herold, a prominent Jewish attorney from Shreveport. Mr. Herold also is the author of the Bill of Rights in the present Louisiana constitution.

He is one of many members of his race who have had
leading rôles in the promotion of liberal movements
in the South. The Jews have never been numerous
below the Potomac, but they have made important
contributions to progressive thought in that area during the past century and a half. The tremendously
able Judah P. Benjamin was the most distinguished
of ante-bellum Jews, but he was a leading defender
of slavery, and hence cannot be catalogued as a liberal.
Other Southern Jews were more liberally disposed,
however, notably Judah Touro, the New Orleans
philanthropist. Touro not only emancipated all his
slaves, but he supplied them with funds with which
to establish themselves independently. He also gave
largely of his ample means to charitable causes without regard to race or creed. On one occasion a Uni-
versalist congregation in New Orleans got into financial difficulties and its house of worship was put up
at auction. Touro bought the building in and returned
it to its previous owners. The spirit of broadminded
tolerance and lofty humanitarianism which he exemplified in the Old South is found today among members of his race in the New South. Such men as Rabbi
Edward N. Calisch of Richmond and Rabbi Henry
Cohen of Galveston are modern leaders whose catholic
sympathies and scholarly attainments have gained
them the admiration of Jew and Gentile alike. It is
also noteworthy that a considerable number of young
Jewish women in the Southern states are interesting
themselves in movements designed to bring about an
amelioration of conditions of labor, especially in the
textile mills.

In summing up, it may be said that while the South is still cursed with a type of narrowness and fanaticism not found in equal measure in any other section of this country, and while it is still sweating under the lash of ecclesiasticism, there is reason to hope that before many years are past it will throw off the dominion of its clerical warlocks and take its place as a thoroughly civilized section of the republic. Members of evangelical sects in ever-increasing numbers are disregarding pastoral injunctions against dancing, card-playing, and theater-going, and there are evidences that they are becoming more rationalistic and less emotionalistic in their attitude toward dry laws, blue laws, and other repressive legislation of a similar nature. One may accordingly venture the prediction that the next generation will see the South definitely out of the land of bondage.

CHAPTER XVII

LABOR AND INDUSTRY IN THE SOUTH

THE LAZY tempo of life in the Old South was not conducive to the development of industry on a large scale. Southern habits of mind fitted much more readily into the agricultural than into the industrial pattern. Almost without exception, the leaders in the Southern states were planters, men who had been reared on the land and who were strongly attached to it, men to whom the song of the mocking bird and the piping of the tree frog were sounds far sweeter than the clangor of the anvil and the forge.

But it was not wholly because they had inherited a love of the soil that the planters were hostile to the building up of a great industrial system. Their opposition also was motivated by the effect the creation of such a system would be apt to have upon the Southern agricultural economy in general and the slave population in particular. The planting class felt, in the first place, that its surplus capital could be more advantageously employed in the purchase of additional land and Negroes than in the erection of factories. It was further of the opinion that large-scale development of industry in the South might result in raising up an economic structure which ultimately would replace the slave system. At the same time, the great slaveholders feared that the factories would employ Negroes—a possibility which both the upper and the lower class whites contemplated with the greatest apprehension, since they believed this would tend to make the blacks dissatisfied with servitude. They also feared that the industries might employ "poor whites," in which event the slaves would perhaps become restless at the sight of thousands of poor but free men earning their daily bread.

The consequence was that until the late nineteenth century the South remained overwhelmingly agricultural. This despite the fact that in the forties and fifties leading Southerners, viewing the industrial superiority of the North with grave concern, became fearful lest their section be reduced to economic vassalage. The exhortations of such men as J. D. B. DeBow and William Gregg at this period resulted in a marked stimulation of industry during the decade immediately preceding the outbreak of the Civil War, but agriculture nevertheless remained supreme.

Several spinning mills had been established in South Carolina as early as 1790, and within two decades such factories had appeared in Georgia, North Carolina, and Virginia. A number of ironworks and other manufacturing plants also had been set up. Then William Gregg of South Carolina published a series of articles in the Charleston *Courier* in 1844, urging upon the South the crying need for adequate industrial development, and the movement was brought to the attention of the Southern people in a manner calculated to enlist rather widespread support.

Gregg, a jewelry merchant in Columbia, saw the

squalor and ignorance which blighted the lives of the "poor whites" of his state. He became convinced that the South's salvation lay in the establishment of factories at strategic points, factories which not only would put an end to the complete industrial dominance of the North, but which at the same time would afford employment and opportunity to the many thousands of underprivileged whites who, he said, were living "in comparative nakedness and starvation." Gregg accordingly established a cotton mill at Graniteville, South Carolina, in 1848. In doing so he laid the foundations of the Southern textile industry.

Graniteville, the first mill of its type in the Southern states, was a pioneering effort of great moment. In the words of Dr. Broadus Mitchell, Gregg's biographer and a leading Southern liberal, it "heralded a new day for the poor whites of the South." While it was paternalistic, almost feudalistic, in character, it was operated in a spirit of such large-hearted benevolence that the paternalism was less objectionable than it would otherwise have been. Gregg required his mill hands who had children between the ages of six and twelve years to keep them in school. Teachers and books were supplied by the company for this, the first system of compulsory education in the South, if not the first in the United States. While the hours were long and the wages low at the mill, they compared favorably with those in effect at the period in the North and in England.

In judging Graniteville and its importance to the subsequent industrial development of the Southern states, it must be borne in mind that hours, wage scales,

and conditions of labor three-quarters of a century
ago were everywhere far less favorable to the worker
than those which obtain today. It would be unreason-
able, therefore, to compare conditions at Graniteville
with such as prevail in the most progressive present
day factories.

In addition to J. D. B. DeBow, to whom reference
already has been made, a man who rendered valuable
assistance to the master of Graniteville in his endeavors
for the promotion of Southern industry was J. H.
Lumpkin of Georgia. Lumpkin shared Gregg's opinion
that the way to provide better living conditions and
more satisfactory educational facilities for the under-
privileged whites was through their employment in
mills and factories.

In view of the fact that most of the textile operatives
in the Southern mills prior to the war were women
and children, one may be permitted to doubt whether
the benefits which Lumpkin and his co-workers envisioned actually materialized. The children, a majority
of whom were between twelve and sixteen years of
age, drew 10 to 20 cents a day, while the women were
paid from 40 to 50 cents. The male employees, a large
percentage of whom occupied clerical or technical
positions, received the munificent per diem of from
50 to 75 cents.

Such was the status of Southern textile manufacture
when the outbreak of hostilities in 1861 forced the
Confederacy to develop this and other industries to a
degree not approached theretofore. No longer able
to depend upon the North for the manufactured
products which they had obtained there in earlier

days, the Southern states were compelled to build up a variety of industrial plants in order to supply the needs of their civilian and military populations. The devastation wrought by the Northern armies in large areas of the Confederacy, the final capitulation of the Southern forces in the field, and the succeeding decade of reconstruction combined to prevent any notable industrial development in the region for some years after Appomattox. During the seventies, however, the industrial revival assumed considerable proportions, and by 1880 the number of spindles in Dixie was almost twice as great as it had been in 1860. Within the next five years the total was doubled again, and in five more years, it was trebled. Contemporaneously with the phenomenal rise of the textile mills came the establishment of tobacco factories in the upper South, molasses and sugar refineries in and near New Orleans, and cottonseed oil and oil cake factories in Texas.

Perhaps the most powerful journalistic voice raised in the post-bellum South on behalf of factory development in the former Confederacy was that of Francis W. Dawson, editor of the Charleston *News and Courier*. Dawson conducted an unrelenting campaign for the building up of Southern industry, and did much to encourage leading citizens to invest their capital in the promotion of industrial enterprises. Another man who played a significant part in the movement in the Palmetto State was H. P. Hammett, whose mill at Garrison Shoals, opened in 1876, was the forerunner of the great Piedmont Mill at that place. Hammett was a paternalist, but a good one. A leading motive with him in his textile operations was his desire to afford employment to the "poor whites" of upstate South Carolina.

In the early eighties D. A. Tompkins settled in Charlotte, North Carolina, and began the practical efforts in the direction of Southern industrial development which were to give him a national reputation. Tompkins viewed the progress of his native section in this field as merely a step toward the reassertion of its former industrial supremacy. He was fond of pointing out that in 1810 the manufactured products of Virginia, the Carolinas, and Georgia were more diversified and were worth more in dollars and cents than those of the whole of New England with New York State thrown in. He called attention to the fact that the South's subsequent preoccupation with other matters caused it to lose its leadership as a center of manufacture. Tompkins was a man of broad vision, with a receptiveness to ideas which fitted him almost perfectly to lead the South's industrial renascence. He is credited with having been in all probability "directly responsible for the building of more cotton mills than any other one man."

While such constructive activity as that promoted by Tompkins and his co-workers was immensely helpful in developing a more optimistic attitude of mind below the Potomac, Walter Hines Page is authority for the statement that as late as 1897 the thoughts of the Southern people were still largely turned to the past. He made a tour in that year with a view to writing a magazine article, but was so depressed by the atmosphere of loneliness and frustration which he encountered almost everywhere, that he determined to abandon the project. Ten years later, however, he traveled through the South again on a similar mission, and found everything completely changed.

"The conversation is not now about reconstruction," he wrote in 1907. "In one place it is about alfalfa, in another it is about stock, in another about corn. . . . I doubt if anywhere in the world there has been so rapid a change in what may be called the fundamentals of good living and of sound thinking and of cheerful work, as the change that has taken place these ten years in many of these rural districts."

The great industrial advance which was one of the principal concomitants of the metamorphosis in Southern attitudes here described, brought many benefits in its train, but it also had its unpleasant side. There was, for example, the tremendous political power wielded by the great corporations. In the same year that Page wrote the article quoted above, Dr. William E. Dodd pointed out that "in Virginia the names of four railway counsellors of high rank appear on the roll of the executive committee of the Democratic party; in North Carolina the American Tobacco Company was able to name the delegates to the last Republican National Convention; and in order to break the hold of J. P. Morgan in Georgia the radical wing of the Democratic party felt constrained to appeal once again to the ever-present race hatred."

A still more deplorable aspect of the Southern industrial revival was to be seen in the atrociously long hours and low wages which obtained in a large percentage of the Southern cotton mills, a state of affairs which had been called forcibly to the attention of the country by Clare de Graffenreid in a moving article published in the *Century Magazine* in 1891. A decade later the matter was taken up by other scribes and given a thorough airing over a period of years. The damning fact that in 1900 more than 234,000 children between ten and fifteen years of age were employed in factories and plants of various kinds in the fifteen Southern and border states, of whom approximately 28,000 were in textile mills, simply could not be explained away. It was pointed out that civilized countries everywhere, including Russia and Japan, had fixed an age limit below which children were forbidden to work in factories, but that a number of Southern states had not even provided this protection for their boys and girls. While many Southern mill men viewed the situation with complacency, others, such as D. A. Tompkins, favored legislation which would correct this condition. It appears quite probable that a considerable percentage of the opposition to such legislation came from New England capitalists who had invested in Southern textile plants.

Edgar Gardner Murphy of Alabama was active in the fight for child labor reform. He received valuable journalistic support from a considerable portion of the Southern press, notably the Columbia *State*. This newspaper's treatment of the child labor question during these years was characterized by him as "the ablest handling of a human industrial issue that our country has known since the period of emancipation."

Conditions in the textile mills were vividly described by Murphy in his valuable survey of the contemporary scene, *The Present South*, which appeared in 1904:

"I have known mills in which for 10 and 12 days at a time the factory hands—children and all—were called to work before sunrise and were dismissed from work only after sunset, laboring from dark to dark. I have repeatedly seen them at labor for 12, 13 and even 14 hours per day. In the period of the holidays or at other 'rush times' I have seen children 8 and 9 years of age leaving the factory as late as 9:30 o'clock at night, and finding their way with their own little lanterns, through the unlighted streets of the mill village, to their squalid homes."

Murphy, together with Dr. Alexander J. McKelway of Virginia and other humanitarians, stirred up such a storm of protest over this dreadful situation that they were able, despite the resistance of a powerful lobby of manufacturers, to secure the adoption, by the end of the year 1903, of child labor laws in practically every industrial state south of Mason and Dixon's Line. These men and others took leading parts in the work of the National Child Labor Committee, formed at this time to safeguard the welfare of children in industry both in the South and elsewhere.

This legislation was merely a beginning, however, for over a long period of years the South has been the most backward section of the country in protecting its children from industrial exploitation. Only a short while ago in North Carolina children from six to ten years old worked on eleven-hour shifts in six industries, including textiles, while in Georgia children aged twelve could be worked ten hours a day and

318 LIBERALISM IN THE SOUTH

those fourteen and a half years old could be worked all night. Even in 1932, Georgia permits its manufacturers to work children fourteen years of age ten hours a day and sixty hours a week, while the same hours prevail in South Carolina, with the exception that the week is fifty-five hours. In Florida and Mississippi conditions are almost as bad. It must be borne in mind, too, that the Southern laws governing labor for both children and adults, unsatisfactory as they are, are not always enforced. This is well illustrated by a recent report of a committee appointed by the South Carolina legislature to investigate enforcement in that state. The committee found the records "replete with instances of violations of the criminal laws of South Carolina in regard to the regulation of working conditions in textile manufacturing corporations." Alabama and Virginia are generally credited with having the best child labor laws in the South.

But if conditions relating to child labor are far from satisfactory at the present time in some of the Southern states, this criticism applies with even greater force to the labor situation as it pertains to adults, especially in the cotton mills. Just as Gregg and Lumpkin and their fellows predicted seventy-five years ago, these mills have tapped the vast reservoir of "poor white" labor for their operatives. Most of these operatives come to the mills from wretched hovels in the mountains, the sand hills, or the pine barrens, where civilized comforts are unknown and where ignorance and degradation are supreme. They belong, in the main, to the great army of several million tenant farmers who move about from cabin to cabin every year or two, with no household effects save a few broken pieces of furniture and battered pots and pans, and with a standard of living lower than is to be found among tenant farmers anywhere else in the civilized world.

It was the hope of the pioneer mill men of the mid-nineteenth century that this great group of down-trodden and unlettered peasants would find in the whirring spindles of the industrial South release from the poverty and destitution of tenant farming, and that they could be given opportunities for education and self-improvement which previously had been denied them. This hope has been realized only partially. If the mills have drawn hundreds of thousands of "poor whites" into the mill villages, and brought them into contact with aspects of modern civilization which formerly they had not known, the mills have also turned a large percentage of them into industrial slaves who can scarcely call their souls their own. Operatives in many of the mill villages are little more than cogs in a vast machine, a machine owned and controlled by the mill, a machine in which all individuality and initiative are stifled. A professor in a North Carolina college who had made a close study of these villages said about a decade ago that during the preceding twenty years not one single person "of county importance" had emerged from among the 300,000 members of mill families in that state.

There is, of course, wide divergence among mill villages. Some are attractively laid out, with well paved streets and well built homes, while others are antiquated, dilapidated and uninviting. But even in the most modern of these settlements there is usually an almost feudalistic relationship between the worker and the company. The worker and his family occupy their home at the pleasure of the company, they deal with the company store, they attend the company church, and if the company does not insist upon having both parents and children in the mill as operatives, the latter attend the company school. The average mill operative in the Southern states seldom leaves the confines of the village, and when he does it is usually to move to another village.

Wages are low and hours are long in the Southern mills, and there is comparatively little legislation for the protection of the workers. Whereas it had been claimed for many years that it was only proper for the Southern textile mills to pay lower wages than the Northern mills, owing to lower living costs in the South, this argument seems to have been exploded by a survey made in 1919 and 1920 by the National Industrial Conference Board, an organization sponsored by the manufacturers. It was found that certain important Southern mill centers had higher living costs than corresponding Northern centers. These conclusions are in harmony with those of Dr. Jennings J. Rhyne, who declared in 1930, following an exhaustive study of the question:

"After making every allowance for welfare work and differences in living costs, it can hardly be claimed that wages paid in the cotton mills in the South are the equivalent of wages paid in New England mills."

It should also be noted that when an employee in a Southern mill is injured the amount he receives under the workmen's compensation law is almost always smaller than he would receive under similar circumstances in the North. And if he is employed in Arkansas, Florida, Mississippi, or South Carolina he receives nothing, for these states have no workmen's compensation laws.

Southern industrialists, it must be said in all fairness, are no more callous toward their employees than industrialists in the North or elsewhere. The explanation for the backwardness of the Southern states in providing protection for workers lies primarily in the fact that the region has been slow to develop in this field, and is now passing through a stage which other sections traversed and left behind them years ago.

Miss Lucy R. Mason of Richmond, Mrs. W. A. Newell of Greensboro, Mrs. Mary O. Cowper of Duke University, and Mrs. A. M. Tunstall of Montgomery are among the prominent Southern women who are coöperating actively and effectively in efforts looking toward the amelioration of working conditions below the Potomac at the present time. Miss Mason points out that "several Southern States give less legal protection to wage earners than any other industrial State or nation of the Western world, and nearly all Southern states fail in important particulars to safeguard wage earners." Alabama and Florida have no laws limiting women's hours of work, while the situation in Georgia, South Carolina and Mississippi is only slightly better. These criticisms apply, in so far as working conditions for women are concerned, to stores, laundries, hotels, restaurants, telephone and telegraph exchanges, bakeries, and other occupations, as well as to cotton mills.

The Southern mill operators, like mill operators in the North and elsewhere under similar conditions, have stubbornly resisted most of the efforts which have been made by outsiders to bring about improvements in hours, wages and working conditions. Some six or seven years ago, for example, the University of North Carolina announced that it contemplated a study of the textile industry in that state, the leading cotton manufacturing state in the Union. The North Carolina Cotton Manufacturers' Association thereupon voted unanimously to refuse permission for the study. David Clark, editor of the *Southern Textile Bulletin* of Charlotte—a reactionary publication which always reflects the point of view of the operators and shares with the Charlotte *Observer* and the *Manufacturers' Record* of Baltimore the dubious distinction of being the most thick-and-thin defender of Southern textile potentates—declared that the mill owners would not "stand for it," as a survey of the industry would breed "radicals and reformers." It should be stated in this connection that Mr. Clark's point of view is wholly at variance with that of his father, the late Chief Justice Walter Clark of the North Carolina Supreme Court, one of the most distinguished liberals in North Carolina history.

But while Southern textile men are at times willing to entertain petitions for better wages and shorter hours, and while there has in fact been substantial shortening of hours in the past two years, owing partly

to the business depression, no Southern textile mag_
nate has as yet come forward to advocate recognition
of the labor unions. Very much to the contrary, the
entire guild of cotton mill operators is grimly united
against the unions in bitter and uncompromising
hostility. These mill men are loud in their protesta-
tions that they have never questioned "the right of
labor to organize," but as a practical matter they
almost invariably seek by every means in their power
to prevent such organization. Employees who are
active in promoting the unions are customarily discharged for their pains.

What Miss Lucy R. Mason has called "the most
hopeful event in the history of the textile industry"
was brought about in 1930 and 1931 through the
efforts of George A. Sloan, president of the Cotton-
Textile Institute, and other prominent textile executives. Mr. Sloan, a Tennessean who is opposed on
principle to night work for women and children, and
other officers of the institute prevailed upon the operators of mills with 80 per cent of the spindles in the
country to limit day operations to fifty-five hours per
week and night operations to fifty hours. They also
persuaded persons controlling nearly 85 per cent of
the spindles to voluntarily abolish night work for
women and for minors under eighteen years of age.
Among the Southern manufacturers who gave a great
deal of time to this movement is Donald Comer of
Birmingham, who also has taken a leading part in
improving conditions of labor for children in Alabama,
and in efforts toward similar improvements for women
in industry. There is considerable danger, however,

that the textile men who have refused to coöperate with the Cotton-Textile Institute, and who have taken advantage of the situation to lengthen hours and lower wages in their own mills, will eventually destroy the effectiveness of what has been done by Mr. Sloan and his fellow workers. This is the opinion of Henry P. Kendall, a Bostonian of unusually liberal tendencies who operates a number of mills in the South.

For many years Southern employers and chambers of commerce boasted of the "docility" of the labor supply in the area. This despite the fact that there had been strikes off and on since the late nineteenth century in connection with efforts to unionize the textile industry. But none of these strikes was as serious as the series of walkouts which began in the spring of 1929, involving many thousands of workers in Tennessee, the Carolinas, and Virginia. While the long hours and low wages were important contributing factors in the launching of these strikes, it was the inauguration of the "stretch-out system" on a wide scale which provided the immediate provocation in most instances. A committee of the South Carolina legislature which investigated this stretch-out system defined it as "putting more work on the employees than they can do." Under the "stretch out," a worker who tends a certain number of machines is given more machines while his pay is not raised in anything like the same proportion and may even be reduced.

The industrial warfare got under way in March, 1929, with the strike of 5,000 rayon workers at Elizabethton, Tennessee. Almost immediately there was disorder, and from that time forward for many months

there were floggings, kidnapings, shootings, and kill-
ings, with both sides guilty of unwarranted violence at
one time or another, but with the courts and law
enforcement agencies almost invaribly aligned against
the strikers. This was particularly true in North Carolina, where the continued conviction of strikers and
the continued acquittal of agents of the mill operators
or their sympathizers gave rise to grave doubts as to
the nature of North Carolina justice.

The first armed clash in that state came at Gastonia,
where Communists were at work. In a gun battle,
Chief of Police O. F. Aderholt was killed. Seven
strikers were charged with the murder, and the prosecution was permitted to introduce their Communist
affiliations in evidence. Communism accordingly became the controlling issue in the trial, and the Communist beliefs of the defendants were emphasized to
such an extent that the facts surrounding the actual
killing became subordinate and secondary. The seven
were given sentences of from five to twenty years.

Some three months after the killing of Aderholt,
Mrs. Ella May Wiggins, a mother of five children who
received $9 for a sixty-hour week in a mill at Gastonia,
was en route to a strikers' meeting called by Communists, when the truck in which she was a passenger
was fired on by a mob. Mrs. Wiggins was killed instantly. Although many witnesses testified at the
subsequent trial that one Horace Wheelus fired the
fatal shot, the Communist issue was injected into the
proceedings by the defense, and Wheelus was acquitted.

Another important center of disturbance in North

Carolina was Marion. Following an extensive walkout, a conference was held between representatives of
two Marion mills and spokesmen for the strikers.
Among the mediators was L. L. Jenkins, wealthy
Asheville textile man and banker. A gentlemen's
agreement was reached, and the strikers went back
to work. A short time thereafter Mr. Jenkins charged
that both companies were violating the terms of the
agreement, and that the honor of the textile fraternity
was being besmirched, a charge which was fully concurred in by the union men who had attended the
conference when the terms were agreed upon.

Within a week or two there was another walkout
in the mill of the East Marion Manufacturing Company. Strikers were picketing the mill gate at dawn,
and were ordered by the sheriff to disperse. They
refused, whereupon tear gas was released by the
sheriff. As the strikers ran from the fumes, volley
after volley was poured into their ranks by the
sheriff's deputies. Twenty-one men fell in the street,
of whom six were mortally wounded. All six were
shot in the back. Not one of the twenty-one was armed.
The sheriff and all his deputies were acquitted when
the case came to trial, and Rignal Baldwin, owner
of the mill, was quoted in the press, without contradiction, as having commended them for being "damn
good marksmen."

When the turmoil in the North Carolina textile
centers simmered down, after an orgy of violence and
brutality extending over many months, it was seen
that whereas nobody had been punished for the killing
of seven unarmed strikers, seven other strikers had

gotten heavy prison terms for the slaying of an officer of the law in a gun battle in which the officer may have been the aggressor. In addition to these major casualties, there was a host of minor ones. Five anti-unionist mobs were charged with flogging, kidnaping, and otherwise maltreating strikers, but in no case was there a conviction. Weimar Jones, writing in *The Nation* for July 2, 1930, summed up as follows:

"In every case where strikers were put on trial strikers were convicted; in not one case where anti-unionists or officers were accused has there been a conviction."

No story of these struggles in North Carolina would be complete, however, without some reference to the gallant efforts of four influential individuals to bring a larger measure of humanity into industrial relationships in that state. These are Gerald W. Johnson, whose work on the editorial staff of the Greensboro *News* antedated the big textile strikes by several years, but which was nevertheless of the utmost importance; Frank P. Graham, who led in the fight for the workers as president of the North Carolina Social Service Conference; and Josephus Daniels, publisher, and Miss Nell Battle Lewis, columnist, of the Raleigh *News and Observer*, both of whom were militant advocates of justice for the strikers.*

From North Carolina the industrial unrest spread a short distance across the Virginia line to Danville, where the largest independent cotton mill in the

---

* Additional information relative to the liberal influence of Mr. Johnson, Mr. Daniels and Miss Lewis will be found in Chapter XX. The work of Dr. Graham is discussed further in Chapter XVIII.

South had begun the application of the stretch-out system and had announced a 10 per cent wage cut. The Danville mill was perhaps the most progressive in the Southern states, with better wages and more humane working conditions than most other plants of a similar nature. Its president, the late H. R. Fitzgerald, was a well-intentioned and benevolent man who had set up what he termed an "industrial democracy." The workers contended, however, that whereas they were given representation in this organization, it was controlled completely by the mill management. When the 10 per cent cut was announced, they urged the abandonment of the company's extensive system of welfare work, in order that wages might be maintained. But Fitzgerald, thoroughly steeped in the old-fashioned paternalistic tradition, took the view that his employees were incompetent to spend higher wages and that they ought to have welfare work instead. The consequence was that the American Federation of Labor organized the mill, a strike was called in September, 1930, and the war was on.

The Danville strike was carried on in much more decent fashion than the strikes in Tennessee and North Carolina. Neither side indulged in the extreme forms of violence which had characterized similar walkouts in neighboring states. Owing to depressed business conditions and other factors, however, it was inevitable from the first that the strike would be lost. It collapsed early in 1931, in an atmosphere of suspicion and distrust of the union organizer in charge which gave the entire movement to unionize the

Southern textile industry a setback from which it will take years to recover.

About twelve months after the failure at Danville, the theater of industrial unrest in the South was transferred to the Kentucky coal fields, where a large number of miners walked out early in 1931, in protest against a 10 per cent wage cut. There followed a carnival of terror, murder, and bloodshed extending over a considerable period, with Communists insinuating themselves into the picture and both sides guilty of violating the law. But the fact that the miners were culpable in some instances does not excuse the Kentucky authorities for the rank discrimination in favor of the coal operators which they have exhibited almost invariably throughout the struggle. Two newspapermen who were sympathetic to the miners went to Harlan, the center of the agitation, and both were shot in the leg. One of them was Bruce Crawford, the able and unterrified editor of *Crawford's Weekly*, published at Norton, Virginia, who had persistently exposed the disgraceful tactics of the operators and the guards they had imported into the coal fields to protect their interests. There were shootings of miners, together with bombings and kidnapings of miners and their sympathizers, but neither the local nor the state authorities could see any occasion for punishing anybody for these crimes. On the other hand, it became an offense against the commonwealth of Kentucky for anyone even to advocate the most elementary justice for the strikers, and more than a hundred strikers and their allies were thrown into jail, many of them on trumped up charges.

In February, 1932, when eleven New York writers, members of a committee for miners' relief, came to Pineville with truckloads of food for the strikers, they were arrested at their hotel on charges of disorderly conduct and escorted to the Tennessee line, where two of them were beaten up.

About six weeks later a group of students from Eastern colleges and universities entered the coal fields for the avowed purpose of "sociological research." County Attorney Walter B. Smith of Bell County, who had ordered the wholly illegal arrest of the New York writers the month before, compelled the students to cross over into Tennessee almost as soon as they arrived in Kentucky. "We shall regard you as malicious intruders until you have proved you are not," Smith told them, thereby reversing the time-honored legal principle that a man must be assumed to be innocent until he is proved guilty. Although the students denied having any Communist affiliations, Smith said he had information to the contrary, and hustled them out of Bell County immediately. Authorities of the neighboring county of Claiborne, in Tennessee, refused to permit them to stop, they said. Student delegations protested in person to Governor Ruby Laffoon of Kentucky `and Governor H. H. Horton of Tennessee that their civil liberties had been grossly violated, but got no consolation. Laffoon replied that they were "too easily bluffed" while Horton bluntly declared: "We don't want a lot of Bolshevists, Communists or anarchists interfering with the dignity of Tennessee."

The complete disregard shown by the authorities

of Harlan and Bell counties for the constitutional rights of the miners and their sympathizers, and the attitude of the governor of the state toward such methods induces the reflection as to what means of redress are open to those who are the victims of this type of persecution—a question which likewise arose in North Carolina during the industrial disorders of 1929. Some liberals are of the opinion that Federal legislation should be enacted permitting the United States government to interfere when local authorities refuse to safeguard constitutional rights. Others feel that even if such a statute were legal, its enactment would be a dangerous invasion of local self-government and might lead to abuses as serious as those which it seeks to remedy. The entire question is one of extreme complexity, and it seems probable that years will pass before there is a satisfactory solution. At present those who have the time and the means can appeal to the courts for relief, preferably the Federal courts, but this is a slow and expensive process quite beyond the reach of a starving miner or a hungry textile worker.

The reign of terror in the Kentucky coal fields is the latest of the clashes between employer and employee which have attended the long struggle of Southern workers for better wages, hours, and conditions of labor. One may venture the prediction that it is not the last.

As for the paternalistic system, once so essential to the development of Southern industry, it has outlived its usefulness, and indications are that it will give way ultimately to unionization. Even where the system is most intelligently applied, as in the admirable villages laid out by George Gordon Crawford for his Birmingham steel mills—villages which are models of their kind, where no racial discrimination is practised and where educational and recreational facilities are the best obtainable—it is impossible to escape the conclusion that paternalism is now an outmoded approach to the problem of industrial adjustment. The feeling is becoming widespread among laboring men that they could well dispense with company welfare work and its attendant control and supervision, in return for higher wages. The laborer, they reason, is as much entitled as any other member of society to own his home, to choose whatever forms of recreation seem good to him, and to spend his wages without reference to any scheme or program forced upon him by his employer. It appears almost inevitable that soon or late this view will prevail in Southern industry.

CHAPTER XVIII

EDUCATION IN THE TWENTIETH CENTURY

DESPITE the tremendous efforts of such men as Curry, Haygood, and McIver, there were fewer than one hundred four-year public high schools in the entire South in 1900. The foundations had been laid, however, for marked progress in public education. The work of the men and women who had toiled during the three decades following the war to provide adequate educational facilities for the masses had culminated in 1898 in the calling of a Conference for Education in the South at Capon Springs, West Virginia, with the Rt. Rev. T. U. Dudley, Episcopal bishop of Kentucky, presiding. This was the first of a series of conferences held annually for the next seventeen years, with the meeting place shifting from state to state and leaders from all parts of the South participating. The stimulating effect of these gatherings can scarcely be overestimated.

Formation of the Southern Education Board in 1901 gave further impetus to the movement at the opening of the new century. The chief purpose of this board was to persuade rural communities to tax themselves for educational purposes. The venerable Dr. J. L. M. Curry, who had only two years of life remaining to him, was chosen supervising director. Then in

1902 John D. Rockefeller established his General Education Board, endowing it lavishly and arranging for substantial aid to high schools and elementary schools, as well as to institutions of higher learning.

The movement for better public schools in the Southern states was greatly accelerated through the activities of these and other agencies operating in the region. Among the individuals whose work at this period was especially noteworthy may be mentioned Dr. H. B. Frissell, successor to General Armstrong as principal of Hampton Institute. Frissell not only took a leading part in the highly important series of Conferences for Education in the South, but at the same time he was able to interest various influential Northerners in the work.

Intensive campaigns for better schools were begun in the several states, and by 1908 they had been held in almost every corner of the South with gratifying results. School revenues for the South as a whole increased more than 100 per cent during the century's first decade, while enrollment, attendance, and equipment all showed similar improvement. In 1913 the George Peabody College for Teachers opened at Nashville, and to its excellent facilities for teacher training may be attributed a goodly share of Dixie's advance in the field of public education since that time.

But while there has been an advance, the rural public school in the South is still considerably below the average for the country as a whole. Terms are shorter, teachers, salaries are lower, and equipment is inferior. Since the former Confederacy is overwhelmingly rural, it is obvious that here is a problem of no little magnitude, one which will require some years for its solution. In the Southern cities, on the other hand, the schools compare favorably with those in the rest of the United States.

In addition to the fact that salaries are distressingly low for rural teachers, the latter at times are made to suffer for their religious beliefs. Teachers have been dismissed because of membership in the Roman Catholic church. There was also the case of the young lady in North Carolina who signed a contract with a school in that state some five years ago in which she bound herself among other things "to take a vital interest in all phases of Sunday-school work," "not to go out with any young men except in so far as it may be necessary to stimulate Sunday-school work," "to remain in the dormitory or on the school grounds when not actively engaged in school or church work elsewhere," "not to fall in love," "to eat carefully" and to "sleep at least eight hours each night." For these services to God and country she was paid at the munificent rate of $85 a month for seven and a half months.

If such facts as these are discouraging to those who have the best interests of the South at heart, one may derive consolation from the work of such a woman as Miss Martha Berry, founder and director of the Berry Schools for mountain children in Georgia. Miss Berry's own fortunate station in life did not blind her to the lack of opportunity afforded the "Cracker" boys and girls who lived in the hills near her home, and with a ramshackle buggy and a one-room log cabin on the Possum Trot Road near Rome she laid the foundations thirty years ago for the great institution which bears her name today. During the past three decades thousands of poor children from the mountains of the Southern states have been educated at the Berry Schools, whose only entrance requirement is poverty. The reputation of the schools—which are now housed in 100 buildings on 20,000 acres of land with 1,000 students and 115 teachers and supervisors—is world wide, and persons of means frequently seek to matriculate their children. But the answer is always the same. Only poor children can be admitted.

The work of such an institution as this in reducing the Southern illiteracy rate is obviously of the first importance. The Berry Schools have some ten thousand alumni, thousands of whom have become teachers. Without the opportunity afforded them by Miss Berry to secure an education free of cost, a large percentage of these under-privileged mountaineers would have remained in ignorance and degradation in the Southern uplands. But in so vast an area as the Southern states, neither one school nor half a dozen schools can possibly take care of the situation. Recognizing that the illiteracy rate there is still far higher than in any other section of the country, a determined effort was launched in 1931 to remedy this condition. This movement is part of a nation wide campaign under the direction of Secretary of the Interior Ray Lyman Wilbur, and is being conducted in the South by Dr. Charles G. Maphis, director of the University of Virginia Institute of Public Affairs. Mrs. Cora Wilson Stewart, famous for her moonlight schools in

Kentucky, is chairman of the national executive committee. Another drive launched of late in the Southern states looking toward the elevation of cultural standards there is the effort begun in 1930 by the American Library Association to equalize library opportunities. Miss Tommie Dora Barker was placed in charge of the campaign, with headquarters in Atlanta.

So much for the progress achieved below the Potomac since 1900 in providing educational facilities for the masses and lowering the illiteracy rate. What of the institutions of higher learning?

Southern colleges and universities labored during the early years of the century under tremendous financial handicaps. One may visualize in some measure the extent of those handicaps when it is pointed out that the total combined annual income available in 1903 for higher education in Virginia, North Carolina, South Carolina, Georgia, Alabama, Mississippi, Louisiana, Tennessee, and Kentucky was less than the yearly income of Harvard University. This state of affairs necessarily made it extremely difficult for Southern seats of learning to pay such salaries to their teaching staffs as would prevent the ablest members of those staffs from accepting more lucrative positions in the North. At the same time, many institutions found themselves forced to lower their entrance requirements in order that they might supplement their meagre funds with income from student tuition fees.

Institutions of higher education in the South also suffered during these years from the unwillingness of many Southerners to allow their schoolmen the enjoyment of complete academic freedom. This attitude was noted by Chancellor Walter B. Hill of the University of Georgia, a distinguished liberal, when he asked:

"Have we freedom of opinion in the South? Must every man who thinks above a whisper do so at the peril of his reputation or his influence, or at the deadlier risk of having an injury inflicted upon the institution or the cause he represents?"

Chancellor Hill sounded "a word of warning against the worst evil in our intellectual, social, political, and religious life, the illiberality that is ready to inflict the urging of rebuke or ostracism as a penalty for difference in opinion."

This tendency was strikingly illustrated by the treatment meted out to Professor Andrew Sledd of Emory College, Georgia, because of an article on the Negro question contributed by him to a Northern magazine.* He stated specifically in the article that the Negro "belongs to an inferior race" and that he had no desire "that the Negro should be the social equal of the white man." He added, however, that the black man has certain fundamental rights which should be respected, and deplored Jim Crow laws and other forms of discrimination against the Negro in the South. Also included in the article was a terrific denunciation of lynching, together with a description of a particularly barbarous episode of this kind which had been witnessed by two trainloads of men and boys who were carried to the scene on special trains provided by an enterprising railroad.

* "The Negro: Another View," *Atlantic Monthly*, July, 1902.

Dr. Sledd, a Virginian by birth, was harshly set upon in the press and termed a "Boston nigger-equality citizen," following publication of his magazine contribution. Tar and feathers were suggested as the proper curative for one with a mentality so diseased, and he was dismissed from the Emory faculty. Two years later he was chosen president of the University of Florida, but was forced to resign in 1909 because the enrollment did not increase with sufficient rapidity. It is only fair to point out that when Emory College became Emory University and was removed from Oxford to Atlanta, Dr. Sledd was reinstated as a member of the teaching staff.

In recent years Emory has been among the most liberal of all Southern institutions. It has established an annual Institute of Citizenship and has sponsored group meetings of Southern economists and political scientists. Dean Edgar H. Johnson of the School of Commerce has been chairman of the board of the Atlanta School of Social Work and with Vice-President T. H. Jack and other members of the staff has given much valuable coöperation to Negro institutions. President Harvey Warren Cox has supported and encouraged the liberalism of his faculty, who have written and published a number of articles on industrial and other important questions. An Interracial Forum has been sponsored by the student body.

The year following Sledd's dismissal from Emory, Dr. John Spencer Bassett wrote an article for the *South Atlantic Quarterly*, of which he was editor, entitled "Stirring up the Fires of Race Antipathy."* In this

* *South Atlantic Quarterly*, October, 1903.

article Dr. Bassett expressed the view that Booker T. Washington was "the greatest man, save General Lee, born in the South in a hundred years." There was an immediate outburst of scurrility and billingsgate from every direction. Editors, professional men, educators, and churchmen from one end of North Carolina to the other joined in clamoring for Bassett's expulsion from the faculty of Trinity College, where he was then serving. Trinity itself was attacked with uncommon ferocity, and was pronounced to be no longer in harmony with "old-fashioned North Carolina Methodism." Josephus Daniels, editor of the Raleigh *News and Observer*, who is today, in some respects, one of the South's most distinguished liberals,† was among those who called for Bassett's dismissal. He distorted the Trinity professor's words, misrepresented his position, and spelled his name "bASSett" in the *News and Observer*.

In view of the well-nigh unanimous demand for Dr. Bassett's head, it seemed reasonable to assume that the Trinity trustees would dispense with his services at once. But at this juncture President John C. Kilgo and the faculty of the college stepped into the breach in defense of their colleague. The principle of academic freedom, they felt, was at stake.

"You cannot hurt this institution more fatally, you cannot deal it a severer blow, you cannot bring upon it more fully the suspicions of just and honorable men than by enthroning coercion and intolerance," President Kilgo told the trustees. "Bury liberty here, and with it the college is buried."

† See Chapters XVII and XX.

Every member of the faculty advised the president privately that he would resign if Bassett was dismissed, and every member signed a public statement which declared:

"Money, students, friends are not for one moment to be weighed in the balance with tolerance, with fairness, and with freedom. . . . We urge you to say of Trinity College what Thomas Jefferson, the founder of American democracy, said of the institution which he established: 'This institution will be based upon the illimitable freedom of the human mind. For here we are not afraid to follow truth wherever it may lead, nor to tolerate error so long as reason is left free to combat it.' . . ."

Despite the tremendous pressure put upon the board by ecclesiastical, journalistic, and other interests throughout the state, it voted 18 to 7 not to dismiss Bassett. The decision represented one of the greatest victories for academic freedom ever won in the United States.

Far less enlightened was the attitude of the University of Florida authorities, who, after ousting President Sledd because he emphasized scholarship above mere numbers, discharged Professor Enoch M. Banks, a Georgian, in 1911 because of sentiments which he expressed relative to the Civil War.* His crime lay in his stated belief that in the war "the North was relatively in the right, while the South was relatively in the wrong," and his further declaration that Abraham Lincoln was a greater man than Jefferson

* *Independent*, February 9, 1911, "A Semi-Centennial View of Secession," E. M. Banks.

Davis. An element of humor was unintentionally injected into the article by Professor Banks when he pointed with pride to the "new spirit of liberality toward opposing views" in Dixie as "perhaps the greatest incipient triumph of the twentieth century South."

The outright dismissal of a professor for the expression of unorthodox opinions on questions of public importance is reprehensible enough, but when the penalty imposed is disguised, when it takes the form of a year's leave of absence without reappointment, the argument may plausibly be advanced that in such a case intellectual honesty has been entirely abandoned. Episodes of this kind rarely get publicity because the parties involved are usually wise enough to confuse the issues and the public learns only that so-and-so has been granted a year's leave of absence to travel in Europe. It is not explained that he is being given a polite dismissal because he has expressed opinions which have brought fire on his institution. A recent case (1928) which appears to belong in this class is that of Dr. Louis Wirth of the Department of Sociology in Tulane University. Dr. Wirth discussed companionate marriage and birth control before a small group in New Orleans. His remarks leaked to the newspapers and the Catholic demand for his resignation was so strong that while in Europe the following year on a fellowship previously granted, he was notified that he would not be reëmployed on his return.*

Other ejections of teachers from Southern institu-

* Dr. Wirth is now associate professor in the University of Chicago and last year was specially cited for the high quality of his instruction of undergraduates.

tions of higher learning might be mentioned, but this is unnecessary. It must be borne in mind, however, that such ejections have certainly been equally common elsewhere. In his *Story of Civil Liberty in the United States* Leon Whipple published a long list of these dismissals for the period from 1893 to 1914, and the number of cases in the North and West far exceeds the total for the South.

In more recent times, the story is the same. The American Civil Liberties Union points out in a pamphlet published in 1931 that more college professors were dismissed or disciplined because of their views in the ten years following the World War than in any other decade in our history. It lists the seven institutions where such things have occurred with greatest frequency, and not one is in the South. It also lists what it deems the eight most flagrant dismissals since 1925, and none of these occurred at a Southern college or university.

Shortly after the union's pamphlet appeared, however, there were two episodes of this kind which might have been included, if they had occurred somewhat earlier. One involved Dr. Carl C. Taylor, dean of the graduate school at North Carolina State College, and the other had to do with Dr. John Earle Uhler of Louisiana State University.

Dr. Taylor's position as dean at North Carolina State was suddenly abolished by the institution's board of trustees at the 1931 commencement, on the recommendation of President E. C. Brooks. Clarence H. Poe, one of the trustees who voted against the move, expressed the opinion that President Brooks had been motivated at least partially in his recommendation by Dr. Taylor's conspicuous activities on behalf of free speech and in the interest of other liberal causes. There had been friction between Taylor and Brooks over a considerable period when Taylor's deanship was abolished. Protests from over a hundred members of the graduating class that he was perhaps the most valuable man on the faculty were unavailing. His eleven years of service with the institution were abruptly terminated.

Dr. Uhler was ousted at Louisiana State following his publication of a novel, *Cane Juice*, which depicted the hypothetical experiences of a Roman Catholic student at that institution. The book fell into the hands of the Rt. Rev. Mgr. F. L. Gassler of St. Joseph's Catholic Church, Baton Rouge. It seemed to Monsignor Gassler that the book reflected upon the "unsullied reputation of our Creole maidens" and was a "monstrous slander of the purest womanhood to be found in the United States." He accordingly circularized prominent citizens of Louisiana and stirred up such a furor that the university's executive board obligingly dismissed Dr. Uhler without a hearing. Six months later he was reinstated, but he should never have been discharged in the first place.

Such an episode as this is disheartening to those who are seeking to build up traditions of academic liberty below Mason and Dixon's Line. Southern institutions of higher learning are sufficiently hampered by inadequate funds without being subjected to the added burden of interference from officious outsiders.

The financial situation is improving measurably,

however. There are still plenty of what Dr. Edwin A. Alderman was fond of calling "monohippic" colleges in the South, but at the same time there are more real universities than ever before. The University of Virginia, the University of North Carolina, and the University of Texas have developed graduate schools of sufficient calibre to meet the severe requirements of the Association of American Universities. It should be remembered, on the other hand, that whereas the South has three universities with sufficiently advanced graduate work and facilities for research to gain admittance to this organization, the North and West have twenty-four.

The University of Virginia, which was generally conceded for the first seventy-five years of its existence to be the leading Southern institution of higher learning, no longer occupies that position of preëminence. This is true despite the fact that it has made remarkable progress in various directions during the past quarter of a century. The failure of the University of Virginia to maintain its undisputed supremacy may be attributed to the extraordinary advances made by other institutions, rather than to any retrogression on its part. The University of Texas, for example, has become immensely wealthy, thanks to a steady stream of gold poured into its coffers by oil gushers. It has a far larger endowment than any other state university in the country and there are nearly twice as many books in its library as are to be found in any other library between Washington, D. C., and the Mexican border. The University of North Carolina has gone forward so rapidly in late years that Harold

J. Laski, the eminent English educator, said recently that it is regarded in Great Britain as one of the half dozen greatest universities in America.

When Dr. Alderman came to Charlottesville in 1904 as president of the University of Virginia, he found an atmosphere of conservatism enveloping that distinguished seat of learning. He set to work at once with a view to developing there a more adequate conception of the university's function as the capstone of Virginia's educational system and a more liberal and progressive outlook. When death overtook him in 1931, the spirit which informed the institution was more consonant with the ideals of its founder than that which had prevailed at the turn of the century. At the same time Dr. Alderman was successful in greatly increasing the enrollment, endowment, and physical equipment, and in building up the university as an outstanding center of research. Some were of the opinion, however, that he laid undue stress upon numerical and financial growth, and he himself declared in an address shortly before his death that educational processes would have to be more selective in the future than they had been in the past.

The manner in which the University of Virginia adheres to Jeffersonian concepts of individual liberty has frequently been noted by observers. When a student is matriculated there the president and faculty assume that he is capable of taking care of himself, and they refrain in so far as they can from interfering with his personal habits. Similarly, the administration of the celebrated honor system is left entirely to the undergraduates.

In addition to its emphasis upon individual freedom, the university stresses Jeffersonian principles of religious liberty. In the presidential campaign of 1928, when the South was engulfed in a wave of religious prejudice, the University of Virginia stood four-square for Governor Smith. Practically every member of the faculty was a Smith partisan, while the attitude of the student body is sufficiently evidenced by its action the day following the election. Religious Intolerance was burned in effigy on the "Lawn," and passers-by found Jefferson's statute shrouded in crepe, with a placard bearing this inscription:

TO THE MEMORY OF JEFFERSONIAN DEMOCRACY AND
RELIGIOUS FREEDOM
DIED IN VIRGINIA, NOVEMBER 6, 1928

While the principle of academic liberty has usually been upheld at the state university of the Old Dominion, the institution's record was besmirched at the height of the World War hysteria, when Professor Leon Whipple was unceremoniously ousted for making a pacifist speech. This is hardly to be wondered at, however, when one considers that the American Association of University Professors went on record officially during the war as advocating the dismissal of any teacher found guilty of such conduct. Harvard University was almost the only institution in the country which managed to maintain standards of complete academic liberty throughout the period of American participation in the world conflict.

Establishment of the Institute for Research in the Social Sciences and the Institute of Public Affairs is a significant development of the past few years at Charlottesville. The former, under the direction of Dr. Wilson Gee, has initiated various research projects of value, while the latter is the leading institute in the country devoting its attention wholly to domestic and Latin-American problems. The Institute of Public Affairs is held for a period of two weeks each summer, when speakers of national and international prominence present subjects of the most controversial nature in a commendable spirit of tolerance and freedom.

Other similar institutes are held in the South, notably at Rollins College, Florida, the University of Florida, Emory University, Louisiana State University, the University of Chattanooga, and the University of Georgia. The last-named institute was founded in 1927, the year the University of Virginia institute was established, and the admirable atmosphere in which it is conducted by Director R. P. Brooks is sufficiently evidenced by an address delivered at the 1929 session by Orville A. Park, Macon attorney and outstanding Southern liberal. Mr. Park said:

"Why will we allow the State's well-being and prosperity to be hampered by our outworn State governmental machinery . . . ? The answer may be expressed in four words—ignorance, inertia, self-complacency, selfishness. A large proportion of our people are too ignorant to know or to appreciate the conditions that exist. A still larger proportion are too lazy to put forth the exertion necessary to change them. Most Georgians have been taught to believe and still think that Georgia is the greatest State in the Union. . . . Our people have been inoculated with the virus of self-satisfaction. We have sung the song of Georgia's greatness, we have shouted from the housetops 'It is great to be a Georgian' until we not only believe it, but we shut our eyes to true conditions and refuse to believe anything else."

An Institute on Human Relations is held by the student body quadrennially at the University of North Carolina, at which distinguished speakers from America and Europe discuss war and peace, industrial and interracial relationships, and other pressing questions of the day. But the establishment of this institute is only one of numerous advances made at Chapel Hill during the past fifteen years.

It was under President Edward Kidder Graham, who took office in 1914, that the University of North Carolina began its phenomenal development in various directions. President Francis P. Venable had done valuable work in emphasizing the necessity of scholarship on the part of both the teaching staff and the student body, but it was Graham, his successor in the chair, who first was able to formulate a nicely articulated program for transmitting the university's dynamic influence to every corner of the state. To an extraordinary degree President Graham enjoyed the confidence of the faculty, the students, and the alumni, and his plans were well on the way to fruition when the influenza epidemic of 1918 carried him off.

He had managed by some miracle of necromancy to secure greatly increased appropriations from the legislature, and Dr. Harry W. Chase, who was chosen to succeed him, was even more fortunate in this regard. President Chase, a native of Massachusetts, proved to be an almost miraculously good selection for the presidency. He was not endowed with his predecessor's gifts of popular leadership, and at the time of his elevation he was scarcely known outside the university, but within a few years he had made a place for himself as one of the great educational executives of America. During his administration the University of North Carolina grew in physical resources, in social vision, and in scholarship, and became the most aggressively liberal of all the Southern institutions of higher learning.

One of the most extraordinary things about the educational *risorgimento* at Chapel Hill has been the productivity of the university's teaching staff in the field of the social sciences and the humanities. This fecundity is undoubtedly traceable in part to the establishment of the University Press and such nationally known journals as *Social Forces* and *Studies in Philology*.

At the same time, the remarkable advance of the State of North Carolina in many directions during the 1920's is attributable in no small degree to the liberal influence of forward-looking scholars at the university. An incomplete list of those who contributed powerfully to this movement would include Dr. E. C. Branson in rural social-economics, Dr. E. W. Knight in education, Dr. Howard W. Odum in sociology, Gerald W. Johnson in journalism, Addison Hibbard, Howard Mumford Jones, and Paul Green in literature and literary criticism, and Dr. Louis R. Wilson in promoting the development of adequate library facilities.

Unfortunately the state expended its funds with

undue rapidity during these years and became heavily involved financially. The consequence was that the university, along with all other agencies of the commonwealth, sustained drastic cuts in revenue. This not only necessitated serious curtailment in some of the most important phases of university activity but it also resulted in the loss of a number of the institution's ablest teachers. In addition, President Chase accepted a call to the University of Illinois, and the trustees were forced to look about for a helmsman who could pilot the school through the storm and stress of financial depression.

At this crisis in the life of the University of North Carolina, a member of its faculty was literally drafted for the presidency. Frank P. Graham, cousin of the late Edward Kidder Graham, sought by every possible means to discourage his selection to the post, but his qualifications were such that the trustees refused to heed his plea. His election was objectionable, it is true, to many operators of textile mills for the reason that in 1929 he had aligned himself uncompromisingly on the side of humanity and justice in the industrial disorders which shook the state, and with Dr. William L. Poteat had led in demanding that those striking for better wages and working conditions be given their constitutional rights. But if the mill operators were against him, all other important elements were enthusiastically for him. The manner in which he has discharged his duties has amply vindicated the judgment of the board in their selection. A man of winning personality and great intellectual force, of liberal viewpoint and uncommon capacity for handling men,

President Graham is triumphing over terrific obstacles in a manner which has elicited widespread admiration.

Another institution in the Old North State which is attracting the attention of the nation is Duke University, which changed its name from Trinity College in 1924 when J. B. Duke provided it with some $40,000,000. Duke University now has a physical plant worth in the neighborhood of $20,000,000, and its great new medical school and hospital were formally dedicated in the spring of 1931. Nothing can prevent this university from taking rank with the foremost in the land if, as it develops physically, it cherishes the ideals which impelled it in 1903, as a small church college, to stand inflexibly for fairness and freedom and justice in the face of furious attacks from demagogues and dervishes.

Duke retains its official connection with the Methodist church, but Vanderbilt University, which originally was affiliated with that denomination, was disowned by the Southern Methodist General Conference after that body had failed in its effort to tighten its grip on the institution with a view to making it more "Methodistic." This long drawn out and acrimonious controversy got under way a few years after the election of Dr. James H. Kirkland as chancellor of the university in 1893. Chancellor Kirkland was carrying on in the liberal tradition of Garland and McTyeire when Dr. E. E. Hoss, editor of the official organ of the church, began a series of attacks on his policies and practices. Dr. Hoss felt that the control of the church over Vanderbilt University should be absolute and that all the professors should be "zealous and active Methodists."

The agitation thus begun culminated in a demand on the part of the General Conference of the church that all trustees of the institution be elected by the conference and, in addition, that the bishops be given powers tantamount to a veto over the decisions of the trustees. This despite the apparently incontrovertible fact that Commodore Vanderbilt had had no intention of endowing a purely denominational university when he founded the institution in 1875, and the further fact that no such rigid control had been sought by the church in connection with any of its other boards or institutions. Chancellor Kirkland and the other university authorities naturally rebelled at this proposal and prepared for a finish fight.

In the early days of the controversy they enjoyed the assistance of three bishops in the Southern Methodist church, R. K. Hargrove, C. B. Galloway, and E. R. Hendrix, but before matters had reached a climax the first two were dead, and Bishop Hendrix was left without an ally in the episcopacy. He fought bravely on, however. When the issue was finally placed in the hands of the courts, the highest tribunal of Tennessee upheld the contentions of the university and overruled those of official Methodism. The decision, rendered in 1914, made it possible for Vanderbilt to go forward under Chancellor Kirkland instead of backward under the Methodist church. That denomination promptly severed all connection with the institution, and left the university at Nashville free to work out its own destiny. How successfully it has done so was apparent in 1925 when Vanderbilt celebrated its semi-centennial by opening a splendid $8,000,000 medical school.

It should be said, however, that while the Vanderbilt medical school is of the first importance, and while the academic faculty boasts some excellent names, notably in its English department, the university, on the whole, has not exhibited the social awareness that has been manifest at other Southern institution in recent years. Dr. Herman Clarence Nixon, an exceptionally liberal member of the Tulane University faculty, pointed this out not long ago when he wrote that Vanderbilt "has lost much of its status of academic leadership in a large part of the South through neglect of aggressive pioneering in the social sciences."

But if the university at Nashville is somewhat unprogressive in this respect, there is a small school farther to the westward which goes to the opposite extreme. Commonwealth College at Mena, Arkansas, is one of the most unusual educational institutions in America. Operated primarily for workers, it has scarcely any native Arkansans among its matriculates, but draws almost all its students from the industrial centers. The most modern and most extreme theories of economics, sociology, history, and other social sciences are studied there in a spirit of untrammeled freedom which is rare, if not unique, in a state which has placed Webster's Dictionary on its *index expurgatorius* and called down a murrain upon the *Encyclopædia Britannica*. Commonwealth College is not "accredited" in the commonly accepted meaning of that term, but it is recognized by such seats of learning as the University of Chicago and the University of Wisconsin. Not the least of its claims to fame is the fact that its faculty serves entirely without salary.

An equally bizarre institution, but one which would appear to be more in harmony with its environment, is Bryan Memorial University at Dayton, Tennessee, opened in 1930 to commemorate the services of William Jennings Bryan to the Fundamentalist cause. All officials and professors must proclaim their unshaken faith in the absolute infallibility of the Scriptures, and the school seeks in every way to perpetuate the antediluvian theological concepts for which the Commoner fought at the Scopes trial. Certainly it is eminently fitting that this institution should be located in Tennessee, the state whose legislature not only adopted an anti-evolution law by overwhelming majorities in 1925, but whose House of Representatives in 1931 voted down by more than four to one a bill repealing that law.

Nothing of importance in the field of scholarship could be expected to originate at Bryan Memorial University, with its background of bigotry and obscurantism, and no one anticipates that it will ever stand for anything but the inerrancy of the Old and New Testaments. The case is different, however, with such an ancient and historic college as William and Mary in Virginia. This oldest of Southern institutions of higher learning numbers among its alumni some of the greatest figures in American history, including three presidents of the United States and four signers of the Declaration of Independence. Yet in 1926 it offered an everlasting affront to these men, and particularly to its most distinguished son, the author of the Virginia Statute for Religious Freedom, by accepting a flag-pole from the Ku Klux Klan. One wonders what the master of Monticello would say if he could revisit his alma mater today and note this pole at the edge of the campus, with a bronze tablet upon its base setting forth its presentation by the Invisible Empire.

An incident of this sort is witnessed with dismay by intelligent Southerners, but it should be borne in mind that the other side of the picture shows such evidences of enlightenment in the former Confederacy as the admirable discussions conducted at the University of Georgia Institute of Public Affairs or the publication by Southern Methodist University of so excellent a journal as the *Southwest Review*.

Thus while the situation as it relates to liberalism in the field of the higher learning below the Potomac at the present time has its disheartening aspects, there are, on the other hand, grounds for optimism. And if various forward-looking colleges and universities have had to curtail or suspend certain activities of late because of the cutting off of appropriations during the business depression, it seems reasonable to assume that these appropriations will be restored with the return of prosperity. Those institutions which were proceeding along liberal lines when the depression began will then be able to resume their upward march.

It should be said in conclusion that many liberals

in the South, as in the North and the West, are beginning to entertain grave doubts as to the validity of the American theory of education. That theory has for many years been predicated upon the thesis that every boy and girl who is not actually of subnormal intelligence is entitled to attend high school and college at State expense. It is a system which calls for the herding together of scholars and dunces into what might almost be termed educational rolling mills, and for excessive standardization of methods and curricula and undue stifling of individuality. Lastly, it entails an annual wastage in the country as a whole of hundreds of thousands, if not millions, of dollars in futile efforts to educate persons who are incapable of profiting by the experience.

An increasingly large proportion of the most progressive schoolmen of today, not only in the South but elsewhere, is endeavoring to formulate a theory of education which will make a more convincing appeal to their pragmatical thinking. It seems to them that while every boy and girl may be entitled theoretically to attend high school and college at the public expense, in practice it is not only harmful to a considerable percentage of those who do so, but it is equally harmful to the institutions concerned. Educators and others who take this view of the matter believe, with Thomas Jefferson, that every young American should be given opportunities for primary schooling and that those who exhibit a reasonable degree of aptitude in the elementary grades should be provided with training in high school and college. But they are convinced that the educational process should be made more selective than it now is; that there should be a raising of standards in the secondary and higher institutions of learning, the setting up of a system calling for less regimentation and more opportunity for the development of individual capabilities and talents, and the placing of added stress upon scholarship among both students and teachers.

It should be emphasized that what has been said here is not in derogation of the men who laid the foundations of our present educational system, except to the extent that they failed to foresee the partial failure of that system. Their motives were of the highest, their sympathies were with the untrained masses, and they envisioned a greater democracy and a greater nation as a consequence of the universal education which they advocated. In so far as the all-important elementary schools are concerned, their program is as valid and as valuable today as they expected it to be. It is only in the field of secondary and higher education that a considerable number of liberals, both North and South, believe that the ideas of the founders need to be modified in the light of experience.

CHAPTER XIX

THE EMANCIPATION OF WOMAN

UNTIL comparatively recent times, woman's position in society was almost invariably subordinate to that of man. Under the Mosaic law, for example, she enjoyed scarcely any legal rights, and under the Roman law her situation at first was similar, although her disabilities were subsequently lightened and indeed virtually abolished by the Christian emperors. The early Christian fathers, on the other hand, seem to have looked upon the ladies with a decidedly jaundiced eye. St. Chrysostom is suspected of having expressed more than his own individual opinion when he pronounced woman "a necessary evil, a natural temptation, a desirable calamity, a domestic peril, a deadly fascination, and a painted ill," for one of his clerical compatriots was so ungallant as to describe her as "the door of hell."

With the advent of the Renaissance, however, woman's status underwent a marked improvement, and this improvement was manifest over a considerable period. Later there was a gradual decline in her position. In eighteenth-century England, for example, she sank to a level not greatly superior to that which she had occupied five hundred years earlier. The disesteem in which she was held is sufficiently evidenced by the attitude of the essayist Addison, who advised her to "content herself with her natural talents, play at cards, make tea and visits, talk to her dog often, and to her company but sometimes."

Prevailing theories as to masculine supremacy were sharply challenged by Mary Wollstonecraft in 1792 with the publication of her *Vindication of the Rights of Woman*, a plea for equality of educational opportunity. But it was to be many years before her plea was granted, either in England or America.

The ante-bellum South placed woman on a lofty pedestal, and Southern Chivalry worshipped at her feet. Southern gentlemen never wearied of hymning the glories of Southern womanhood. When, for example, a celebration of the one hundredth anniversary of the founding of Georgia was held at Athens in the early 1830's, numerous toasts were drunk, but the one which brought twenty rousing cheers, nearly twice the number accorded any of the others, was to "Woman!!! The center and circumference, diameter and periphery, sine, tangent and secant of all our affections!"

In the Old South there were no women's "rights," as these are known today. George W. Bagby, the Virginia writer, described the status of woman at the period in the following words: "To feed, to clothe, to teach, to guide, to comfort, to nurse, to provide for and to watch over a great household and keep its complex machinery in noiseless order—these were the woman's rights which she asserted, and there was no one to dispute; this was her mission, and none ever dared to question it."

Miss Ellen Glasgow comments in more acidulous vein in her novel *Virginia* upon the rôle occupied by Southern womanhood before the war. The heroine's education, Miss Glasgow wrote, was "founded on the simple theory that the less a girl knew about life, the better prepared she would be to contend with it," and was designed "to paralyze her reasoning faculties so completely that all danger of mental 'unsettling' or even movement was eliminated."

Such was the situation in Dixie under the beneficent régime of chivalry. So chivalrous, indeed, was the ante-bellum South that its women were granted scarcely any rights at all. Everywhere they were subjected to political, legal, educational, social, and economic restrictions. They took no part in governmental affairs, were without legal rights over their property or the guardianship of their children, were denied adequate educational facilities, and were excluded from business and the professions.

This is not to say, however, that the women of "before the war" were lacking in capabilities of a high order. For if they were not always learned in books, they often exhibited executive and administrative ability in the management of large households. It is quite likely, too, that those who did possess a measure of "book learning" were frequently reluctant to disclose the fact, lest they be accused of indulgence in intellectual exercises unbecoming a Southern gentlewoman.

When Frances Wright of Scotland came to America in 1820, the agitation for the emancipation of woman in this country began. Then about a decade later the anti-slavery movement got under way, and the two causes were in large measure joined. Many who objected to slavery also felt that the subordinate position of woman could never be justified on logical grounds. In 1840 the temperance movement was launched in earnest, and a third group of agitators sprang up, a group which included numbers of those who also were working against slavery and for woman's rights. Thus by the middle years of the century these three mutually coöperative crusades were well under way, each led by women of great determination.

Two of the principal reformers were the Grimké sisters of Charleston, South Carolina, who had left their native state in 1819 in protest against the slave system, and had become active anti-slavery workers in the North. Angelina Grimké's marvelous oratorical powers have been noted in an earlier chapter. The novel spectacle of a Southern gentlewoman speaking to immense throngs on political topics and swaying them with her eloquence did much to undermine the theory that the arena of public affairs should be reserved exclusively for men. The Grimkés were attacked in the North by the General Association of Congregational Ministers, which charged them with seeking to entice "women from their proper sphere and loosening the foundations of the family." This brought forth a vigorous defense of the sisters from John G. Whittier in his poem "The Pastoral Letter."

But while there was opposition throughout the country to the efforts of the feminists, that opposition was strongest in the Southland. There the twin institutions of chivalry and slavery combined to thwart the equal

rights movement at every turn. Miss Nell Battle Lewis
has pointed out in a discriminating series of articles
in the Raleigh *News and Observer** that slavery operated
in various ways to prevent the liberation of Southern
womanhood. Miss Lewis calls attention to the fact
that the close relationship between the feminist movement and the anti-slavery movement was severely
prejudicial to the cause of equal rights in the South.
At the same time, she says, the argument was advanced
that if the franchise were granted to women, Negro
women might get the vote and there would also be
danger of "social equality." She also advances the
contention that the very presence of the institution
of slavery "acted to dull the South's conception
of individual liberty as the greatest boon of all mankind and made the lack of such liberty in the case of
women seem less important and less deplorable than
it otherwise might have appeared."

When Harriet Martineau visited this country in the
middle thirties, she found only seven occupations open
to women, namely, teaching, needlework, keeping
boarders, working in cotton mills and in book bind-
eries, typesetting, and household service. These forms
of employment were available in the United States
as a whole to women of all classes, but the last four
on the list and perhaps others were not regarded as
suitable for women of the Southern aristocracy. These
gentlewomen conducted numerous private schools,
and in the late forties and the fifties they held positions
in the public schools, notably in North Carolina, where
Superintendent Calvin H. Wiley succeeded in procur-

* April 19 and 26, May 3, 10, 17, and 24, 1925.

ing for female teachers with certificates the highest salaries in the nation. In addition, women of the upper class sometimes wrote for the magazines or the newspapers, and occasionally there was a woman novelist, although Miss Martineau displayed no awareness of this fact. Publications which were especially hospitable to feminine contributors during the two decades immediately preceding the war include the *Southern Literary Messenger*, the Charleston *Literary Gazette*, and the Louisville *Courier*.

There were practically no facilities for the higher education of women at the opening of the nineteenth century, either in this country or in England. Even in Boston girls were barred from all public school grades above the primary, and they were not permitted to receive primary instruction except from April to October, a situation which obtained until 1825.

The Old South was unable to boast of a worker in the field of women's education to rank with Emma Willard or Mary Lyon in the North, but the educational facilities offered to women below the Potomac were not greatly inferior to those provided contemporaneously in other sections. Genuine collegiate work was not available to "females" anywhere in the United States until the founding of Vassar College in 1865. Most of the so-called institutions of higher learning for women in the pre-war era were seminaries offering courses in music, art, etiquette, and English literature, with an occasional excursion into French and the classics.

Outstanding among the earliest of these schools to be established in the Southern States was Salem Female Academy, founded by the Moravians at Salem, North Carolina, in 1802. Four years later the Rev. John Lyle, a Presbyterian divine, opened the first female seminary in what was then the West, at Paris, Kentucky. He was able to build up an enrollment of two hundred or more, but in 1809 or 1810 he closed the school permanently because certain of its officials objected to the public reading of the Bible there.

The need for better educational facilities for women was recognized in Mississippi earlier than in many of the other states. Elizabeth Female Academy was founded in 1818 at Washington, and twelve years later Mississippi College, a coeducational institution, was opened at Clinton. Through the efforts of Miss Sallie E. Reneau and Governor John J. McRae the state legislature voted the establishment of a State Female College in 1856, but as no endowment was provided, this gesture was rather futile. It is obvious, however, that the attitude of a substantial element in Mississippi toward woman's position in society was decidedly advanced for the period. When in 1839 Mississippi granted to married women the control over their own property, it was the first state in the Union to do so.

Alabama, too, displayed an awareness of the need for higher learning for women rarely found in the first quarter of the nineteenth century. As early as 1820 the Alabama legislature, in establishing the state university, provided for a branch which would offer "female education." Two years later the number of such branches was increased to three. Unfortunately this broadly comprehensive plan was never put into operation, probably owing to lack of adequate finances.

Duncan G. Campbell was the pioneer agitator for better educational facilities for women in Georgia. After his death, Daniel Chandler took up the cudgels, and it was largely through his efforts that the Georgia Female College at Macon was chartered by the State in 1836. This institution, now known as Wesleyan College, claims to have been the first college for women in the country to give the B. A. degree. The difficulties under which it labored in the early years of its existence may be at least partially envisioned in the answer given by "a gentleman of large means and liberal views" when asked to contribute to its support.

"No, I will not give you a dollar," this liberal gentleman declared. "All that a woman needs to know is how to read the New Testament, and to spin and weave clothing for her family."

A Vermonter named Zelotes C. Graves was the guiding spirit behind the establishment in 1850 of the Mary Sharp College at Winchester, Tennessee, originally known as the Tennessee and Alabama Female Institute. Graves sought to provide as thorough collegiate training for the women of Tennessee as was available to the men. He claimed that Mary Sharp was the first college for women in America to require both Latin and Greek for the B. A. degree, and the claim appears to have been well-founded if one excludes coeducational institutions from the category of "colleges for women." The educational work done by Graves in the ante-bellum South was genuinely significant, and it is unfortunate that his college fell upon evil days in the eighties and was forced to suspend operations not long afterward.

Almost simultaneously with the establishment of Mary Sharp College in Tennessee, Charles Lewis Cocke, who at nineteen years of age had expressed a fixed intention to devote his life to the cause of higher education for women, took charge of Hollins Female Institute near Roanoke, Virginia, the first chartered institution for girls in the Old Dominion, now Hollins College. The opening of this school in 1852 doubtless was in some measure the result of the agitation for better educational opportunities for women begun years before by Thomas Ritchie in the columns of the Richmond *Enquirer*.

While there were other colleges for women in the Old South, those which have been mentioned are perhaps the most important. But if there was an appreciable amount of sentiment below the Potomac for equal educational facilities for women, there was practically none for equal political rights. The activities of Susan B. Anthony, Elizabeth Cady Stanton and their fellow-workers in the North on behalf of the enfranchisement of their sex were frequently greeted with hoots and jeers and sometimes with insults and physical violence. It appears certain that these ladies would have been given an equally inhospitable reception if they had extended their operations to the slave states, for both of them were as strongly hostile to slavery as they were favorable to women's rights, and Miss Stanton had been active in the anti-slavery crusade.

After Appomattox the militant suffragettes of the North were indignant at the enfranchisement of the illiterate freedmen in the former Confederacy by a government which had steadfastly turned a deaf ear to their own pleas for the ballot. But there was still little or no interest on the part of Southern women in the vote, and several decades were to elapse before any such interest could be aroused.

Meanwhile the women of the South were manifesting no little concern for the progress of educational movements, whether designed for the exclusive benefit of their own sex or not. So marked had this interest become, in fact, by the early nineties, that the Rev. A. D. Mayo, a New Englander who spent twelve years in educational work in the Southern states after the war, declared that the greatest single educational force in the area was to be found in its womanhood.

As in the case of the men's colleges, however, too much emphasis was placed upon the number of institutions. Many were led to believe that because there were more women's colleges below the Potomac than were to be found above it, the facilities for educating Southern women were superior to those provided for Northern women. In the early eighties no fewer than 111 of the 142 "higher institutions for women" in the country were in the Southern and South Central states, and of 904 degrees conferred on women in 1882, a total of 684 were conferred in those states. It need hardly be said, however, that the type of training provided at such colleges as Vassar, Wellesley, and Smith was far superior to anything offered at the period in the South.

Men like Governor W. Y. Atkinson of Georgia and Charles D. McIver of North Carolina were active in their respective states on behalf of improved educational opportunities for women, while J. L. M. Curry was zealous in the cause throughout the South. Atkinson, as a member of the Georgia legislature, urged the establishment of the State Normal and Industrial College for Girls at Athens, and after he entered the governor's chair, appointed a board composed entirely of women for the school. McIver was the greatest advocate of improved education for women in North Carolina. One of his favorite sayings was: "When you educate a man you educate one person; when you educate a woman, you educate an entire family." McIver devoted most of his adult life to this crusade, and he was chiefly instrumental in founding the State Normal and Industrial College at Greensboro.

Walter Hines Page jolted many citizens of North Carolina and other Southern states out of the *laissez faire* state of mind which had characterized their attitude on this question with his address on "The Forgotten Man" at the Greensboro college in 1897.

"I have thus far spoken only of the forgotten man," Page declared on that occasion, "but what I have come to speak about is the forgotten woman. . . . Let any man whose mind is not hardened by some worn-out theory of politics or of ecclesiasticism go to the country in almost any part of the state and make a study of the life there, especially of the life of the women. He will see them thin and wrinkled in youth from ill prepared food, clad without warmth or grace, living in untidy houses, working from daylight till bedtime at the dull round of weary duties, and the slaves of men of equal slovenliness, the mothers of joyless

24

children—all uneducated, if not illiterate. Yet even
their condition were endurable if there were any hope,
but this type of woman is encrusted in a shell of dull
content with her lot."

In Mississippi the prolonged campaign of Miss
Sallie E. Reneau both before and after the Civil War
for the establishment of a state female college was unsuccessful, and Miss Reneau finally removed to Tennessee. Mrs. Annie C. Peyton then took charge of the
movement. Largely as a result of her efforts, extending
over a considerable period, the Mississippi Industrial
Institute and College, the first school of its kind in the
country, opened its doors in 1885 with nearly 350
students.

But if Mississippi was willing to make this concession
to its feminine population, it was by no means ready
to entertain new-fangled theories having to do with
"women's rights." President Richard W. Jones of the
State Industrial Institute and College made this plain
when he declared shortly after his inauguration:

"We are not teaching woman to demand the 'rights'
of men nor to invade the sphere of men. The conditions are supplied here for that high training of the
mind, of the sensibilities, of her æsthetic faculties, of
the moral and religious parts of her being which fits
her for the ways of modest usefulness, for works of true
benevolence, and which invests her with that true
womanly character and those beautiful Christian
graces that constitute her the charm of social life and
the queen of home."

By 1892 the state universities of Arkansas, Kentucky,
Texas, and Mississippi admitted women on the same

basis as men, but the movement for equal political rights was barely under way in the region. Long cherished ideas concerning Southern chivalry made the average male living below the Potomac and the Ohio instinctively hostile to the equal rights program. Evidence of the strong hold of the chivalric tradition upon the young men of the South in the elegant nineties may be seen in the flamboyant dedication of the University of Virginia annual for 1895:

TO

SOUTHERN WOMANHOOD,

EVER THE INSPIRATION AND SUPPORT OF SOUTHERN

CHIVALRY, THIS VOLUME IS DEDICATED

WITH PRIDE IN HER PATRIOTISM,

REVERENCE FOR HER PURITY,

LOVE FOR HER MATCHLESS TENDERNESS,

AND TRUST IN HER UNFADING TRUTH.

Such lofty sentiments were not entertained beyond the Mississippi, however, and four far Western states gave the ballot to the ladies before the turn of the century.

Below Mason and Dixon's Line suffragists not only had to contend with the widespread beatification of woman, but they found it necessary at the same time to combat powerful groups with selfish interests to serve. These included exploiters of women and children in industry and men with money invested in the liquor business, elements which feared that an aroused and enfranchised womanhood would quickly force them to the wall. But if the brewers and distillers sought to thwart the movement, workers for equal rights found a valuable ally in the Woman's Christian Temperance Union, an organization enjoying particular puissance in the former Confederacy.

By 1915, eleven states, all west of the Mississippi River, had granted full suffrage to women, while Illinois had conferred upon its feminine population the right to vote in presidential elections. Advocates of enfranchisement were able to point to the accomplishments of women voters in the West in securing the passage of much liberal legislation, including laws having to do with factory inspection and child labor, juvenile courts, institutions for delinquents, improved educational facilities, and so on.

The movement made such progress that Woodrow Wilson endorsed suffrage for women in principle in 1916, provided it was conferred upon them through action of the individual states, and Charles E. Hughes, his opponent in the presidential campaign of that year, placed the stamp of his approval upon the proposed Federal amendment. Two years later President Wilson urged the Congress to pass the suffrage amendment to the constitution as a measure "vital to the winning of the war," and this was done in June, 1919. The amendment was then submitted to the states for ratification.

The suffragist drive had gathered such momentum in the years immediately preceding that Arkansas and Texas had granted the ballot to their womenfolk on virtually the same terms as their menfolk before the amendment was submitted, while Tennessee had done likewise, in so far as presidential and municipal elections were concerned. Arkansas had led the way in

1917 by passing a law permitting women to participate in Democratic primaries on the same basis as
men, an enactment which was practically tantamount
to complete enfranchisement, since the Democratic
party is almost always overwhelmingly dominant in
that state. Texas adopted similar legislation the following year and then in 1919 Tennessee conferred the
ballot on women desiring to participate in presidential and municipal contests.

Shortly thereafter the Federal amendment was submitted to the states, and ratification began. One legislature after another fell into line, until thirty-five had
done so. Only one more was needed when the Tennessee assembly convened in 1920. Realizing the cru-
cial importance of capturing the Volunteer State, each
side marshaled all the forces at its command. Nationally known suffrage leaders joined in the fight at Nashville and urged the legislature to complete the political
emancipation of American womanhood by ratifying
the amendment. Leading opponents invoked the ancient chivalric shibboleths and proclaimed that the
supremacy of the white race would be jeopardized
and the pillars of the social edifice undermined if
women were given the ballot. After an epic struggle,
the Tennessee assembly approved the amendment by
a narrow margin, and the nineteenth amendment became a part of the organic law of the nation. The rock-
ribbed conservatism of much of the South is evidenced,
however, by the fact that the amendment was never
ratified by the legislatures of Virginia, the Carolinas,
Georgia, Florida, Mississippi, or Louisiana. This is of
course attributable in some measure to the opposition

of large numbers of prominent Southern women to the enfranchisement of their sex.

The result in Tennessee was due in part to strong journalistic support from Luke Lea's Nashville *Tennesseean*, George Fort Milton's Chattanooga *News* and other leading dailies. In the neighboring state of Kentucky, the Lexington *Herald*, owned and edited by Desha Breckinridge, supported the suffrage cause from the opening of the twentieth century, and partially offset the fulminations of "Marse Henry" Watterson's Louisville *Courier-Journal* against those whom he contemptuously termed "silly Sallies and crazy Janes." W. T. Anderson's Macon *Telegraph*, usually conspicuously liberal, was the only important paper in Georgia which fought the suffragists. In Mississippi the Jackson *Daily News*, edited by Frederick Sullens, was as vigorously favorable to the enfranchisement of women as the Macon *Telegraph* was opposed to it.

Pro-suffragist editors in the South enjoyed the assistance and coöperation of many remarkably able women in the fight for enfranchisement. Some of these women were at the same time staunch advocates of other important liberal causes. For example, Mrs. Madeline McDowell Breckenridge of Kentucky not only devoted a large part of her attention to furthering the suffragist movement, but her activities also extended into the fields of child labor and compulsory school attendance legislation and into public health and family welfare work. In Virginia Mrs. Lila Meade Valentine was a pioneer worker on behalf of better public welfare and public education, as well as an ardent advocate of votes for women, and she was ably

assisted in her feminist endeavors by Miss Mary Johnston, who sought in her novel *Hagar* to further the
emancipation of Southern womanhood, and who
worked indefatigably in various ways for the cause.
Other important suffragist leaders include Mrs. Min-
nie Fisher Cunningham of Texas, Mrs. Ella C. Chamberlain of Florida; Mrs. Elizabeth Lyle Saxon, Mrs.
Caroline E. Merrick, and Miss Kate M. Gordon of
Louisiana; Mrs. Mary Latimer McLendon of Georgia,
and Mrs. T. Palmer Jerman of North Carolina. Occasionally, too, an intrepid male stood up and fought
to give the opposite sex the ballot, braving the criticism and ridicule which was sure to be visited upon
any one who was conspicuous in the movement. Several journalists who did so have already been mentioned, but no list of the men who gave their time,
their money and their influence to the effort for enfranchisement would be complete without a reference
to Chief Justice Walter Clark of North Carolina. The
devotion of this eminent jurist to the suffragist cause
is all the more striking when it is recalled that he was
a Confederate veteran steeped in the traditions of the
Old South.

We have noted the activities of Southern women in
the educational field both in the ante-bellum and the
post-bellum eras. While their influence was especially
pronounced in the decades following the Civil War,
the valuable services of the women of the former Confederacy to education in the early years of the twentieth century should under no conditions be overlooked. Women were active in the long series of annual
Conferences for Southern Education which had their

inception at Capon Springs, West Virginia, in 1898. In addition they were almost wholly instrumental in the formation of School Improvement Leagues throughout the South. These organizations, which were designed to promote the common schools, originated in Virginia, largely through the efforts of Mrs. Beverley B. Munford of Richmond and other leaders in the Cooperative Education Association of Virginia. Mrs. Munford has been the ablest and most conspicuous advocate of better educational facilities for the women of the Old Dominion, and her influence on behalf of this and other liberal causes has extended far beyond the borders of that commonwealth.

Another woman who has been widely influential in the South is Dr. Orie Latham Hatcher, founder and executive head of the Southern Woman's Educational Alliance, an organization which is doing a pioneer work in providing vocational and educational training for Southern women, particularly in rural areas.

Many other women throughout the South have been prominent since 1900 in efforts looking toward the improvement of educational opportunities for their sex, particularly in the field of the higher learning. There is among them, however, a growing awareness that equality of opportunity does not necessarily imply absolute identity of courses and curricula. Now that they have won the right almost everywhere to the same grade of education as is enjoyed by members of the opposite sex, they are viewing the matter more objectively and are coming to a realization that the educational requirements of men and women are at times somewhat divergent. Yet the fact remains that while educational facilities have been tremendously broadened in the Southern states during the past three decades, those states are still the most laggard of all in providing collegiate instruction for women.

Virginia was the last state in the Union to provide such instruction. College doors were first thrown open to women by that commonwealth in 1918, when the College of William and Mary became coeducational. Two years later the University of Virginia amended its regulations sufficiently to permit women who are over twenty years of age and who have had two years of collegiate training to enter the graduate and professional schools and the department of education.

Although women were not made eligible for matriculation in the University of Georgia until 1918, several women's colleges had been operated by the State of Georgia for many years prior to that time. Consequently Georgia was well ahead of Virginia in providing educational facilities for its womanhood.

In this connection it is interesting to note that the University of Florida was the last state university in America to admit women. It did not do so until 1925, at which time it allowed them to enter subject to much severer requirements than were provided for male students. On the other hand, we should bear in mind that Florida has had a State College for Women since 1905.

One of the major interests of Southern women is in the work of women's clubs and similar organizations. Outstanding among club women below Mason and Dixon's Line may be mentioned Mrs. Percy V. Pennybacker of Austin, Texas, and Mrs. Samuel M. Inman of Atlanta, both of whom are known and respected over a wide area. During the past decade, however, and especially during the past five years, the typical women's clubs have given way in the South, as elsewhere, to societies, associations, or clubs of a more specialized and more selective nature. These include Business and Professional Women's Clubs, the various Leagues of Women Voters, study groups of one sort or another, alumnæ groups, and so on.

There are numerous ways in which the Southern woman can earn a livelihood, but the South is still reluctant to accept her in such professions as law or medicine. In fact she must be equipped in the highest degree with respect to both training and personality to succeed in either of these callings. Her chances are considerably better in such comparatively new occupations as social service, public health, or library work, or in home economics or business. In industry, as has been pointed out in an earlier chapter, she is frequently exploited.

It should be stated that present-day Southern women who seek careers are apt, like Southern men, to be a bit more alive to human values and a bit less willing to surrender completely to the pull of professional ambition at the expense of the amenities of life, than those who achieve careers in the North or West.

Members of the various Southern women's clubs and other related groups are often active in promoting such liberal causes as better international relationships, improved public health, more humane systems of penology, and a more balanced attitude toward labor. They are particularly zealous in the sphere of interracial endeavor, where the work of Mrs. Jessie Daniel Ames of Atlanta, Miss Louise Young of Scarritt College, Nashville, and Mrs. W. A. Newell of Greensboro is deserving of high praise.

In conclusion it may be said that the liberal leadership which the women of the former Confederacy are exhibiting today in a number of important fields is one of the most significant phenomena of the Southern scene. These women who are scarcely a generation removed from the chivalric era and who have emerged only recently from the penumbra of sanctity which previously enveloped them, are unquestionably among the most substantial liberalizing forces in the Southern states.

CHAPTER XX

LITERATURE AND JOURNALISM BELOW
THE POTOMAC

DESPITE excursions into realism on the part of such writers as George W. Cable and Joel Chandler Harris, Southern fiction at the opening of the twentieth century was for the most part mellow and moon-drenched. And where it was not compounded wholly of handsome colonels and their raven-haired ladies, of shuffling "darkies" and despised "poor white trash," it was often strongly partisan in its attitude toward the North. The romantic novels and stories of Thomas Nelson Page are typical of the former genre, while the writings of Thomas Dixon, Jr., exhibit all the bellicosity and animus of the latter.

But if Page's glamorous and delicately wrought tales of the Old South are properly subject to criticism on the score that they present only one side of the ante-bellum canvas, the works of Dixon are sadly lacking in literary distinction and are definitely pernicious as well. Dixon had been a sensational politician, preacher, and lecturer before he made his début as a sensational novelist in 1902 with the publication of *The Leopard's Spots*. This book, which sought to foment discord and strife between the North and the South, was followed by such works as *The Clansman* and *The*

Traitor, novels conceived in a similar spirit of venom and prejudice. Over and above the harmful effect which these widely read works had on intersectional relationships was the manner in which they seriously disturbed the growing feeling of cordiality between the whites and the blacks by inculcating the doctrine that the solution of the Negro problem was to be found in the extermination of the Negroes.

Yet Dixon's works were greatly admired in the former Confederacy. Among their staunchest partisans was Miss Mildred Lewis Rutherford of Georgia, who likewise esteemed "Parson" Weems as a leading Southern historian. Miss Rutherford devoted nearly seven pages of panegyric to Dixon's writings in her *The South in History and Literature*, published in 1906. She also took occasion in this book to extol slavery as a "God-given right," and to declare that the Negro had been "better off physically and morally under the institution of slavery" than he was after forty years of freedom.

Far different was the point of view exhibited by Professor W. M. Baskervill of Vanderbilt University shortly before his untimely death at the turn of the century, when he wrote concerning the considerations which should govern the attitude of those undertaking to speak authoritatively on the subject of Southern literature and Southern civilization:

"Truth demands that the complete picture shall be given, though silly scribbler or narrow bigot may accuse the author of trying to cater to Northern sentiment. Every now and then some Southern writer is subjected to this unmanly and ignoble insult, though much less frequently than formerly. Mr. Maurice Thompson's poem and Mr. Henry Watterson's speech on 'Lincoln,' Mr. James Lane Allen's lecture on 'The South in Fiction,' and Mr. W. P. Trent's 'Life of William Gilmore Simms' seem to produce a mild form of rabies in certain quarters. . . . Shutting one's eyes to facts removes them neither from life nor from history."

Something of the liberalism which informed the literary criticism of Baskervill is present in the *Reminiscences of the Civil War* which General John B. Gordon, the "Chevalier Bayard of the Confederate Army," published at that period. The most noteworthy feature of the volume is its complete lack of partisanship and rancor, its tolerance toward the Northern people and the Northern viewpoint.

William Garrott Brown's *The Lower South in American History*, which appeared almost simultaneously, is another example of the revival of the critical spirit below the Potomac. A scholarly book, written in an excellent literary style, it makes no concessions to Southern prejudices, and treats the Southern scene with candor and realism. Brown soon came to be regarded as perhaps the most promising historical writer in Dixie. In his death at the age of forty-five years his native section suffered a serious loss.

But if the historical writings of Brown and the literary criticism of Baskervill were liberalizing forces below the Potomac as the century opened, the novels of Miss Ellen Glasgow were also important factors in the South's literary advance. Miss Glasgow had revolted in her first book from the genteel tradition, a product

of the Puritan conscience which had found a congenial
soil in the South. She was the first Southern novelist
to write of the South as a part of the civilized world
rather than as a lost province. As she herself has remarked, she has written not of Southern nature but
of human nature. The first to unite the Southern scene
with a cosmopolitan point of view, she is a liberal in
the sense that she has escaped from local prejudices
and conditions to universal problems.

But while her interests are as wide as humanity itself, and while she is an artist rather than a reformer,
the general effect of Miss Glasgow's nineteen novels
upon Southern habits of mind has been liberalizing
in the highest degree. She has shown herself to be
completely independent of many of the inhibitions
which formerly encumbered and embarrassed writers
of fiction in the South. She did not hesitate, for example, to draw her heroes from among the "poor
whites," an element which had customarily appeared
in the lowly rôle of hangers-on or flunkeys to the
aristocracy. She revealed the absurdity of the notion
that women are fragile and ethereal beings fit only
for the adoration of chivalrous males. She turned the
keen edge of her wit against many a hollow pretense
and empty sham and withered it under a barrage of
scintillating epigrams. She paraphrased Bismarck by
calling for additional "blood and irony," "blood"
signifying courage and "irony" a sense of humor which
would enable human beings to laugh at themselves
on all proper occasions. In her three latest novels she
has revealed an increasingly critical point of view.

A liberal of a rather different type is James Branch

Cabell, also of Richmond. Whereas Miss Glasgow concerns herself to a considerable degree with questions of large social significance, Mr. Cabell troubles himself scarcely at all with such matters. Aloof in his ivory tower, this scrupulously conscientious artist and master ironist views the passing scene with supreme detachment, content to "write perfectly of beautiful happenings" and to let fall now and then a sardonic comment upon the inanities and puerilities of that "ape reft of his tail and grown rusty at climbing" who now amuses, now dismays him.

"As I grow older," he writes in his most recent book, "I find I am more than usual calm . . . as to all questions of large social import. I burn with generous indignation over the world's pigheadedness and injustice at no time whatever. I do not expect any one to be intelligent or large-hearted. . . ."

But if Mr. Cabell is no crusader, if no iron of righteous indignation has entered into his soul, he has done much to popularize the critical viewpoint in Southern life and letters. An æsthetic and intellectual liberal, his saturnine observations upon the state of civilization below the Potomac have been a civilizing force in the region. He has turned his barbed and polished shafts against the chivalric tradition of the Old South and the pruderies and imbecilities of the New South with devastating effect.

Mr. Cabell and Miss Glasgow were the only Southern writers of fiction who made significant contributions to liberalism from the death of Joel Chandler Harris in 1908 until the early 1920's, if we except Miss Mary Johnston, whose *Hagar* is a ringing appeal for women's rights, and Mrs. Corra Harris, some of whose work is in the realistic and iconoclastic tradition. George W. Cable and Charles Egbert Craddock had done their most important work long before, and their writings during these years were comparatively inconsequential.

But at the opening of the century's third decade, when Southern letters were at a low ebb, the South felt the revivifying force of the liberal movement which followed the World War. Its effects were reflected in the literatures of both America and England, and even in that of Russia. It was impossible, therefore, for the South to remain untouched, and one may assume that the literary burgeoning which occurred below the Potomac in the post-war era is attributable in large measure to the powerful currents which were then sweeping through the world.

The publication of Mr. Cabell's *Jurgen* and the establishment of the *Reviewer* were significant events indicative of the new tendency in Southern literature, while the appearance of H. L. Mencken's celebrated polemic, *The Sahara of the Bozart*, added impetus to the movement.

The *Reviewer* was founded in 1921 by Emily Clark and Hunter Stagg, two impecunious Richmonders who embarked upon the quixotic and apparently hopeless task despite the croakings of multitudinous Cassandras that the project would be a dismal failure. But so far from being a failure, it was an extraordinary success. This was due as much to the fact that the *Reviewer* represented a serious effort on the part of Southerners to contribute something of value to the national letters as to the intrinsic merit of its contents. Observers were soon expressing astonishment that a periodical of this type was possible in the Southern states. True, the *Sewanee Review*, the *South Atlantic Quarterly*, the *Double Dealer* and the *Texas Review* were being published during these years, but none of them was attracting much attention nationally. The appearance of the *Reviewer* was the occasion for much favorable comment in the North.

This little magazine was operated on such a miraculously small budget that it was unable to pay anything to contributors, remuneration, according to an editorial announcement, being "in fame, not specie." Yet, astonishingly enough, Miss Clark found it possible to obtain contributions from many of the foremost literary figures in America. Mr. Mencken was generous in his commendation and assistance, while Carl Van Vechten, Ernest Boyd, Joseph Hergesheimer, Hugh Walpole, Gertrude Stein, and other nationally known writers helped to promote the fortunes of the magazine in various ways. Mr. Cabell and Miss Glasgow were at all times glad to give time and encouragement to the enterprise, which enjoyed its greatest prosperity under the managing editorship of Russell B. De Vine.

But even more significant than Miss Clark's ability to obtain manuscripts or counsel from authors whose reputations were already established is the fact that she was able to introduce the work of various talented writers who were then unknown, but who were shortly to achieve national fame. This latter group included Mrs. Julia Peterkin, Miss Frances Newman, Gerald

W. Johnson, and DuBose Heyward. To mention these names is to state that during its brief existence, the *Reviewer* was a liberalizing force of unusual significance, and that it carved for itself an important niche in the literary history of the South.

Its first issue contained a review of Mr. Mencken's *Sahara of the Bozart*, a blistering essay on the decay of Southern civilization. This roweling broadside infuriated many of the natives and caused them to describe its author with considerable variety and picturesqueness as a polecat, a cockroach, a hyena, and a jackass, but it set others to wondering whether, after all, there was not a good deal of truth in what he had to say. The ultimate effect upon Southern attitudes was distinctly salutary. Authors and journalists below the Mason and Dixon Line began taking a more forthright and intelligent view of Southern problems and *mores*, a tendency traceable in part to the action of the Gentleman With the Meat-Ax in forcing upon them an awareness of the fact that all was not well in Dixie.

For a decade or two prior to 1920 the bulk of the writing done south of the Potomac and the Ohio had been the work of those "right-minded authors" whom Anatole France has described as "authors without any minds." Most of these littérateurs were lacking in both courage and capacity, and they concerned themselves with ephemera rather than with fundamentals. But, as already set forth, the impact of post-war liberalism upon American literary attitudes had its inevitable effect in the South, and an extraordinary revival of polite letters began in that region almost at once. Not only so, but this movement has acquired additional momentum with each passing year, until the South is now able to point to as large a body of intelligently critical writing as any other section of equal population.

One of the fields in which the new spirit is most apparent is in the South's literary treatment of the Negro. Whereas in earlier fiction the blackamoor was customarily given a subordinate and secondary place, and was made to bathe in the reflected glory of his "white folks," this point of view is now almost wholly outmoded. Southern novelists whose work is done in the new mood treat the Negro as a human being in his own right.

Mrs. Julia Peterkin, for example, has written with tenderness and beauty in a series of novels of the lives of Southern blacks, and DuBose Heyward whose *Porgy* is an unforgettable study of a poor Negro cripple, also has helped to popularize this point of view. Paul Green has given us a number of plays in which he has pictured the struggles of the rural Negroes of North Carolina with stirring power. His *In Abraham's Bosom*, like Mrs. Peterkin's *Scarlet Sister Mary*, was awarded a Pulitzer prize. Howard W. Odum's *Rainbow 'Round My Shoulder* sets forth with fidelity and craftsmanship the inner workings of Negro psychology, while T. S. Stribling's *Birthright* is a courageous and competent study of the educated Negro's position in the South. George Madden Martin and Roark Bradford also have made important contributions to the interpretation of the black race.

In their assaults upon the genteel tradition Mr.

Cabell and Miss Glasgow have been aided substantially by Isa Glenn, whose *Southern Charm* proclaims Southern womanhood's emancipation from charm, that elusive feminine quality without which the entire chivalric ritual falls to the ground. Stark Young, despite his deep nostalgia for older forms of culture, is an intellectual liberal, a fact made manifest in his *River House*. Fielding Burke's *Call Home the Heart* is a boldly conceived and poignantly written story of the unsuccessful struggles of a mountain woman to find happiness in a mill village. Although it has faults, it is a work of unusual social significance. Other contemporary writers of fiction below the Potomac whose work is in the liberal tradition are Elizabeth Madox Roberts, Mary and Stanley Chapman, William Faulkner, Evelyn Scott, John Peale Bishop, Caroline Gordon, Thomas Wolfe, Jonathan Daniels, Erskine Caldwell, and Roy Flannagan. The critical essays of Sara Haardt also are noteworthy.

The *Fugitive* group of poets centering in Nashville and taking its name from the small magazine which it published for some years, and the South Carolina Poetry Society, led by DuBose Heyward, have been important factors in raising Southern poetry from the doldrums into which it had lapsed. The Nashville group was responsible, it is true, for the publication of the recent symposium *I'll Take My Stand*, a volume which celebrates the virtues of agrarianism as opposed to industrialism and inculcates a rather reactionary social philosophy. But if one may dissent from many of the opinions expressed in that work, one may at least be grateful for the emphasis which it places upon the need for an adjustment in our educational system and for the warning which it sounds against the dangers of excessive commercialization. Important contributors to the book who also were leaders in the *Fugitive* group are John Crowe Ransom, Donald Davidson, and Allen Tate. In addition to the substantial services which they rendered in helping to bring on the revival of poetry in the South, Messrs. Davidson and Tate have done valuable work in the field of literary criticism, and the latter has published several notable biographies of Southern leaders of the Civil War period.

The late Dr. C. Alphonso Smith issued a plea in 1920 for the building up of more adequate critical standards in the former Confederacy. "There must be developed in the South a finer and more standardized critical sense," he wrote. "Criticism, ceasing to be provincial, must become balanced, just, liberal and unafraid. Southern writers ask no critical favors and should receive none."

That appeal was accorded a generous response. It is doubtful, indeed, if in late years any other section has produced a more brilliant coterie of critics of literature and life than Burton Rascoe, Joseph Wood Krutch, Laurence Stallings, Gerald W. Johnson, Herschel Brickell, and the late Frances Newman. At the same time Stark Young has achieved a place in the front rank of American commentators on the drama, and Irita Van Doren, as literary editor of *The Nation* and the New York *Herald Tribune*, also has been an important liberal influence. While it is true that almost all of those in the foregoing list are now living in the North—the only portion of the country, apparently, where they are able to obtain rewards commensurate with their abilities—the fact remains that they were born in the South and that most of them received their training and education there.

Another Southerner who has made an important contribution to the revival of the critical spirit below the Potomac is Dr. John D. Wade, whose life of A. B. Longstreet created a sensation upon its appearance in 1924. Because Dr. Wade was fearless enough to tell the truth about Longstreet and the civilization of which Longstreet was a part, he was denounced by a goodly number of professional Southerners. Not long afterward Dr. Edwin Mims published *The Advancing South*, in which he set forth in an effective way the progress of various liberal movements during the first quarter of the twentieth century. As Dr. Mims is a "middle-of-the road" liberal, and his book exemplifies that attitude, he was the recipient of metaphorical brickbats from persons of more advanced views as well as from ultra-conservatives. Still another Southerner whose writings have contributed to the revival of liberalism in the region is Dr. Broadus Mitchell. His work has been done largely in the field of industrial relations, where in books and magazine articles he has effectually exposed the tergiversations of grasping employers. The writings of Robert W. Winston also are deserving of especial mention as being imbued with a liberal spirit.

In the domain of historical scholarship the South has produced a respectable body of sound and unbiased writing, especially in late years. Whereas un-

392   LIBERALISM IN THE SOUTH

discriminating local patriotism was dominant below
the Potomac, as elsewhere, until comparatively recent
times, a fact which had its inevitable effect upon the
work of most Southern historians, this condition no
longer exists to any considerable extent.

Reference has been made to the untimely death
some two decades ago of William Garrott Brown,
whose scholarship and courage were of a high order.
At about the same time several Southern pupils of
Professor William A. Dunning at Columbia University
executed studies of the reconstruction period which
practically revolutionized prevailing theories relative
to the ten-year period following Appomattox. Included in this list were books dealing with reconstruction in North Carolina, Alabama, and Texas by Drs.
J. G. deRoulhac Hamilton, Walter L. Fleming and
Charles W. Ramsdell, respectively, men who also
have done other work of an historical character which
has added dignity to the South's standing in this field.

Dr. Ulrich B. Phillips is a Southern historian who
combines brilliant scholarship with an excellent style,
and whose judgments as to American Negro slavery
and plantation life in the Old South are accepted
everywhere as authoritative. Dr. William E. Dodd is
a man of liberal outlook who unites literary ability
with facility in research. Dr. Thomas J. Wertenbaker
has done work of the first importance in a series of
books on colonial Virginia. The late Dr. John Spencer
Bassett did much to further our knowledge of the history of his native North Carolina, and as secretary
of the American Historical Association for nearly a
decade was a leading force in the promotion of schol-

arship in this country. The late Dr. John H. Latané made a distinct contribution to our knowledge of international relations. Dr. Dumas Malone, who is directing the preparation of the *Dictionary of American Biography* in a manner which has been widely acclaimed, is publishing in this national work of reference a quantity of material contributed by Southerners, and is himself the author of a life of Thomas Cooper which was well received by the critics.

Unfortunately each of the men listed in the foregoing paragraph has found it desirable for one reason or another to leave the South. Among those of recognized distinction who still remain may be mentioned Dr. William K. Boyd and Professor R. D. W. Connor, authorities on the history of North Carolina and the South as a whole; Dr. H. J. Eckenrode, who has produced several excellent works in the field of Virginia history and in biography; and Dr. E. C. Barker, widely known for his studies in the history of the Southwest.

Many of these historians have contributed significant papers to the various Southern periodicals, a number of which, in addition to the *Reviewer*, have been established since the turn of the century.

First of these in point of time is the *South Atlantic Quarterly*, founded at Trinity College in 1902 with John Spencer Bassett as editor. While the influence of this journal has not been great in recent years, its contents have generally been decidedly liberal in tone. And if its most liberal period was during the three years of Bassett's editorship, the magazine's policies did not change appreciably under Professors Edwin Mims and W. H. Glasson, who took charge after Bassett's resignation. Upon the occasion of the *South Atlantic's* tenth anniversary, *The Nation* commented as follows:

"It has kept free from the narrower sectionalism, its columns being open to writers from all parts of the country, and it is today one of the few journals in which vital subjects can be treated seriously and without some yielding to the popular clamor and superficial interest."

The circulation of the *South Atlantic Quarterly* has now shrunk to a few hundred, and while it has manifested unusual openmindedness on the Negro question of late and has published several articles by prominent members of the black race, its contents have not been notable in other respects.

The *Texas Review,* founded at the University of Texas in 1915 with Stark Young as editor, was a commendable effort. Nine years later it was moved to Southern Methodist University, and its name was changed to the *Southwest Review.* That periodical has appeared under the direction of Drs. Jay B. Hubbell, John H. McGinnis and others, and has been influential in shaping opinion in its portion of the South. Its tone has been admirably progressive and forward-looking, and it has published important articles of a critical nature on matters relating to the Southwest, a field in which it specializes. When the moribund *Reviewer* became too much of a burden to the group at Chapel Hill which took it over after it had run its course in Richmond, the *Southwest Review* gave it a decent burial by absorbing it in 1926.

That was also the year in which the *Double Dealer*

expired, after struggling along without adequate support from the Southern public from the time of its establishment in New Orleans in 1921. The *Double
Dealer* was devoted almost exclusively to fiction and
poetry and essays on subjects of a literary nature. Its
liberal purposes and policies are sufficiently indicated
in an editorial in an early issue, calling for less sentimentality and more virility and vitality in Southern
literature. Among the guiding spirits behind the
magazine were Basil Thompson, John McClure, and
Julius Weis Friend.

Establishment at the University of North Carolina
of the *Journal of Social Forces*, which various authorities have pronounced the foremost sociological journal in the country, was a forward step of the greatest
importance during these years. Questions deeply affecting the Southern states have been considered with
the utmost freedom in its pages, thanks to the competent editorial direction supplied by Dr. Howard W.
Odum, who was responsible for founding the magazine in 1922, and who has been in charge of it since
that time. During the first few years of its existence
Social Forces was attacked in scathing fashion by various elements. These assaults proceeded mainly from
clergymen and textile magnates who were outraged
at the frankness with which it discussed questions
having to do with religion and industry. *Social Forces*
was termed atheistic, socialistic, and communistic, and
literature denouncing it as a public menace was widely
circulated. The magazine managed to survive these
onslaughts without undue difficulty, however.

The most significant periodical of a general nature

to make its appearance below the Potomac since the Civil War is the *Virginia Quarterly Review,* published at the University of Virginia. The *Sewanee Review* under Trent and the *South Atlantic Quarterly* under Bassett were more militantly liberal, particularly when one takes into consideration the period in which they were published, but neither of these journals has enjoyed a list of contributors at any time since its establishment comparable to that of the *Virginia Quarterly.* Combining a balanced liberalism with a high literary standard, this magazine is in a class by itself among publications of its type in the Southern states. To President Edwin A. Alderman goes a large share of the credit for its establishment in 1925, and to Dr. James Southall Wilson, the capable and discerning first editor, may be attributed much of its general excellence. Since Dr. Wilson's relinquishment of the editorial reins, his place has been ably filled by Stringfellow Barr.

It goes without saying that the presence in the South of the various periodicals mentioned in the foregoing paragraphs has aided in bringing on the Southern literary revival. This revival also has been furthered by the encouragement offered to writers by the Duke University Press, the University of North Carolina Press, and the Southwest Press at Dallas. Each of these presses has been scholarly and unafraid, and each has specialized in the publication of books dealing with themes which are peculiarly Southern.

So much for the major factors which have influenced the building up of a more liberal literature below Mason and Dixon's Line since 1900. The movement made slow progress and found its inspiration in the work of a very few writers until the twenties, when there was a spurt forward as the number of liberals doubled and trebled within a brief period. But having accomplished the demolition of sentimentality during the twenties, liberal thinkers in the thirties are turning away from the old battlefields. Whereas Southern liberalism was formerly largely destructive in character, a substantial element is now changing front and is endeavoring by the erection of a finer and a better culture upon the foundations of the Southern past to avoid the complete obliteration of that past.

But if the former Confederacy is able to point to extraordinary progress since 1900 in the field of literary liberalism, its advance in the realm of journalistic liberalism has been equally remarkable. At the close of the nineteenth century the tone of the average Southern newspaper was narrowly provincial and egregiously partisan. And while there were exceptions to this generalization, some of which have been noted in an earlier chapter, it is none the less true that the Southern press as a whole was far less independent than it now is. This condition is in large measure attributable to the fact that the passions and prejudices engendered by the Civil War had not entirely cooled.

Politics was easily the chief interest of the editors of that era, but such a phenomenon as a paper which was politically untrammeled was so rare in the majority of Southern states as to be almost non-existent. Practically the entire press was so violently and virulently Democratic that the Republican party got little except abuse, both in the editorial and the news columns. There was also much denunciation of the North, and any Northerner who presumed to speak in critical fashion of the South was in danger of being pilloried as "an object of distaste to all decent people" and a "blue-abdomened miscreant"— phrases applied by a Jackson, Mississippi, newspaper to an outlander who was so thoughtless as to visit Mississippi in the early 1900's after expressing himself in an unfavorable manner concerning certain aspects of Southern civilization. In addition to the strong sectional bias exhibited by a large percentage of editors in the region, few of them showed any disposition to tackle thorny problems of large social significance, such as the relationship between capital and labor, the disgracefully long hours and low wages in important Southern industries and other cognate questions.

But if this was the prevailing attitude of newspapers below the Potomac and the Ohio at the opening of the twentieth century, a gradual change has made itself manifest during the succeeding years. Slowly but surely Southern journalists have been shaking themselves free of the inhibitions and tabus which formerly shackled them, until today the press of the South equals, if indeed it does not surpass, that of any other section of the United States in forthrightness and in liberalism. This fact is unknown to most persons living outside of Dixie, for Southern newspapers do not circulate in the North or the West to any appreciable extent, but it must be borne in mind by every student of the Southern scene. Such manifestations of intolerance and stupidity as the revival of the Ku Klux Klan and the launching of the anti-evolution movement have drawn the fire of many editorial sharpshooters, while newspapers have frequently led in efforts to secure better conditions for workingmen, improved educational facilities, more cordial relationships between the races, and better treatment for Negroes.

Consider, for example, the character of public service rendered by such a daily as the Montgomery *Advertiser*, one of the oldest and most influential journals in the Southern states. Founded more than a hundred years ago, the *Advertiser* was an organ of the Jacksonian Democracy. After the Civil War, with Major W. W. Screws as its editor, the paper sought to reconcile the differences between the sections and to put an end to bitterness and dissension. At the present time under the ownership of Frank P. Glass and the editorial direction of Grover C. Hall, it is a thorn in the side of the politico-ecclesiastics and the KuKluxers, the Heflinites and the Fundamentalists. While it has been unable to purge the Alabama statute books of the grotesque enactment which bans all forms of liquid refreshment which look or smell like beer and all bottles having any resemblance to a beer bottle or a whisky flask, it has many substantial accomplishments to its credit. Its brilliant editor was awarded the Pulitzer prize for his devastating attacks on the Klan. Mr. Hall played a large part, too, in bringing about the defeat of Senator Heflin, and he was instrumental in securing the nomination and election of Governor Miller, who is now in office and whose victory put an end to the Klan's power in Alabama. He assailed a ruling of the Alabama Court of Appeals that the dying testimony of an atheist was not admissible in an Alabama court, and that tribunal reversed itself. It is undoubtedly due in some measure to his influence that Montgomery is as yet unconvinced that prohibition is an experiment noble in motive.

While the conspicuous success of the *Advertiser* may be attributed in part to the policy of its owner, who is wise enough to give his editor free rein, Mr. Glass was not the publisher of the paper at the time Mr. Hall made the fight on the Klan which won the Pulitzer prize. He had relinquished his interest temporarily to Victor H. Hanson, also publisher of the Birmingham *News* and Birmingham *Age-Herald*. These two papers coöperated with the Montgomery *Advertiser* in its campaign against the hooded order, and like all the other dailies in the state, they made war on William Jennings Bryan and his anti-Darwinian disciples.

Another Southern newspaper honored by the Pulitzer committee for its attacks on the sheeted band of self-styled hundred per cent Americans was the Memphis *Commercial-Appeal*, edited by the late C. P. J. Mooney—who, however, was a blown-in-the-bottle Fundamentalist—while the Columbus, Georgia, *Enquirer-Sun* conducted a similar campaign under Julian Harris which likewise earned a Pulitzer award. The prize did not go to Mr. Harris solely because of his anti-Klan crusade, however. His gallant onslaughts against legislation outlawing the evolutionary hypothesis and his uncompromising fight for justice for the Negro also were taken into consideration.

Mr. Harris and his talented wife, Julia Collier Harris, took charge of the *Enquirer-Sun* in 1923. The Klan was already a tremendous political force in Georgia and throughout the United States, and was gaining daily in membership and influence. The fact did not deter the Harrises. They opened up on the organization at once and kept up their bombardment despite the loss of a large percentage of their subscribers and ugly threats of physical violence. With the aid of the New York *World* they exposed Governor Clifford Walker's membership in the order. When the Rev. Caleb Ridley, Atlanta cleric and Chief Kludd of the Klan, came to Columbus and partook too freely of the vine, the *Enquirer-Sun* chronicled the fact for the delectation of its readers. When Governor Walker tried to get himself elected chancellor of the University of Georgia, the paper helped to thwart the plan.

The story of the *Enquirer-Sun* under Julian Harris is one of the most inspiring in American journalism. Here was a man who valued principle above pelf, who scorned to remain silent in the face of iniquity. Practically every other paper in Georgia was cowering before the Klan when the Harrises launched their offensive but they carried on, heedless of the consequences. Circulation and advertising declined alarmingly, but the *Enquirer-Sun* was undaunted. In the end the paper went to the wall, but not until it had earned the admiration of self-respecting and honest men both in Georgia and elsewhere.

The published statement has been made, however,

that this journal was the only one in Georgia to attack the Klan over a period of three years. This is far from true. The Macon *Telegraph* assailed the organization from the moment of its inception. Years before Julian Harris acquired the paper at Columbus, the *Telegraph* was pouring hot shot into the Invisible Empire. Not only so, but it dealt savagely with the Supreme Kingdom, exposed the racketeering methods which were being used by the sponsors of that sainted enterprise, and practically destroyed it. Then when the Black Shirts appeared on the horizon Publisher W. T. Anderson and his able associate and managing editor, Mark Ethridge, loosed a ferocious assault which put these panderers to race prejudice out of business.

Thus it will be seen that the liberalism of the *Telegraph*, while not quite so widely publicized as that of the *Enquirer-Sun*, is just as militant as that of Julian Harris's lamented journal. The paper not only has been fearless in unmasking various moronic movements which originated in Atlanta, but it also has been zealous in its advocacy of a more enlightened social attitude on the part of Southern industrialists.

True, it once made an attack on Laurence Stallings because Stallings referred in print to a Negro novelist as "Mr." so-and-so; but it is not given to such outbursts, and has long been a staunch friend of the blacks. In fact it has published a special edition for Negroes for the past eighteen years in which the members of that race are regularly spoken of as "Mr." and "Mrs." The *Telegraph* enjoys the same happy combination as is found on the Montgomery *Advertiser*, namely a publisher who is courageous and intelligent and who at the same time allows his extremely competent chief editorial writer the utmost freedom.

But if the Klan was strong in Georgia, as it certainly was in the middle 1920's, it was equally so in Texas, where the membership totaled well into the hundreds of thousands. And nowhere in Texas did the order thrive more lustily than in Dallas. Yet the Dallas *Dispatch*, risking its very existence, unleashed an editorial cannonade against the Kluxers which was as brave as it was effective. The campaign was conducted by Glenn Pricer of the *Dispatch's* editorial staff, who was not deterred by the physical danger involved. When the campaign was over the Klan's hold on Dallas had been broken.

During this same period the El Paso *Times* also dealt the order some lusty thwacks. The pungent pen of Duncan Aikman was an important factor in this fight, as in various other assaults launched by the *Times* on clericalism, bigotry, and kindred blights. The paper was outspokenly liberal except toward industrial and economic progressivism. The El Paso *Herald* likewise took pleasure in tweaking ecclesiastical noses, as is evidenced by its assertion that the action of the state authorities in censoring the school books in order to bring them into conformity with prevailing Fundamentalist theology "is evidence of political cowardice and social irresponsibility in the face of stupid fanaticism and the malice that always accompanies it." The *Herald* went on to aver that "progressive Texas fears no dark age, and only asks that Texas clowns be not taken seriously."

Another newspaper in the Lone Star State which rendered a conspicuous service to the cause of liberalism is the San Antonio *Express*. It conducted an inquiry into the penal system of Texas which resulted in sweeping reforms. The *Express* pursued its objective without regard to consequences, and turned up some startling facts. Thanks to the coöperation of the Dallas *News*, it was able to get these facts before a large section of the state, and legislative action followed shortly thereafter.

A Tennessee paper with a long tradition of liberalism behind it is the Chattanooga *Times*. This journal was acquired more than half a century ago by Adolph S. Ochs, who subsequently purchased the New York *Times* as well. The Chattanooga *Times*, edited during the first twenty-five years of the Ochs ownership by Colonel J. E. MacGowan, made a notable fight on the railroads in 1891, when they were the most powerful element in the American plutocracy, and forced them to grant Chattanooga better rates.

In 1903, upon the death of Colonel MacGowan, Mr. Ochs placed Lapsley G. Walker in charge of the editorial page, and Mr. Walker has been chief editorial writer ever since. He has carried out in an admirable way the principles laid down by the publisher when he took over the paper in 1878. At that time Mr. Ochs announced that the aim of the *Times* was "to be sound—or as nearly sound as possible—in the expression of opinions on all current events touched on—national, local, political, social, and religious."

The services of this newspaper in fighting the baleful clerical influence which has so degraded Tennessee and other sections of the South, have been particularly noteworthy. Bigotry and intolerance have no more resolute foe than the Chattanooga *Times*, and it has jousted with all varieties of ecclesiastical meddlers. When Bryanism engulfed Tennessee, the paper buckled on its armor on behalf of the freedom of the schoolroom, and when the embattled enemies of the Pope took the field against Governor Alfred E. Smith in 1928, it espoused the cause of the Democratic nominee with enthusiasm. It stood with Wilson in 1912 when he launched his program of economic liberalism, and it has always denounced high tariffs as placing a burden upon the masses for the benefit of the classes. And if it opposed the ratification of the suffrage amendment because it believed that this constitutional provision infringed upon the rights of the states and was out of harmony with the ideas of the founders, it fought the prohibition amendment on the same ground.

Mississippi is able to boast a daily which is liberal in most respects. This is the Jackson *Daily News*, edited by Frederick Sullens. It is true that Mr. Sullens raves almost in the manner of a bedlamite at the mere mention of Mr. Mencken's name; and it is reported that he succumbed some years ago to the witchery of the Rev. Gypsy Smith, Jr., and that this led him to publish William Jennings Bryan's Sunday school lessons in his paper for a time. But this latter emotion apparently has passed. Frederick Sullens has always been a tigerish foe of Mississippi's political zanies, he assails the parsons of the state whenever the occasion seems to require it, he has denounced the Mississippi anti-evolution law, and he has fought for justice for the Negro.

No Southern state boasts a more liberal press than North Carolina. If the Charlotte *Observer* has abandoned the principles of Tompkins and Caldwell and become a mouthpiece of Bourbonism and reaction, and if the *Southern Textile Bulletin* of the same city is even worse, there are other journals in the Old North State which stand for decency and intelligence.

Foremost among them, perhaps, is the Greensboro *News*, edited by Earle Godbey. This paper is notable for the enlightenment of its views no less than for the urbanity of the language in which those views are expressed. When Gerald W. Johnson was on its editorial staff, the *News* held undisputed sway in the state, and was the mouthpiece of North Carolina liberalism. Mr. Johnson finally resigned to become professor of journalism at Chapel Hill and, incidentally, to contribute to leading magazines many brilliantly penetrating critiques dealing with various aspects of Southern civilization. Subsequently he joined the editorial staff of the Baltimore *Evening Sun*, where he is not only continuing his journalistic work, but at the same time is contributing frequently to periodicals and publishing characteristically provocative biographical studies of Southern figures. The loss of Mr. Johnson, whose contribution to liberal causes in the South during the past dozen years has been of the first importance, was naturally a heavy one for the Greensboro *News*. But Mr. Godbey is carrying on in the same liberal tradition, and his editorial page is read today by those who enjoy a combination of sound writing with equally sound ideas.

Josephus Daniels's Raleigh *News and Observer* has been metamorphosed since it led the pack against John Spencer Bassett nearly thirty years ago. It is still erratic in some respects, and its publisher's relationship with the Democratic party causes it to be astonishingly naïve at times in its analyses of political issues. On the other hand the *News and Observer* is probably the most fearless paper in the South in its attitude toward economic and industrial questions. The textile and tobacco interests, the two most powerful commercial groups in North Carolina, are treated as cavalierly by Mr. Daniels as if they controlled no advertising. In his advocacy of the right of laboring men to organize in unions and his excoriation of the reactionary textile element, he has exhibited independence of the highest order. He has been fortunate, too, in having on his staff Miss Nell Battle Lewis, whose Sunday column has been a widely read feature of the paper for a good many years. In Miss Lewis's keenly discriminating mind are combined boldness and intelligence, unwavering resolution and open-minded tolerance. Her liberal influence has extended beyond the confines of her native state.

Robert Lathan, who presides over the editorial page of the Asheville *Citizen*, was formerly with the Charleston, South Carolina, *News and Courier*, where his "The Isolation of the South" won a Pulitzer prize. This editorial set forth courageously and sanely the need for adequate political leadership below the Potomac.

Two smaller papers in North Carolina which are deserving of attention are the Elizabeth City *Independent*, edited by W. O. Saunders, and the Chapel Hill *Weekly*, edited by Louis Graves. Mr. Saunders has a *penchant* for clowning, but he is in many ways a man of sense. Mr. Graves is a balanced liberal whose weekly paper has a distinctive flavor.

The neighboring state of Virginia also has a Pulitzer prize winner in Louis I. Jaffé, editor of the Norfolk *Virginian-Pilot*. The award went to him for his open espousal of the cause of justice for the Negro over a period of some years. Mr. Jaffé began calling for more equitable treatment of the weaker race when such an attitude was widely regarded in Norfolk as tabu. He fought for better recreational facilities for the blacks, and was prominent in the movement which led to the passage of the Virginia anti-lynching bill. He was the first editor in the Old Dominion to assail the Klan upon its rise to prominence following the World War, and he ridiculed the "red" hunts conducted at the same period under the ægis of Attorney-General A. Mitchell Palmer. Intolerant parsons and oafish politicians have no more relentless foe than Louis Jaffé; and his editorials are done in a bravura style which adds greatly to their effectiveness.

Dr. Douglas S. Freeman, editor of the Richmond *News Leader*, is another inveterate foe of meddlesome clerics and demagogic psuedo-statesmen. One of his outstanding editorial utterances relative to the officious interference of ecclesiastics in temporal matters was a stinging reply to the Methodist ministers of Richmond who had issued a ukase demanding the reëlection of a certain judge. Few editors in the South are so consistent in their championship of the Negro, or belabor the patrioteers and the industrial Bourbons with greater regularity. The *News Leader's* prestige is further augmented by virtue of the fact that its publisher is John Stewart Bryan, one of Virginia's foremost citizens.

Under the editorial direction of Mr. Bryan and Dr. Freeman the *News Leader* has become increasingly liberal in late years. The Atlanta *Constitution*, on the other hand, once a liberal voice in the South, has taken the opposite course and has grown more and more conservative. The fine traditions established there by Henry W. Grady and Joel Chandler Harris appear to be only a memory today, and not a particularly vivid memory either, in the office of that prosperous and plutocratic journal. The *Constitution* can get tremendously excited over the state of the weather or the misdeeds of the Abyssinians, but when a nauseous thing like the Black Shirts parades under its nose it is as silent as a clam. True, it was awarded a Pulitzer prize recently for its work in cleaning up a ring of grafters in the city government of Atlanta, but it has done little else of late to belie the prevailing conviction that it is intellectually moribund.

Thus the *Constitution*, like the Charlotte *Observer*, has abandoned many of the causes for which it once fought so valiantly. The same is true to a large degree of the Louisville *Courier-Journal*. Under Watterson that paper had an editorial page which was conspicuously intelligent. Not so today. Few ideas are manufactured currently in its sanctum, and the liberal leadership in Kentucky journalism has passed to Desha Breckinridge's Lexington *Herald*.

It is gratifying to record, however, that the Columbia, South Carolina, *State* continues to cherish the principles upon which it was founded more than forty years ago by the Gonzales brothers. Liberalism has been an enduring tradition in the Gonzales family, a tradition which William E. Gonzales, as editor of the *State*, is upholding today. Until a few years ago he had a worthy rival in R. Charlton Wright, who gave the Columbia *Record* a powerful and widely quoted editorial page. Mr. Wright has recently retired from active journalism.

There are seven Scripps-Howard newspapers in the Southern states, and while they joined with the rest of this ordinarily liberal newspaper chain in its incomprehensible support of Herbert Hoover in 1928, they can usually be counted on to fight reaction in whatever form it manifests itself. The Knoxville *News-Sentinel*, for example, has shown admirable courage in denouncing the recent atrocities in the mining section of Kentucky, and the other Southern members of the chain are often fearless in their attitude toward matters of public concern. These other papers are the Birmingham *Post*, Memphis *Press-Scimitar*, Houston *Press*, Fort Worth *Press*, El Paso *Herald-Post*, and Covington *Kentucky Post*.

In addition to the newspapermen mentioned above as contributing to the journalistic prestige of the South, Marshall Ballard, editor of the New Orleans *Item* and New Orleans *Tribune*, exhibits a flair for transcending conventional *laissez faire* attitudes toward

economic and industrial problems. There are column-
ists, too, whose work is sufficiently outstanding to
merit attention. Thomas Lomax Hunter, a relentless
foe of buncombe, contributes a column to the Richmond *Times-Dispatch* in which he dissects the politico-
ecclesiastics with a master hand. C. T. Davis enlivens
the editorial page of the Arkansas *Gazette*, while Clay
Fulks and Charles Morrow Wilson are other Arkansans
whose writings are in the liberal tradition. No survey
of liberal journalism in the South would be complete,
however, without a reference to the balance, the
sanity, and the general excellence of the Norfolk
Journal and Guide, a Negro paper edited by P. B.
Young.

A striking illustration of the increasing independence of Southern newspapers may be seen in the
position which almost all of them took in the Smith-
Hoover presidential campaign of 1928. Here was a
contest in which from Washington, D. C., to El Paso,
Texas, the paramount issue was religious freedom.
Hundreds of thousands of Southern Democrats were
bolting the nominee of their party because of his
Catholicism. Hundreds of thousands were indulging
in calumny and slander concerning his religious faith
and his private life. There was in this disgraceful
state of affairs a challenge to fundamental American
principles; and from that challenge the Southern
press did not shrink. Almost without exception the
leading dailies stood up and fought for Governor
Smith. The Democratic papers were far more outspoken in their stand than the Democratic politicians,
although their obligation to support the nominee was

much less imperative than that of the officeholders. In Virginia, for example, the Richmond *Times-Dispatch* saw that a large percentage of the senators, representatives and assemblymen were anxious not to commit themselves either for or against Mr. Smith. It accordingly asked every one of them whether or not he was supporting the nominee. All replies were published, together with the names of those who made no answer. In this way the politicians were smoked out and made to stand on the firing line.

The attitude of this and scores of other Southern papers in that campaign is only one of various indications that there is untrammeled and unterrified journalism in Dixie. True, the percentage of newspapers which are liberal under virtually all circumstances is by no means as high as the percentage which supported Governor Smith in 1928. But the press of the South makes a respectable showing, none the less, when compared with that of any other section.

In summing up it may be said that the Southern press as an entity has become vastly more liberal since 1900. Even since 1920 the metamorphosis in some localities has been complete. Editorial attitudes which would have been looked upon a comparatively short time ago as dangerously radical or alarmingly subversive now occasion only passing comment.

It is to the more forthright and intelligent newspapers, indeed, that Southern liberalism must look in the future for much of its aggressive leadership. The effort to lift the former Confederacy out of the morass of ignorance and illiteracy, of zealotry and narrowness in which it has long been marooned—an

effort which hitherto has been only partially successful—may well be entrusted to the South's more
enlightened authors and editors, its progressive institutions of higher learning, and its organizations of
alert and socially minded women. These are the
elements which are carrying the burden of the liberal
movement in the South today. Perhaps in the coming
years they will be able to win for that storied land a
future which will be in some measure worthy of its
splendid heritage.

CHAPTER XXI

SUMMARY AND CONCLUSION

IN THE foregoing chapters an effort has been made to portray Southern liberalism in its major outlines in terms of specific persons, organizations, episodes and movements. The approach, on the whole, has been descriptive rather than analytical, although there has been a measure of interpretation and an endeavor to avoid the placing of undue emphasis upon surface phenomena. It may be well, in conclusion, to assess and to summarize the achievements of Southern liberals for the past century and a half, and to present a brief appraisal of current tendencies.

First, in the light of the events and movements recorded in the foregoing chapters, let us reëxamine our definition of "liberalism" so that we may see more clearly the interrelationship of these events and movements. The definition of the term from the pen of Lord Morley, quoted in part in the Introduction, will serve as our starting point:

"Respect for the dignity and worth of the individual is its root. It stands for the subjection to human judgments of all claims of external authority, whether in an organized church, or in more loosely gathered societies of believers, or in books held sacred. In law-

making it does not neglect the higher characteristics
of human nature, it attends to them first. In executive
administration, although judge, gaoler, and perhaps
the hangman will be indispensable, still mercy is
counted a wise supplement to terror. . . . It is worth
noting that a strange and important liberalizing
movement of thought had awakened the mind of
New England with Emerson for its noble and pure-
hearted preacher in 1837. The duty of mental detachment, the supreme claim of the individual conscience,
spread from religious opinion to the conduct of life
and its interwoven social relations. . . . If government
and order are of the very essence, so, too, are conscience, principle, the thinker, the teacher, the
writer. . . ."

It is about the all-important concept of the dignity
and worth of the individual, stressed in the foregoing
paragraph, that much of the liberal creed revolves.
An abiding respect for the dignity and worth of the
average man is, indeed, an even more essential in-
gredient of a liberal society than a lively concern for
the right of the individual to freedom of thought and
action. For while there is no implication here that
freedom of thought and action are non-essentials under
a liberally constituted government, it must be borne
in mind that any government which respects the
individual inevitably grants him liberty of conscience
and independence of movement.

Let us now recapitulate the results of liberal thought
below the Potomac during the past century and a half.

It need scarcely be said that the great advances
made by liberal movements during the fifty years

which followed the outbreak of the American Revolution are of the utmost importance, not only to the South but to the country as a whole. These include the enunciation of numerous fundamental rights in the Bill of Rights and the Declaration of Independence, the abrogation of landed privilege through the abolition of entails and primogeniture, the disestablishment of the Episcopal Church, and the elimination of the legal slave trade with Africa in the year 1808, this last having been accomplished with the coöperation of Northern liberals. At the same time the franchise was broadened, and many discrepancies in representation which favored the lowlanders as against the uplanders were eliminated. On the other hand, these gains were partially offset by the South's failure to provide educational facilities for the masses to the extent that the North provided them, although in the field of the higher learning it made some substantial contributions to educational thought. In literature there were no conspicuous liberals during this period, with the exception of a few writers on political and economic themes, while the number of liberal journalists was limited, owing partly to the scarcity of newspapers.

During the three decades immediately preceding the Civil War, openly-avowed liberalism was virtually extinct below Mason and Dixon's Line. The large number of Southerners who had sought to abolish slavery in earlier days lapsed into silence or became active defenders of the system. The political parties, the educational institutions, the religious denominations and the editors and writers coöperated almost without exception in saying no word which might be construed as lending aid and comfort to the hated abolitionists of the North. Free speech was stifled, and the nerves of the principal actors on both sides of the Potomac became so jangled under the strain of the growing enmity between the sections that they sometimes indulged in harsh and unseemly personalities. There were, it is true, important advances in the public school systems of two Southern states during these years. To this should be added the further fact that Edgar Allan Poe, whom the South claims as an adopted son, made his highly significant contributions to literature and criticism in the thirties and forties.

Viewed from the liberal standpoint, the great failures of the Old South are to be found in its retention of the slave system and its neglect of the economic, educational, and social well being of the large group of unfortunates known as "poor whites." While the collapse of the anti-slavery movement in the South after 1830 is attributable in part to the violently denunciatory harangues of the abolitionists, other leading factors, such as the invention of the cotton gin, must under no conditions be overlooked. It should be noted, however, that neglect of the under-privileged whites was an almost inevitable corollary of slavery, for as long as the individualistic and well-nigh feudalistic social order of the ante-bellum era prevailed, the large class of yeomanry as well as the "poor whites" were almost sure to occupy a minor place in the Southern scheme of things.

The Civil War not only brought about the liberation

27

of the Negroes but the leveling processes which accompanied the abolition of the slave system were psychologically effective in inducing a broader attitude in the mind of the average Southerner toward questions of large social import. It is possible, indeed, that a considerable share of the responsibility for the postwar revival of humanitarianism in the South may be traced to this psychological factor. The period saw the emergence of an important group of educators who labored mightily in the fields of primary, secondary, and higher education; it produced notable workers for interracial amity and intersectional good will, and it witnessed the rise of the common man to a position of political dominance. At the same time, liberal journalism and literature prospered in gratifying fashion. True, almost all the principal religious denominations became active in the quest for heretics, but this condition was not confined to the Southern states.

With the arrival of the twentieth century and the accompanying upturn in agriculture and commerce, further impetus was given the Southern educational movement, with the result that the public schools increased markedly in number and efficiency, while at the same time the colleges and universities expanded both physically and intellectually. Southern womanhood, long handicapped by virtue of the adoration heaped incontinently upon it by worshipful Southern males, finally achieved its emancipation. In the fields of literature and journalism the South went forward with astonishing rapidity, once the country's third decade had been reached. There were significant gains, too, in the building up of more cordial interracial relationships and in the opening up of wider vistas of opportunity to the Negroes, although race prejudice appeared all too frequently in virulent form, and lynchings, although substantially reduced in number, could not be completely eradicated.

Southern politics, on the other hand, has remained provincial and reactionary since 1900, under the blighting influence of the one-party system, with statesmanship all too rare and quacks and clowns holding the spotlight. And while conditions in Southern industry are improving slowly, under the pressure of public opinion, liberalism has been unable to secure for Southern textile workers and coal miners the right to affiliate with labor unions; nor has it been able to prevent the grossest sort of discrimination in recent years on the part of the local authorities and the courts of at least two states in favor of employers and against employees whenever serious clashes between the two have occurred. In the religious realm the South has been afflicted with a larger percentage of Fundamentalist zealots and anti-Catholic fanatics than any other section, and the evangelical pastor has long held dominion over his flock to a degree not equaled in other portions of the republic.

Just at this point it should be noted, however, that the South has lately given indisputable evidence of a desire to free itself from the yoke of ecclesiasticism. Long regarded as the stronghold of prohibition—despite the fact that the quality and quantity of its

moonshine whisky is unequaled from coast to coast—
the South is at last proclaiming its emancipation from
Anti-Saloon League domination. This is not to say
that the league has been completely bereft of its
authority in Dixie, for in a good many sections it still
manages to speak with something of its pristine assur-
ance. On the other hand, there are unmistakable
signs that its days of power below the Potomac are
numbered. The wave of anti-prohibition sentiment
which swept over the country with such compelling
force during the spring and summer of 1932 engulfed
more than one Southern state, and there were other
indications that prohibition as we have known it for
the past twelve years is doomed.

But the fact that the existing policy of liquor control
apparently is to be changed in the not distant future
is less important, for the purposes of this discussion,
than the fact that the omniscience of the Southern
parson is being challenged as it has seldom been
challenged before. When the Southern dominie no
longer is able to speak *ex cathedra* upon matters of
science and politics, we may expect the elimination
of legislation designed to sustain the inerrancy of the
Scriptural theory of the creation and the liberalization of existing Sabbatarian enactments, as well as
the modification or repeal of the liquor regulations
which we now enjoy. Similarly we may hope for a
cessation of the political proscription by the evangelicals of persons whose religious affiliations are not to
their liking.

When these desiderata are achieved, Southern
liberalism will claim and will deserve the credit; for

an insistence upon a reasonable degree of separation between church and state has always been a tenet of cardinal importance in the creed of American liberals, both North and South. It is true that those who are alive to the realities are aware that the complete separation of the secular and the religious arms is a goal so utopian as to be unattainable in the civilization which we know. All that can be done is to discover the nature of each and to find a relationship between them which will inure to the public benefit.

And just as absolute separation of church and state is recognized by pragmatists as being impossible of attainment, so are these same realists aware that the rights insisted upon by liberals sometimes amount to no more than mere figments of the imagination. These rights, indeed, cannot always be maintained where bread and butter are necessary to life, where different opinions may be honestly held, and where employers, whether trustees of a university or directors of a business establishment, can hardly be expected to give employment to persons whose viewpoint they consider dangerous. It is important to note, too, that one of the greatest hindrances today to the free exercise of the individual conscience in relation to problems involving ethical considerations is to be found in the dependence of the individual on the good will of his employer. For no matter how efficient an employee or workman may be, if he happens to be a Socialist or some other type of radical, he will usually find it personally advantageous to keep his opinions on economic and political questions to himself. In-

LIBERALISM IN THE SOUTH

numerable men and women earning wages or salaries

numerable men and women earning wages or salaries who have minds of their own are forced into a cynical silence because a frank expression on their part would cause them to be thrown out of employment.

But if today we are far from achieving the right to freedom of speech, we are much nearer the goal than those who lived when the pronouncements of kings and popes were law. What we have was won by liberal thought and action, and the most pressing task of present day liberalism is to promote those conditions necessary to the further development of individual inquiry and self-expression. It might be said, indeed, that the individual wins reality for himself only as he takes part in this intense search of the modern age for more genuine and complete liberty.

In so far as freedom of speech is concerned, one right not yet woven into our organic law is of an even more fundamental nature. This is the right to a job and a living wage. If a man is willing to work and the system under which he lives does not give him a job at a living wage, talk of his dignity and worth becomes mere twaddle. Since the right to work for an adequate return is necessary to the establishment of individual dignity and worth, it is of prime significance, and we should make such changes in our present economy as are necessary to the achievement and maintenance of that right.

These are considerations which liberals cannot afford to ignore. And just as the relationship between church and state is under close scrutiny today, so is the relationship between business and the state. Never in recent times has there been a livelier interest in the problem of economic adjustment, never have the brains of the civilized world been concentrated more completely upon the search for an adequate formula for economic recovery. The question of the interconnection between business and government looms large in the thinking of those who are addressing themselves to this problem, and there is a strong suspicion among liberals that fundamental maladjustments in the relationships between these two agencies are responsible for a goodly share of the world's ills.

In seeking a way out, liberalism is intelligent enough and open-minded enough to welcome the closest scrutiny of the existing economic order. While recognizing that in such systems as those in Russia and Italy there are elements which cannot be reconciled with certain major implications of the liberal thesis, it holds, none the less, that these experiments are worthy of the most careful study. Liberalism merely laughs when professional alarmists quake at the thought of Communism; for although liberalism repudiates instinctively the regimentation of opinion and the repression of civil rights which are such important concomitants of Soviet rule, it holds that America after all may learn something of value from present-day Russia.

Certainly the time has come for bold pioneering in the fields of business and government. The capitalistic system has been shaken to its roots, and an ailing world cries out for statesmen who will lead it back to prosperity and peace. Here in America the dearth of leadership since the great crash in 1929 has been appalling. President Hoover's do-nothing policy of vacillation and equivocation finally gave way to belated suggestions for relief, most of which suggestions would have been more effective had they been advanced a year or two earlier. Congress likewise has failed to rise above pettiness and politics in its bungling efforts to cope with the situation.

As for Southern liberalism, it has had little to contribute to the solution of the problems which so perplex the world in the present crisis. This, it is hardly necessary to point out, is in direct and startling contrast to the situation which obtained a century and a half ago, when Southern statesmen furnished the major part of the leadership which carried America successfully through a bloody revolution, and at the same time produced the Bill of Rights, the Declaration of Independence and the Federal constitution. Since the post-revolutionary era, however, practically nothing of permanent importance has been contributed by anyone, North or South, to our political thinking.

The grave emergency precipitated by the depression has served to emphasize the fact that there is a serious lack of clarity and coherence in our political and social concepts, and has brought into prominent relief the need for a reëxamination of many hypotheses which we had previously regarded as axiomatic. Herein lies an almost unexampled opportunity for Southern liberalism to reassert itself as a vital force in our national life. By furnishing an adequate answer to some of the principal questions raised by the existing economic distress, Southern statesmanship can establish itself once more as a controlling factor in the national councils. At the same time it should thereby be able to give to the dignity and worth of human beings everywhere a greater measure of reality.

In its efforts to achieve an added measure of dignity and worth for the average citizen, Southern liberalism, like liberalism elsewhere, is cautious before breaking definitely with the past, for it holds that experience is the safest guide. But if it is unwilling to discard established modes of thought until they have been found to be clearly destructive of individual rights and individual responsibility, it has the courage to strike out along new paths when such a course is found to be desirable. There is nothing of intellectual anchylosis in the liberal point of view, for liberalism welcomes suggestions from every quarter in its search for answers to the questions which confront it. Such a study, as for example, *I'll Take My Stand*, receives the attention of liberals not because they agree, necessarily, with its authors in their fervent devotion to older forms of culture, but because they are aware that the viewpoint which the contributors to this symposium express is deserving of thorough scrutiny. And as a matter of fact the attitude of the "Nashville group" toward the problems of the present South is one which liberalism cannot properly disregard. For if the emphasis of the Nashvillians upon the past is excessive, it is nevertheless an emphasis not without value in this materialistic and mechanistic age. Many Southern liberals, indeed, incline to the view that the rawness and crudeness of much of the New South might well be tempered with something of the beauty and charm of the Old South; that there is no serious incompatibility between a concern for the dignity and worth of the individual Southerner of today and a desire for the preservation of the grace and good manners which often characterized the Southerner of a hundred years ago.

The accomplishments of Southern liberalism for the past century and a half may, on the whole, seem rather unimpressive. Yet except during the three decades preceding the Civil War, liberal tendencies appear to have been equally as pronounced below the Potomac as elsewhere in the republic. Who can say that any other people, saddled with slavery almost from the day that their first settlements were established, and possessing an agricultural economy which made its elimination difficult, would have gone farther in the direction of liberal achievement than the people of the ante-bellum South? Who will assert without fear of contradiction that the inhabitants of some other region, conquered and humiliated as was the South, would have exhibited a greater measure of liberalism than the South exhibited after 1865? And if the New South has given us Harlan and Gastonia, lynchings and peonage, we should bear in mind that California, where for some years human rights have been in serious disrepute, furnished the locale for the Mooney-Billings case; that Massachusetts took the lives of Sacco and Vanzetti; that the atrocities perpetrated by the Pennsylvania coal and iron police are notorious, and that Herrin is in Illinois.

Liberalism is under fire today in some quarters as inadequate to the needs of the hour. An object of scorn both to radicals and to conservatives, it is criticised on the one hand as being feeble and ineffectual and on the other as constituting the advance guard of red revolution. But liberalism, for its part, regards the utopian schemes of extreme radicalism and the authoritarian doctrines of ultra-conservatism with equal suspicion. It seeks to strike a reasonable average between the two, and thus to build up a system of social theory by means of which it may achieve a larger measure of dignity and worth for the individual.

It cannot be said, however, that liberalism in itself is a system of social theory in the sense that Capitalism or Fascism, Socialism or Communism are systems of social theory. Liberalism has been an important living force under Capitalism and is not necessarily inimical to Capitalism. It lies at the basis of Socialism, and some of its elements are present in Communism and Fascism. Liberalism is not a complete system but merely the foundation upon which other systems may be erected.

If pausing to consider is a weakness, and it sometimes is, then liberalism is weak. But if the welcoming of new ideas, if full and free discussion and readiness to reform are signs of strength, then liberalism has a large measure of strength. Many regard it, indeed, as fundamental to all social progress, and an examination of the genuinely important movements in the history of the world reveals that liberalism has been a prime factor in most of them.

Certainly in the Southern hagiology the liberals are entitled to the most commanding place, for to them may be attributed almost everything that has been done in the Southern states in building up a broader and more humane civilization, in developing the potentialities of the average man and in striking the shackles from the human spirit. The South may well rejoice that the social attitudes of its leaders and its people are coming to be more and more shot through with liberalism. In that fact lies the South's chief hope of future greatness.

BIBLIOGRAPHY

BOOKS

Adams, Herbert B. *The College of William and Mary*. Washington, D. C., 1887.
———— *Thomas Jefferson and the University of Virginia*. Washington, D. C., 1888.

Alderman, Edwin A., and Gordon, Armistead C. *J. L. M. Curry, A Biography*. New York, 1911.

Ambler, Charles Henry. *Thomas Ritchie, A Study in Virginia Politics*. Richmond, Va., 1913.
———— *Sectionalism in Virginia From 1776 to 1861*. Chicago, 1910.

Anthony, Susan B., and others. *The History of Woman Suffrage*, Vols. IV and VI. Rochester, N. Y., 1902, and New York, 1922.

Armes, William Dallam. *The Autobiography of Joseph Le Conte*. New York, 1903.

Ashe, Samuel A'Court. *History of North Carolina*. Two vols., Greensboro and Raleigh, N. C., 1925.

Bagby, George W. *The Old Virginia Gentleman and Other Sketches*. New York, 1910.

Baker, Ray Stannard. *Woodrow Wilson: Life and Letters*. Two vols., Garden City, N. Y., 1927.

Bancroft, Frederic. *Slave-Trading in the Old South*. Baltimore, 1931.

Barnes, Harry Elmer. *The Twilight of Christianity*. New York, 1929.

Baskervill, William Malone. *Southern Writers*. Two vols., Nashville, Tenn., 1897 and 1902.

Bassett, John Spencer. *Anti-Slavery Leaders of North Carolina*. Baltimore, 1898.

Bates, Ernest Sutherland. *This Land of Liberty*. New York, 1930.

Blandin, Mrs. I. M. E. *History of Higher Education of Women in the South Prior to 1860*. New York, 1909.

Bleyer, Willard Grosvenor. *Main Currents in the History of American Journalism*. Boston, 1927.

Boucher, Chauncey Samuel. *The Nullification Controversy in South Carolina*. Chicago, 1916.

Bowers, Claude G. *The Tragic Era*. Boston, 1929.

Brawley, Benjamin. *Doctor Dillard of the Jeanes Fund*. New York, 1930.

Brown, William Garrott. *The Lower South in American History*. New York, 1903.

Brownlow, W. G. *Sketches of the Rise, Progress and Decline of Secession*. Philadelphia, 1862.

Bruce, Philip Alexander. *The Rise of the New South*. Philadelphia, 1905.

Bush, George Gary. *History of Education in Florida*. Washington, D. C., 1889.

Cable, George W. *The Silent South*. New York, 1885.

———— *The Negro Question.* New York, 1890.

Cambridge History of American Literature, Vols. I-IV, inclusive. New York, 1917, 1918, 1921.

Carpenter, Jesse T. *The South as a Conscious Minority.* New York, 1930.

Carson, William J., ed. *The Coming of Industry to the South.* Philadelphia, 1931.

Chafee, Zechariah, Jr. *Freedom of Speech.* New York, 1920.

Claiborne, J. F. H. *Mississippi as a Province, Territory and State.* Jackson, Miss., 1880.

Clark, Emily. *Innocence Abroad.* New York, 1931.

Clark, Willis G. *History of Education in Alabama.* Washington, D. C., 1889.

Cobb, Sanford H. *The Rise of Religious Liberty in America.* New York, 1902.

Cole, Stewart G. *The History of Fundamentalism.* New York, 1931.

Collins, Winfield H. *The Truth About Lynching and the Negro in the South.* New York, 1918.

Cooke, John Esten. *Virginia: A History of the People.* Boston, 1893.

Coulter, E. Merton. *College Life in the Old South.* New York, 1928.

Dieffenbach, Albert C. *Religious Liberty: The Great American Illusion.* New York, 1927.

Dodd, William E. *The Cotton Kingdom.* New Haven, Conn., 1919.

———— *Statesmen of the Old South.* New York, 1911.

———— *The Life of Nathaniel Macon.* Raleigh, N. C., 1903.

Dorchester, Daniel. *Christianity in the United States.* New York, 1895.

Drewry, John E. *Some Magazines and Magazine Makers.* Boston, 1924.

Du Bois, W. E. Burghardt. *The Souls of Black Folk.* Chicago, 1909.

———— *Darkwater.* New York, 1920.

Dyer, G. W. *Democracy in the South Before the Civil War.* Nashville, Tenn., 1905.

Faulkner, Harold Underwood. *The Quest for Social Justice—1898-1914.* New York, 1931.

Fay, Edwin Whitfield. *The History of Education in Louisiana.* Washington, D. C., 1898.

Fish, Carl Russell. *The Rise of the Common Man, 1830-1850.* New York, 1927.

Forrest, W. M. *Do Fundamentalists Play Fair?* New York, 1926.

Fortier, Alcée. *A History of Louisiana.* Four vols. New York, 1904.

Gaines, Francis Pendleton. *The Southern Plantation.* New York, 1924.

Garrison, George P. *Texas, A Contest of Civilizations.* Boston, 1903.

Graves, J. R. *The Great Iron Wheel.* New York, 1858.

Green, Fletcher M. *Constitutional Development in the South Atlantic States, 1776-1860.* Chapel Hill, N. C., 1930.

Gruening, Ernest, ed. *These United States.* Two vols. New York, 1923 and 1924.

●Hall, Thomas Cuming. *The Religious Background of American Culture.* Boston, 1930.

Hansen, Allen Oscar. *Liberalism and American Education in the Eighteenth Century.* New York, 1926.

Harris, Joel Chandler, ed. *Joel Chandler Harris' Life of Henry W. Grady. Including His Writings and Speeches.* New York, 1890.

Harris, Julia Collier, ed. *Joel Chandler Harris, Editor and Essayist.* Chapel Hill, N. C., 1931.

Hart, Albert Bushnell. *The Southern South.* New York, 1910.

Haworth, Paul Leland. *America in Ferment.* Indianapolis, 1915.

Hecker, Eugene A. *A Short History of Women's Rights.* New York, 1911.

Helper, Hinton Rowan. *The Impending Crisis of the South.* New York, 1857.

Hicks, John D. *The Populist Revolt.* Minneapolis, 1931.

Hobhouse, L. T. *Liberalism.* New York, no date. [1914]

Hudson, Frederic. *Journalism in the United States From 1690 to 1872.* New York, 1873.

Jackson, Helen Hunt. *A Century of Dishonor.* Boston, 1885.

Jackson, Jerome K., and Malmberg, Constantine F. *Religious Education and the State.* New York, 1928.

Johnson, Charles S. *The Negro in American Civilization.* New York, 1930.

Jones, Charles Edgeworth. *Education in Georgia.* Washington, D. C., 1889.

Kirbye, J. Edward. *Puritanism in the South.* Boston, 1908.

Knight, Edgar W. *Public Education in the South.* Boston, 1922.

Krock, Arthur, ed. *The Editorials of Henry Watterson.* New York, 1923.

Lane, J. J. *History of Education in Texas.* Washington, D. C., 1903.

Langdon-Davies, John. *A Short History of Women.* New York, 1927.

Lee, James Melvin. *History of American Journalism.* Boston, 1917.

Lewinson, Paul. *Race, Class, and Party.* London and New York, 1932.

Lewis, Alvin Fayette. *History of Higher Education in Kentucky.* Washington, D. C.. 1899.

McElroy, Robert McNutt. *Kentucky in the Nation's History.* New York, 1909.

Macy, Jesse. *The Anti-Slavery Crusade.* New Haven, Conn., 1919.

Malone, Dumas. *The Public Life of Thomas Cooper.* New Haven, Conn., 1926.

Martin, Everett Dean. *Liberty.* New York, 1930.

Maury, Reuben. *The Wars of the Godly.* New York, 1928.

Mayes, Edward. *History of Education in Mississippi.* Washington, D. C., 1899.

Mayo, A. D. *Industrial Education in the South.* Washington, D. C., 1888.

————— *Southern Women in the Recent Educational Movement.* Washington, D. C., 1892.

Meriwether, Colyer. *History of Higher Education in South Carolina.* Washington, D. C., 1889.

Merriam, Lucius Salisbury. *Higher Education in Tennessee.* Washington, D. C., 1893.

Milton, George Fort. *The Age of Hate.* New York, 1930.

Mims, Edwin. *The Advancing South.* New York, 1925.

————— *Sidney Lanier.* Boston, 1905.

Mitchell, Broadus. *William Gregg, Factory Master of the Old South.* Chapel Hill, N. C., 1928.

Mitchell, Broadus, and Mitchell, George Sinclair. *The Industrial Revolution in the South.* Baltimore, 1930.

Moses, Montrose J. *The Literature of the South.* New York, 1910.

Moton, Robert Russa. *What the Negro Thinks*. New York, 1929.

Mott, Frank Luther. *A History of American Magazines, 1741-1850*. New York, 1930.

Munford, Beverley B. *Virginia's Attitude Toward Slavery and Secession*. New York, 1909.

Murphy, Edgar Gardner. *Problems of the Present South*. New York, 1904.

Nevins, Allan. *The American States During and After the Revolution, 1775-1789*. New York, 1924.

———— *The Emergence of Modern America, 1865-1878*. New York, 1927.

Niebuhr, H. Richard. *The Social Sources of Denominationalism*. New York, 1929.

O'Connor, Mary D. *Life and Letters of M. P. O'Connor*. New York, 1893.

Odum, Howard W., ed. *Southern Pioneers in Social Interpretation*. Chapel Hill, N. C., 1925.

———— *An American Epoch*. New York, 1930.

Page, Kirby. *Jesus or Christianity*. New York, 1931.

Page, Thomas Nelson. *The Old South*. New York, 1903.

Page, Walter H. *The Rebuilding of Old Commonwealths*. New York, 1905.

Parrington, Vernon Louis. *Main Currents in American Thought*, Vols. II and III. New York, 1927 and 1930.

Patton, John S. *Jefferson, Cabell and the University of Virginia*. New York and Washington, 1906.

Payne, George Henry. *History of Journalism in the United States*. New York, 1920.

Phelan, James. *History of Tennessee*. Boston, 1888.

Phillips, Ulrich B. *American Negro Slavery*. New York, 1918.

———— *Life and Labor in the Old South*. Boston, 1929.

Poteat, William Louis. *Can a Man Be a Christian Today?* Chapel Hill, N. C., 1926.

Putnam, Emily James. *The Lady*. New York, 1910.

Rhyne, Jennings J. *Some Cotton Mill Workers and Their Villages*. Chapel Hill, N. C., 1930.

Riley, I. Woodbridge. *American Philosophy: The Early Schools*. New York, 1907.

———— *American Thought From Puritanism to Pragmatism*. New York, 1915.

Robertson, William J. *The Changing South*. New York, 1927.

Rogers, Edward Reinhold. *Four Southern Magazines*. Richmond, Va., 1902.

Rowe, Henry Kalloch. *The History of Religion in the United States*. New York, 1924.

Rutherford, Mildred Lewis. *The South in History and Literature*. Atlanta, 1906.

Schaper, William A. *Sectionalism and Representation in South Carolina*. Washington, D. C., 1901.

Shinn, Josiah H. *History of Education in Arkansas*. Washington, D. C., 1900.

Shipley, Maynard. *The War on Modern Science*. New York, 1927.

Simkins, Francis Butler. *The Tillman Movement in South Carolina*. Durham, N. C., 1926.

Sinclair, Upton. *The Goose Step*. Pasadena, Cal., 1923.

———— *The Goslings*. Pasadena, Cal., 1924.

Skaggs, William H. *The Southern Oligarchy*. New York, 1924.

Smith, Arthur D. Howden. *The Real Colonel House*. New York, 1918.

Smith, C. Alphonso. *Southern Literary Studies*. Chapel Hill, N. C., 1927.
Smith, Charles Lee. *The History of Education in North Carolina*. Washington, D. C., 1888.
Smith, Rembert Gilman. *Politics in a Protestant Church*. Atlanta, 1930.
Smith, William Benjamin. *The Color Line*. New York, 1905.
Snowden, Yates. *History of South Carolina*. Two vols. Chicago and New York, 1920.
Southern Reporter, May 19, 1932, pp. 195-221, inclusive, full text of opinions of the Alabama Supreme Court in the Scottsboro, Ala., cases.
South in the Building of the Nation, The, Vols. I-XII, inclusive. Richmond, Va., 1909.
Sprague, William B. *Annals of the American Pulpit*, Vol. III. New York, 1868.
Stearns, Harold. *Liberalism in America*. New York, 1919.
Sweet, William Warren. *The Story of Religions in America*. New York, 1930.
Tannenbaum, Frank. *Darker Phases of the South*. New York, 1924.
Tassin, Algernon. *The Magazine in America*. New York, 1916.
Taylor, James Monroe. *Before Vassar Opened*. Boston, 1914.
Thompson, Holland. *The New South*. New Haven, Conn., 1919.
Thwing, Charles F. *A History of Higher Education in America*. New York, 1906.
Tippett, Tom. *When Southern Labor Stirs*. New York, 1931.
Trent, William P. *William Gilmore Simms*. Boston, 1892.
————— *Southern Statesmen of the Old Régime*. New York, 1897.
————— *Southern Writers*. New York, 1905.
Twelve Southerners. *I'll Take My Stand*. New York, 1930.
Underwood, Oscar. *Drifting Sands of Party Politics*. New York, 1928.
Van Doren, Carl. *James Branch Cabell*. New York, 1925.
Wade, John Donald. *Augustus Baldwin Longstreet*. New York, 1924.
Washington, Booker T. *Up From Slavery*. New York, 1907.
Watterson, Henry. *"Marse Henry," An Autobiography*. Two vols. New York, 1919.
Weeks, Stephen B. *Southern Quakers and Slavery*. Baltimore, 1896.
Weigle, Luther A. *American Idealism*. New Haven, Conn., 1928.
Whipple, Leon. *Our Ancient Liberties*. New York, 1927.
————— *The Story of Civil Liberty in the United States*. New York, 1927.
White, Andrew D. *A History of the Warfare of Science With Theology in Christendom*. Two vols. New York, 1896.
White, Walter. *Rope and Faggot*. New York, 1929.
Whitfield, Theodore M. *Slavery Agitation in Virginia, 1829-1830*. Baltimore, 1930.
Wilson, Henry. *History of the Rise and Fall of the Slave Power in America*, Vols. I and II. Boston, 1872.
Withrow, W. H. *Religious Progress in the Century*. Nineteenth Century Series, London, Eng., 1903.

ARTICLES, PAMPHLETS, TRACTS, ETC.

The complete files of the *Texas Review*, 1915-1924, and the *Reviewer*, 1921-1925, have been examined, as well as every issue of the *Sewanee Review*, the

28

South Atlantic Quarterly, the *Southwest Review* and the *Virginia Quarterly Review* from the establishment of each of these periodicals through 1931.

"A Carolinian." "Southern Sidelights," *Sewanee Review*, May, 1896.

Aikman, Duncan. "Politics and Ma Ferguson in Texas," *Independent*, December 19, 1925.

Alderman, Edwin A. "Education in the South," *Outlook*, August 3, 1901.

———— "Thomas Jefferson," radio address, April 14, 1930, published in University of Virginia *Alumni News*, May, 1930.

Anderson, D. R. "A Jeffersonian Leader: William Branch Giles," *Sewanee Review*, January, 1913.

———— "The Teacher of Jefferson and Marshall," *South Atlantic*, October, 1916.

Angoff, Charles. "The Higher Learning Goes to War," *American Mercury*, June, 1927.

Armstrong, Orland Kay. "Bootleg Science in Tennessee," *North American Review*, February, 1929.

Bacon, Nathaniel T. "The Real Southern Question Again," *World's Work*, May, 1902.

Baird, William. "The South in the Intellectual Development of the United States," *Southern Magazine*, January, 1894.

Baker, Ray Stannard. "Following the Color Line," *American Magazine*, April-August, inclusive, 1907.

———— "The Tragedy of the Mulatto," *American Magazine*, April, 1908.

———— "An Ostracized Race in Ferment," *American Magazine*, May, 1908.

———— "The Black Man's Silent Power," *American Magazine*, July, 1908.

———— "What to do About the Negro," *American Magazine*, September, 1908.

Banks, Enoch Marvin. "The Passing of the Solid South," *South Atlantic*, April, 1909.

———— "A Semi-Centennial View of Secession," *Independent*, February 9, 1911.

Bassett, John Spencer. "The Reign of Passion," *South Atlantic*, October, 1902.

———— "Stirring up the Fires of Race Antipathy," *South Atlantic*, October, 1903.

———— "The Task of the Critic," *South Atlantic*, October, 1904.

———— "William Garrott Brown," *South Atlantic*, April, 1917.

Bean, William G. "An Aspect of Know Nothingism—The Immigrant and Slavery," *South Atlantic*, October, 1924.

Bingham, Robert. "Sectional Misunderstandings," *North American Review*, September, 1904.

"B. J. R." "Features of American Slavery," *Sewanee Review*, August, 1893.

Black Justice, pamphlet published by American Civil Liberties Union, New York, May, 1931.

Bond, Albert Richmond. *Southern Baptists and Illiteracy*, pamphlet published by education board, Southern Baptist Convention, March 26, 1928.

Bond, Horace M. "Negro Leadership Since Washington," *South Atlantic*, April, 1925.
———— "A Negro Looks at His South," *Harper's*, June, 1931.
Bowers, Claude G. "Jefferson, Master Politician," *Virginia Quarterly*, July, 1926.
Boyd, Thomas. "Defying the Klan," *Forum*, July, 1926.
Boyd, William Kenneth. "Southern History in Southern Universities," *South Atlantic*, July, 1902.
Brackett, Jeffrey R. "Democracy vs. Aristocracy in Virginia in 1830," *Sewanee Review*, May, 1896.
Brewton, William W. *The South Must Publish Her Own Books*, pamphlet published by the author, Atlanta, 1928.
Brown, William Garrott. "The South in National Politics," *South Atlantic*, April, 1910.
Bruce, Philip Alexander. "Evolution of the Negro Problem," *Sewanee Review*, October, 1911.
Brydon, G. MacLaren. *The Established Church in Virginia and the Revolution*, pamphlet published by Virginia Diocesan Library, Richmond, Va., 1930.
Butterick, Wallace. "Education in the New South," *Review of Reviews*, April, 1926.
Cain, James M. "The Solid South," *Bookman*, November, 1928.
Carnathan, W. J. "The Proposal to Reopen the African Slave Trade in the South, 1854-1860," *South Atlantic*, October, 1926.
Cason, Clarence E. "The Mississippi Imbroglio," *Virginia Quarterly*, April, 1931.
———— "Is the South Advancing?" *Yale Review*, Spring, 1931.
Centennial Remembrance Book of Colonel John Forsyth, Mobile, Ala., 1912.
Clark, Emily. "Mr. Jefferson's University," *American Mercury*, February, 1930.
Coulter, E. Merton. "The Genesis of Henry Clay's American System," *South Atlantic*, January, 1926.
Creel, George. "What Have Women Done With the Vote?" *Century*, March, 1914.
Crowell, Chester T. "Strange News From Texas," *American Mercury*, March, 1925.
———— "Journalism in Texas," *American Mercury*, April, 1926.
Curry, J. L. M. "Education in the Southern States," *Review of Reviews*, August, 1889.
Dabney, Richard Heath. "Virginia's Attitude Toward Slavery and Secession," *Sewanee Review*, April, 1910.
Dabney, Virginius. "Virginia," *American Mercury*, November, 1926.
———— "Governor Byrd of Virginia," *Nation*, June 6, 1928.
———— "Bishop Cannon Wins an Award," *Nation*, April 17, 1929.
———— "Negro Barbers in the South," *Nation*, July 16, 1930.
Davenport, Walter. "Yes, Your Excellency!" *Collier's*, December 13, 1930.
Davidson, Philip E. "Industrialism in the Ante-Bellum South," *South Atlantic*, October, 1928.
Dillard, James Hardy. "Liberalism," *South Atlantic*, January, 1917.

———— "Fourteen Years of the Jeanes Fund," *South Atlantic*, July, 1923.

Dodd, William E. "The Place of Nathaniel Macon in Southern History," *American Historical Review*, July, 1902.

———— "Some Difficulties of the History Teacher in the South," *South Atlantic*, April, 1904.

———— "Freedom of Speech in the South," *Nation*, April 25, 1907.

———— "The Dilemma of Democracy in the United States," *Virginia Quarterly*, October, 1925.

———— "The Declaration of Independence," *Virginia Quarterly*, July, 1926.

Dowd, Jerome. "Child Labor," *South Atlantic*, January, 1902.

Eaton, Clement. "The Freedom of the Press in the Upper South," *Mississippi Valley Historical Review*, March, 1932.

Eaton, G. D. "Harriet Beecher Stowe," *American Mercury*, April, 1927.

———— "The Heart Beneath Legree's Shirt," *Plain Talk*, April, 1928.

Eckenrode, H. J. "Sir Walter Scott and the South," *North American Review*, October, 1917.

Edgerton, John E. "Labor," address at University of Virginia Institute of Public Affairs, August 5, 1930, published in mimeographed form by the Institute.

Ellis, H. M. "Puritanism and Conformism," *South Atlantic*, October, 1918.

Embree, Edwin Rogers. "A Kentucky Crusader," *American Mercury*, September, 1931.

Ethridge, Willie Snow. "Southern Women Attack Lynching," *Nation*, December 10, 1930.

Few, W. P. "Southern Public Opinion," *South Atlantic*, January, 1905.

Fight for Civil Liberty, 1930-31, The. Published by American Civil Liberties Union, New York, June, 1931.

"Free Speech in the South," by a Northern Woman, *Independent*, January 15, 1903.

Frissell, H. B. "Educational Progress in Virginia," *South Atlantic*, July, 1903.

Gag on Teaching, The. Published by American Civil Liberties Union, New York, May, 1931.

Gambrell, Herbert. "James Stephen Hogg: Statesman or Demagogue?" *Southwest Review*, Spring, 1928.

Garner, James W. "Recent Agitation of the Negro Question in the South," *South Atlantic*, January, 1908.

———— "The Dismissal of Professor Banks," *Independent*, April 27, 1911.

Gee, Wilson. "The Contribution of the Countryside," *South Atlantic*, July, 1924.

Gewehr, Wesley M. "The Rise of the Popular Churches in Virginia, 1740-1790," *South Atlantic*, April, 1928.

Gilman, Daniel C. "The Launching of a University," *Scribner's*, March, 1902.

Glasgow, Ellen. "The Novel in the South," *Harper's*, December, 1928.

Granbery, John C. "What is a Liberal?" *Southwest Review*, Autumn, 1929.

Gray, Virginia Gearhart. "Activities of Southern Women, 1840-1860," *South Atlantic*, July, 1928.

Greever, Garland. "Southern Leadership Since the Civil War," *North American Review*, August, 1910.

Guerry, William A. "Harriet Beecher Stowe," *Sewanee Review*, July, 1898.

Hall, Grover C. "We Southerners," *Scribner's*, January, 1928.

Harman, Henry E. "Sidney Lanier—A Study," *South Atlantic*, October, 1915.

Hawes, Ruth B. "Slavery in Mississippi," *Sewanee Review*, April, 1913.

Haygood, Atticus G. "The South and the School Problem," *Harper's*, July, 1889.

Henderson, Archibald. "Democracy and Literature," *South Atlantic*, April, 1913.

Henneman, J. B. "Ten Years of the *Sewanee Review*: A Retrospect," *Sewanee Review*, October, 1902.

Herring, Harriet E. "Cycles of Cotton Mill Criticism," *South Atlantic*, April, 1929.

Herzberg, Max J. "Thomas Jefferson as a Man of Letters," *South Atlantic*, October, 1914.

Hesseltine, W. B. "Look Away Dixie," *Sewanee Review*, January-March, 1931.

Hibbard, Addison. "Literature South, 1924," *Reviewer*, January, 1925.

Hicks, Granville. "The Past and Future of William Faulkner," *Bookman*, September, 1931.

Hubbell, Jay B. "On 'Southern Literature'," *Texas Review*, October, 1921.

————— "The New Southwest," *Southwest Review*, October, 1924.

Hudson, John B. "The Spoils System Enters College," *New Republic*, September 17, 1930.

Hughes, Robert W. *Editors of the Past*, lecture before Virginia Press Association, published at Richmond, 1897.

Hugins, Roland. "Confusion Among the Liberals," *American Mercury*, December, 1928.

Hunt, Gaillard. "James Madison and Religious Liberty," annual report, *American Historical Association*, 1901, Vol. 1.

Institute of Public Affairs and International Relations: Bulletin, University of Georgia, Vol. xxx, November, 1929, No. 2.

Jacob, Cary F. "The South That Never Was," *Sewanee Review*, April-June, 1927.

Jaffé, Louis I. "Al Smith and the Democracy," *Virginia Quarterly*, July, 1927.

Johnson, Gerald W. "The South Takes the Offensive," *American Mercury*, May, 1924.

————— "The Battling South," *Scribner's*, March, 1925.

————— "The Dead Vote of the South," *Scribner's*, July, 1925.

————— "A Tilt With Southern Windmills," *Virginia Quarterly*, July, 1925.

————— "Journalism Below the Potomac," *American Mercury*, September, 1926.

————— "Southern Image-Breakers," *Virginia Quarterly*, October, 1928.

————— "Chase of North Carolina," *American Mercury*, June, 1929.

————— "The Cadets of New Market," *Harper's*, December, 1929.

Jones, Charles C., Jr. "Dr. Lyman Hall, Governor of Georgia, 1783," *Magazine of American History*, January, 1891.

Jones, Howard Mumford. "The Southern Legend," *Scribner's*, May, 1929.

————— "Is There a Southern Renaissance?" *Virginia Quarterly*, April, 1930.

————— "On Leaving the South," *Scribner's*, January, 1931.

Jones, M. Ashby. "The Negro in the South," *Virginia Quarterly*, January, 1927.

Jones, Weimar. "Southern Labor and the Law," *Nation*, July 2, 1930.

Kendall, Henry P. "Cotton Textiles," *Survey Graphic*, March, 1932.

Kennedy, Fronde. "Russell's Magazine," *South Atlantic*, April, 1919.

Kilgo, John Carlisle. "Some Phases of Southern Education," *South Atlantic*, April, 1903.

Kirkland, J. H. "Freedom of Speech in the South," *Independent*, January 29, 1903.

Kirkland, Winifred. "Slavery in the South Today," *Century*, July, 1929.

Knauss, James O. "The Farmer's Alliance in Florida," *South Atlantic*, July, 1926.

Knight, Edgar W. "Some Fallacies Concerning the History of Public Education in the South," *South Atlantic*, October, 1914.

————— "Can the South Attain to National Standards in Education?" *South Atlantic*, January, 1929.

Latané, John Holladay. "Problems of the American College," *South Atlantic*, January, 1910.

Law, Robert Adger. "The Texas Review," *Southwest Review*, October, 1924.

Lewis, Nell Battle. "The Woman Movement," series in Raleigh, N. C., *News and Observer*, April 19 and 26, May 3, 10, 17 and 24, 1925.

————— "The University of North Carolina Gets Its Orders," *Nation*, February 2, 1926.

————— "North Carolina," *American Mercury*, May, 1926.

Leyburn, John. "An Interview With General Robert E. Lee," letter in *Century*, May, 1885.

Lovejoy, Owen R. "Dr. Alexander Jeffrey McKelway, 1866-1918," *Child Labor Bulletin*, published by National Child Labor Committee, May, 1918.

Lowrey, Flora. "The Dallas Negro Players," *Southwest Review*, Spring, 1931.

McBryde, John M. Jr. "Womanly Education For Women," *Sewanee Review*, October, 1907.

McCulloch, J. E., ed. *The Human Way*, addresses on race problems at Southern Sociological Congress, Atlanta, 1913, published by the Congress, Washington, D. C., no date.

Maier, Walter A. "The Jeffersonian Ideals of Religious Liberty," address at University of Virginia Institute of Public Affairs, August 9, 1930; published in mimeographed form by the institute.

Malone, Dumas. "A Challenge to Patriots," *Virginia Quarterly*, October, 1928.

Mann, Dorothea Lawrence. "Ellen Glasgow: Citizen of the World," *Bookman*, November, 1926.

Marley, Howard P. "The Negro in Recent Southern Literature," *South Atlantic*, January, 1928.

Mason, Lucy Randolph. *Standards For Workers in Southern Industry*, pamphlet published by National Consumers' League, New York, November, 1931.

Mayo, A. D. "William Preston Johnston's Work For a New South," *Report of the Commissioner of Education, 1898-1899*, Vol. 11.

Mecklin, John M. "Vardamanism," *Independent*, August 31, 1911.

——— "The Black Codes," *South Atlantic*, July, 1917.

Mellen, George Frederick. "New England Editors in the South," *New England Magazine*, February, 1903.

Meyer, Adolph E. "Advocatus Diaboli," *American Mercury*, September, 1927.

Miller, Kelly. "Have the Civil War Amendments Failed?" *South Atlantic*, April, 1928.

Milton, George Fort. "Democracy—Whither Bound," *Virginia Quarterly*, January, 1926.

——— "Planks in a Liberal Platform," *Outlook*, March 31, 1926.

——— "Black Ballots in the White South," *Forum*, December, 1927.

Molyneaux, Peter. "Land of Cotton," *Southwest Review*, Summer, 1931.

Moncure, John. "John M. Daniel: Editor of *The Examiner*," *Sewanee Review*, July, 1907.

Murphy, Edgar Gardner. "The Task of the Leader," *Sewanee Review*, January, 1907.

Mussey, Henry Raymond. "Garrison, Breaker of Chains," *Nation*, January 7, 1931.

Nixon, Herman Clarence. "DeBow's Review," *Sewanee Review*, January-March, 1931.

Oglesby, T. K. *The Britannica Answered and the South Vindicated*, pamphlet, Montgomery, Ala., 1891.

Parker, Lewis W. "Science in the Development of the South," *South Atlantic*, April, 1910.

Parkins, A. E. "The Antebellum South: A Geographer's Interpretation," *Annals of the Association of American Geographers*, Vol. xxi, No. 1, March, 1931.

"Passing of Two Notable Men, The," editorial, *South Atlantic*, January, 1906.

Pearson, C. Chilton. "William Henry Ruffner: Reconstruction Statesman of Virginia," *South Atlantic*, January, 1920.

Pekor, Charles F., Jr. "An Adventure in Georgia," *American Mercury*, August, 1926.

Poe, Clarence H. "Lynching: A Southern View," *Atlantic*, February, 1904.

Proceedings of the Institute of Public Affairs, Bulletin, University of Georgia, Vol. xxxi, March, 1931, No. 4.

Ramage, B. J. "The Dissolution of the Solid South," *Sewanee Review*, August, 1896.

Ransdell, Hollace. *Report on the Scottsboro, Alabama, Case*. Published by American Civil Liberties Union, New York, May 27, 1931.

Reed, John C. "Reminiscences of Ben Hill," *South Atlantic*, April, 1906.

——— "The Recent Primary Election in Georgia," *South Atlantic*, January, 1907.

Report of Commission on Religious Prejudices, Supreme Council, Knights of Columbus, 1915, 1916 and 1917.

440 BIBLIOGRAPHY

Richardson, Eudora Ramsay. "The Case of the Women's Colleges in the South," *South Atlantic*, April, 1930.

Scottsboro Case, The. Mimeographed report on the case published in May, 1931, by the Commission on Interracial Coöperation, Atlanta, Ga.

Shepherd, H. E. "Higher Education in the South," *Sewanee Review*, May, 1893.

Shipley, Maynard. "Growth of the Anti-Evolution Movement," *Current History*, May, 1930.

Shoup, Francis A. "Uncle Tom's Cabin Forty Years After," *Sewanee Review*, November, 1893.

Sledd, Andrew. "The Negro: Another View," *Atlantic*, July, 1902.

—————— "The Dismissal of Professor Banks," *Independent*, May 25, 1911.

Smith, C. Alphonso. "The Possibilities of the South in Literature," *Sewanee Review*, July, 1898.

Smith, Charles Forster. "Southern Colleges and Schools," *Atlantic*, October, 1884, and December, 1885.

Snyder, Henry N. "John H. Carlisle—Educator," *South Atlantic*, January, 1910.

Stemons, James Samuel. "Negro Suffrage in the South," *Southwest Review*, Winter, 1931.

Stephenson, Gilbert T. "Education and Crime Among Negroes," *South Atlantic*, January, 1917.

Story of Civil Liberty, 1929-30, The. Published by American Civil Liberties Union, New York, May, 1930.

Strother, French. "The Governors Ferguson of Texas," *World's Work*, September, 1925.

"Studies in the South," series of ten unsigned articles, *Atlantic*, January-December, inclusive, 1882.

Tait, Samuel W., Jr. "The St. Louis *Post-Dispatch*," *American Mercury*, April, 1931.

Trent, William P. "Dominant Forces in Southern Life," *Atlantic*, January, 1897.

—————— "Tendencies of Higher Life in the South," *Atlantic*, June, 1897.

"Trinity College and Academic Liberty," anonymous, *South Atlantic*, January, 1904.

Van Doren, Dorothy. "Eight Who Must Not Die," *Nation*, June 3, 1931.

Van Horne, John Douglass. "The Southern Attitude Toward Slavery," *Sewanee Review*, July-September, 1921.

Wade, John Donald. "Jefferson: New Style," *American Mercury*, November, 1929.

Wallace, D. D. "Henry Laurens of South Carolina," *Texas Review*, April, 1916.

"Washington's Words on a National University," *Old South Leaflets*, Vol. IV, No. 76, Boston, no date.

Watterson, Henry. "George Dennison Prentice," *Library of Southern Literature*, Vol. IX.

White, John E. "The Need of a Southern Program on the Negro Problem," *South Atlantic*, April, 1907.

White, Owen P. "Workers in the Vineyard," *Collier's*, October 6, 1928.

Wilson, Edmund. "The Freight-Car Case," *New Republic*, August 26, 1931.

Wilson, James Southall. "Breaking the Solid South," *Virginia Quarterly*, January, 1929.

Winston, Robert W. "Rebirth of the Southern States," *Current History*, July, 1925.

———— "The North and the South Today," *Current History*, November, 1927.

Wood, George A. "The Black Code of Alabama," *South Atlantic*, October, 1914.

Woodberry, George Edward. "The South in American Letters," *Harper's*, October, 1903.

World's Work, June, 1907, special Southern number.

INDEX

A*bolition Intelligencer* (Shelbyville, Ky.), 91
Abolitionists, 103 ff.
Academic freedom, 338 ff.
Adams, Herbert Baxter, 53
Adams, Governor J. H., 119
Adams, John, 28
Adams, John Quincy, 106
Adams, John Quincy II, 158
Addison, Joseph, 360
Aderholt, O. F., 325
Advancing South, The, 391
Advertiser (Montgomery), 229, 258, 399-400, 402
Agrarianism, 10, 310
Agricultural Wheel, 205
Aikman, Duncan, 403
Ainsworth, W. N., 284
Alabama, 19, 148, 249, 272-73, 281, 365-66
Alderman, Edwin A., 176, 180-81, 345-46, 396
Alexander, W. W., 251
Alien and Sedition Acts, 16
Allen, James Lane, 382
Allston, Colonel R. F. W., 147
Alston, Joseph, 20
American Anti-Slavery Society, 103, 112
American Association of University Professors, 300
American Civil Liberties Union, 279, 343
American Facist [*sic*] Association and Order of Blackshirts, 261
American Federation of Labor, 328
American Historical Association, 392
American Library Association, 337
American Revolution, 1 ff.
American Telephone and Telegraph Company, 278
American Tobacco Company, 315
Ames, Mrs. Jessie Daniels, 379
Anderson, W. T., 374, 402
Anglican church, 25, 26 ff., 28, 62

Anglican clergy, 43
Anglicans, 32, 55, 56
Anthony, Susan B., 367
Anti-Catholic movements, 282-83
Anti-evolution bills, 281
Anti-evolution legislation, 289 ff., 295 ff., 300-01, 406
Anti-lynching bill, 408
Anti-prohibition, 420
Anti-Saloon League, 280-81, 420
Anti-slavery societies, 71-72
Archive, 263
Arkansas, 296-97, 321, 372-73
Armstrong, Samuel Chapman, 167-68
Arnold, Benedict, 267
Asbury, Francis, 38
Association of American Universities, 345
Association of Southern Women for the Prevention of Lynching, 250
Atkinson, Governor W. Y., 175, 368
Atlanta Board of Education, 298
Atlanta School of Social Work, 339
Atlantic Monthly, 167, 185, 236
Aycock, Charles B., 181, 275

Bache, B. F., 87
Bagby, George W., 360
Baker, Ray Stannard, 247
Baldwin, Abraham, 45-46
Baldwin, Rignal, 326
Ballard, Marshall, 410
Baltimore, 199
Baltimore, Lord, 24
Banks, Enoch M., 341
Baptist church, 281, 296, 301
Baptist General Association of Virginia, 306
Baptist Ministers' Conference of Richmond, 306
Baptists, 26-27, 30-31, 32, 35, 38 ff., 39, 66, 113 ff., 194, 195, 282, 291-92
Baptists, Hardshell, 39
Baptists, Primitive, 39
Barker, E. C., 393

29